# THE PORNOGRAPHY OF REPRESENTATION

# FEMINIST PERSPECTIVES
## SERIES EDITOR: MICHELLE STANWORTH

*Published*
Barbara Sichtermann, *Femininity: The Politics of the Personal*
Julia Swindells, *Victorian Writing and Working Women*

# The Pornography of Representation

Susanne Kappeler

University of Minnesota Press, Minneapolis

Published by the University of Minnesota Press 2037 University Avenue Southeast, Minneapolis MN 55414.
Published simultaneously in Canada by Fitzhenry & Whiteside Limited, Markham.
Printed in Great Britain.

Library of Congress Cataloging-in-Publication Data

Kappeler, Susanne, 1949 —
    The pornography of representation.

    (feminist perspectives)
    Bibliography: p.
    1. Pornography–Social aspects.    2. Representation.
    (Philosophy)    3. Feminism.    I. Title.    II. Series.
HQ471.K36  1986          363.4'7          86–6981
ISBN 0–8166–1543–8
ISBN 0–8166–1544–6 (pbk.)

The University of Minnesota
is an equal–opportunity
educator and employer.

# Contents

# Acknowledgements

My thanks to all the sisters and their work. Very special thanks to Diane DeBell, Lisa Jardine and Julia Swindells, who have been and are true interlocutors. Thanks also to Michelle Stanworth, sister and editor, and to Helen Pilgrim, Jane Katjavivi and Ann Hall.

And thanks to my Moroccan friends, students and colleagues, among whom I wrote this book.

The author wishes to thank the following for permission to reprint previously published material in this book:

Mother Jones and Deirdre English for extracts from Deirdre English, 'The Politics of Porn: Can Feminists Walk the Line?', Mother Jones (April 1980);
Mother Jones and Henry Schipper for extracts from Henry Schipper, 'Filthy Lucre: A Tour of America's Most Profitable Frontier', Mother Jones (April 1980);
Writers and Readers Publishing Cooperative Society and John Berger for extracts from John Berger, About Looking, published by Writers and Readers Publishing Cooperative, 144 Camden High Street, London NW1 ONE, UK;
Macmillan, London and Basingstoke, and Jane Gallop, for extracts from Jane Gallop, Feminism and Psychoanalysis: The Daughter's Seduction, published in the UK by Macmillan; and Cornell University Press and Jane Gallop for the same extracts from The Daughter's Seduction: Feminism and Psychoanalysis, published in the USA by Cornell University Press.

A major portion of Problem 7 appeared in slightly different form in Feminist Review 16.

# Preamble

A feminist critique of pornography needs first of all to engage with the terms in which pornography is discussed. Pornography is not a given entity in the world, but the construct of particular discourses. It is notorious that there exists no clear-cut definition of pornography; instead, different dicussions identify different characteristic elements as their basis for a discussion of the phenomenon.

The opposition to pornography, whether feminist or otherwise, has almost unanimously argued its case in terms of an assumption that pornography is a special case of sexuality. Feminists and anti-pornography lobbyists alike slip easily from discussing the goings-on inside pornographic representations to discussing goings-on in the world. Their concern is that practices portrayed in pornography may become practices in our lives. The traditional emphasis is on 'obscenity': the immoral or 'dirty' quality of the sex portrayed. Feminist argument has shifted the focus on to violence: the violent quality of the sex portrayed. In this respect, the feminist emphasis has not so much introduced new ways of dealing with the problem of pornography as a new basis for morality.

On the other side of the argument, censorship experts and advocates of free pornography deny that a link between pornography and criminal sexual practice in reality can be proven. They assert a fundamental difference between fantasy and reality. Pornographic representations, for them, belong to the separate realm of fantasy and fiction. We should therefore look at this pure realm of fantasy, how it has come about, and where exactly it lives if it is not part of reality.

It is my contention that the feminist argument about

pornography would significantly advance if we were to shift the ground of the argument. Pornography is not a special case of sexuality; it is a form of representation. Representation, therefore, not 'real-life sex', should be the wider context in which we analyse this special case of representation: pornography. The traditional debate has focused on 'porn' at the expense of 'graphy', an emphasis duly reflected in the customary abbreviation to 'porn'. 'Porn', in this slippage, has gradually come to mean 'obscene sex' or 'violent sex' – forms of sexuality we disapprove of. We do not like them (or would not like them) in real life, therefore we do not want them represented.

The object of this study is pornography, that is representations, word- or image-based, or, to be more precise, representational practices, rather than sexual practices. The fact of representation needs to be foregrounded: we are not just dealing with 'contents'. Sex or sexual practices do not just exist out there, waiting to be represented; rather, there is a dialectical relationship between representational practices which construct sexuality, and actual sexual practices, each informing the other.

Forms of representation have their own histories, yet we have become so accustomed to representations in many media that the media and their conventions have become naturalized, 'transparent', apparently giving a key-hole view on make-believe reality, reflections of reality. Literature and the visual arts are the expert domains of representation, and they embody the history of the naturalization of the medium. Their concepts of realism have fostered our commonsense attitude of dividing representations into form and content, medium and represented reality. The aim of realism is to obliterate our awareness of the medium and its conventions and to make us take what is represented for a reflection of a natural reality. Realism sees itself as holding up a mirror to life. The mirror, if not transparent, reflects, and it is above all 'faithful'. The question should never arise as to who is holding the mirror, for whose benefit, and from what angle; at least it should not arise in terms which would make this concept of the mirror – and hence of reality – problematical.

Within the disciplines of the study of art and literature, cinema and photography, the analysis of realism and of the relationship between form and content has long significantly advanced beyond this simple sketch. Yet the notions of 'realism' and of 'form and content' still have a firm hold upon our commonsense responses. They are at the bottom of the content orientation towards pornography (the focus on sex). They are at the bottom of our easy division into fact and fiction. And they are at the bottom of official newspaper policy, of professional organizations of editors and journalists claiming to produce neutral, unbiased, objective or transparent reporting – to hold up the mirror of events to the reading public. It is for this reason that a more elaborate analysis of representation needs to be brought to bear in a feminist analysis of pornography.

Representations are not just a matter of mirrors, reflections, key-holes. Somebody is making them, and somebody is looking at them, through a complex array of means and conventions. Nor do representations simply exist on canvas, in books, on photographic paper or on screens: they have a continued existence in reality as objects of exchange; they have a genesis in material production. They are more 'real' than the reality they are said to represent or reflect. All of these factors somehow straddle the commonsense divide between fiction and fact, fantasy and reality.

So a first shift of ground, for a feminist critique of pornography, involves moving from a content orientation to an analysis of representation. This move however takes us out of the comfortable seclusion of the Arts – the storehouses of (respectable) representations – and leads us to look at the functions of representations in society. Crucial factors of representation are the author and the perceiver: agents who are not like characters firmly placed within the representation as content. They are roles taken up by social beings in a context. This context is political: a question of class, race, gender. This context is cultural: a question of the relationship of representations to a generalized concept of culture (and 'reality'). And this context is economic: a question of the relationships of cultural production and exchange. None of these questions of course is independent of the others, which poses a problem of how to present them.

The procedure in this study will be two-fold: on the one hand I shall be clearing the ground, challenging a plethora of concepts that appear as the givens of the debate on pornography; on the other, I shall build up the concepts and methods necessary for a feminist critique of pornography and patriarchal culture.

# Fact and Fiction

*The Guardian Weekly*, in its first issue of 1984, carried an article entitled 'A Murder in Namibia'. A white farmer, van Rooyen, aged 24, had tortured and killed the 18-year-old Thomas Kasire, a new black worker on his farm. The history is as follows: on account of the language Kasire speaks and the area he comes from, his white boss accuses him of being a supporter of the national liberation movement SWAPO (South Western African People's Organisation). He

> throws a heavy chain around the throat of Thomas Kasire. For two days the white farmer keeps Thomas chained fast in his farmyard. Eventually, Thomas is killed as van Rooyen's drinking pals applaud and take pictures. This happens on a farm, in Namibia, in 1983.[1]

Three pictures accompany the article, one showing the murderer 'as he appeared in court', wearing a suit and tie. The other two pictures are from the 'scene' of crime: a close-up of Kasire's head, bleeding, one ear half cut off, a heavy iron chain around his neck, with the white left arm of his torturer holding on to the chain, intruding from the left into the middle foreground of the picture. The third photograph has the caption: 'The victim is forced to pose with a clenched fist (SWAPO salute), while a friend of the murderer takes photos.'[2] The murderer himself is in the picture, towering over the young black man whom he holds by the chain. He is wearing farm clothes and a cap (they could also be paramilitary gear) and he is facing the camera. The young black man looks as if he were held up on his feet chiefly by the chain the white man holds.

The event is a curiosity in criminology, for the pictures

were the damning evidence. Without them, the court would in all probability have acquitted [van Rooyen]. The explanations given by him and his white friends would have outweighed the statements of black witnesses. So safe are the whites in their dominant position within the apartheid system that, incredibly, the whole event was photographed at van Rooyen's request.[3]

The coincidence of this kind of violence and its representation is no accident. It is no curiosity in the domain of representation. The pictures are not documentary evidence, snapped by a journalist or observer by chance in the right place at the right time. The pictures are compositions, deliberate representations, conforming to a genre. The victim is forced to 'pose'; the perpetrator of the torture positions himself in the other picture with reference to the camera. Another white man is behind the camera, framing the picture. The picture may remind us of those taken by fishermen and hunters posing with their catch, smiling into the camera. But the catch is a human being, a victim, and thus the picture also reminds us of some of the darkest photographic memories of the Vietnam war, those pictures which break the documentary mould and where a temporary victor briefly poses for the camera with his victim vanquished, acknowledging the presence of the camera, drawing it into complicity. The picture may also remind us, or some of us, of pornography, a woman in the place of the black man, the white men in their respective positions – in the picture, behind the camera – unchanged.

The written report, too, cannot but align itself with the existing literary tradition of the genre:

Sunday afternoon – two white guests arrive at the farm. Thomas has now stood, bound, for two days without food or water. Van Rooyen suggests to his friends that they should have some drinks and soon they begin celebrating the capture of a young 'terrorist'.

The victim is fetched and forced to pose whilst one of the guests borrows van Rooyen's Instamatic camera. A short time after the pictures are taken there is an almost inaudible sob from Thomas Kasire. After a faint shudder he falls backwards – lifeless.[4]

For 'Thomas' – the 'boy'[5] put 'Justine' or 'Emanuelle' or 'O' – the victim already designated by reduced identity, a first name, no family name. For 'farm' put 'chateau', retain the aristocratic patronym of its owner and you have the perfect scenario of sadean libertinism, the classic paradigm of the genre.

Experts on pornography, obscenity and censorship, experts of the law as well as experts of the arts, will argue that the issue of real violence, physical violence to people as in 'A Murder in Namibia', is irrelevant to the question of pornography. Real violence is a case for the courts and the criminologists: it is fact, not fiction.

Experts in law are for the most part concerned with fact, although with cases of threat, libel and with the question of censorship they are themselves concerned with a realm of representation that relates ambiguously to the realm of fact. Experts of the arts are now virtually exclusively concerned with fiction, since the modern understanding of art and literature highlights the creative and imaginative as the defining elements, coupled with an evaluative criterion of 'excellence'.[6] When the issue is pornography, both sides offer themselves as the obvious experts while at the same time effectively disowning it. Thus the arts experts, while coyly refraining from claiming pornography as an art (not 'excellent' enough), nevertheless recognize its affinity with their own subject and, moreover, have memories of the law interfering in the arts proper with its censorship arm, as in the famous literary obscenity trials.[7] They claim, as it were, the other side of the boundary between fiction and pornographic fiction (without apparently any contradiction). Liberalism is in favour of a clear separation of expertise and of restricting the law to unambiguous fact. The law, increasingly complying, restricts its concern to the possibility of a factual relation between fiction (potential fact) and actual fact, thus placing pornography itself outside its proper domain.

Hence the present situation where protectors as well as critics of pornography face each other over the (law's) problem of refuting or proving a causal relationship between the consumption of pornographic fiction and the perpetration of sexual crimes: does represented content lead to content being acted out? Did a sexual assailant get his crime out of a book, film or magazine? Representation itself, pornography itself, is already no longer in question, in this search for a match between contents. Sociology provides statistics: they prove nothing. Perhaps it is rather a case for the psychologists, and there are psychiatric estimates: 'no correlation'.[8] What is clear from this division of domains and competencies is that representation itself is not considered a part of the real; as fiction it is opposed to fact, and it does not apparently involve any acts, activity, action, save fictional ones in its content.

In the murder of Thomas Kasire, 'posing' for pictures was an integral part of his torture; in fact, it was the final cause of death. In the murdering of Thomas Kasire, taking pictures was an integral part of the act of torture and an integral part of the enjoyment of the act of torture. This particular form of violence has two parts: doing it and enjoying it, action and appreciation. Today, we loosely call it sadism. Enjoyment, according to Sade, requires a sophisticated intellectual structure, beyond sheer gratification. It requires an audience. With an audience, torture becomes an art, the torturer an author, the onlookers an audience of connoisseurs. This sophisticated structure is manifest in the present case: there is a host, the owner of the farm, and there are guests. One white man, the host, is the *maître de cérémonie*,[9] also acting as torturer in the content of the picture, another white man, a guest, behind the camera, acting in the production of the picture. The two look at each other. The one in the picture will come out of the picture and take the place of the man behind the camera, looking at the scene he has framed. The host and his guests mingle and merge in the audience, they become one as the audience, but the host is the author of the party, and they are 'celebrating'.

The victim does not come out of the picture, the victim is dead. In this case literally, in the general case of representation virtually, or functionally, as there is no designated role in the world, and in the continued existence of the representation, for the victim to take up. If the person filling the role of victim is not actually dead, s/he should be. In the words of the Marquis de Sade:

> There's not a woman on earth who would ever have had cause to complain of my services if I'd been sure of being able to kill her afterwards.[10]

An interesting use of the word 'cause'.

The white men's party, their action of representing the torture and death of Thomas Kasire, is disregarded by both camps of experts. In the face of the 'real', factual violence involved in the production of the representation, the arts experts deem that the representation ceases to be fiction and a relative of the arts. The case is handed over to the courts, where the representation becomes 'evidence', a chance windfall for the prosecution, who treats it as a mirror reflection of reality, the reality of the crime. Van Rooyen is tried for murder; his action of producing pornographic representations, relatives of the snuff-movies, goes unnoticed and untried.

Experts on fiction and art will say that this incident does not count, because the incident was real (the victim really died). Fiction, of course, has always had a troubled relationship with reality, its investment in realism motivated by a concern with authenticating its own enterprise in an increasingly secular culture, guaranteeing a certain relevance. But it wants no part *in* reality, it is the Other to the real. It is the surplus of the real, it need have no function in the real, it need serve no purpose. It is the leisure and the pleasure which complements the work and utility of the real. That is its beauty, the beauty and privilege of the arts. Gratuitousness becomes the trademark of the arts' sublimity.

Gratuitousness is the mark of the murderer's photography. It is for sheer surplus pleasure, as is the torture itself, which has nothing of course to do with fighting so-called terrorists or any other utility in the world. It serves the leisure and the pleasure of the white man (the incident happens at a weekend, Friday–Sunday),[11] it is a form of his free expression of himself, an assertion of his subjectivity.

Van Rooyen's production of pictures is fiction *par excellence*. The pictures are *made* (fiction from *fingere* = to form), careful compositions according to the laws of aesthetics and representation. The fiction exceeds fact in its representation of reality: Thomas Kasire lives on in his representation, though Thomas Kasire is dead. The fiction continues its existence in reality.

# Problem 2

# Human Rights

In its present, received position, the case of pornography is unanswerable. Radicals and conservatives are confused about on which side of the fence they are or ought to be; only liberals and intellectuals know their place is firmly on it. The problem, as they all see it, is that pornography is about sexuality: radicals and some liberals are 'for' it, and for its 'liberation'. Conservatives are against liberation, and very concerned about 'public morality'. There is a further problem, and this is freedom of expression. Liberals and intellectuals become almost radical when it comes to this question. Conservatives are not too sure freedom is good for everyone, and are in favour of regulating it. All of them thus happily agree that the problem of pornography is one of morality and censorship, or sexual liberation and freedom of expression, depending on the colour of the vocabulary. Feminists – radicals from the point of view of patriarchy – slot themselves uneasily into the debate in these terms: depending on their other allegiances they may come down on either side of the fence. Radically opposed to pornography, they may find themselves pleading with Mary Whitehouse for its 'abolition', for censorship. With an investment in intellectual liberalism or the arts (not to mention the 'sexual liberation' of the sixties) they may argue that pornography is not really an issue.

The Minneapolis City Council narrowly approved a new ordinance on 30 December 1983, which declares that 'certain kinds of pornography violate women's civil rights.'[1] The importance of this new ordinance – for the drafting of which the City Council had consulted two feminists, Catharine MacKinnon, a lawyer, and Andrea Dworkin, teacher and author of a book on pornography – is that it shifts the issue of pornography from its traditional place of obscenity and censorship to a question of civil rights: the civil rights of women. What is further interesting is how this vote split up the conventional categories of conservative, liberal and radical (although in American parlance 'liberal' already covers a spectrum from centre to left). The *Minneapolis Star and Tribune* staff writers report:

> If [the Mayor] vetoes it, the proposal will come up before the new council, which takes office Tuesday. Supporters [of the new ordinance] said they fear the new council will be less favorable to the proposal.
>
> The new council members are widely viewed as *more liberal*, particularly in the area of civil liberties, and not as amenable to the ordinance.[2] (My emphasis)

Being more liberal, expecially in the area of civil liberties, apparently renders council members less amenable to the civil rights of women. The report continues:

> Yesterday's vote was basically an alignment of council *feminists* and people who are *conservative morally*. However, two feminists . . . opposed it. And two *men* who generally vote for conservative moral issues . . . voted against it.
>
> The Minnesota Newspaper Association released a statement opposing it and the Minnesota Civil Liberties Union also has said it will challenge the ordinance. Both are worried about censorship.[3] (My emphasis)

Pornography has here become an issue of the civil rights of women, though some (most) conservatives still see in it an issue of morality and vote accordingly. Thus they vote along with feminists, who are for the radical proposition of enshrining civil rights for women in law.

However, two *women* ('feminists') oppose the ordinance; one 'said that while she's a feminist "I'm concerned what this does to the fight for human rights . . . It's censorship".'[4] It is not, in fact, censorship, as a woman would sue the purveyors or producers of pornography in a civil suit. But for this woman, it is a case of women's civil rights versus 'human rights', and her allegiance to the latter overrides her commitment to the former, without apparently any contradiction. Two *men*, who as conservatives would normally vote for the ordinance (for morality), vote against it. Their allegiance to patriarchy (the rights of men, 'human rights') overrides their conservative moral interests. One of them says that he and his advisers, 'dozens of people, lawyers, civil rights commission members, a judge' (note: experts), are 'all concerned about pornography, but they don't think this is the way to go . . . There would be a perception in the country if we lost that the city couldn't do anything about pornography.'[5] The need to succeed is more important than the cause that might be attempted; the need to *be seen* to succeed by the rest of the country a concern beyond the civil rights of women. 'There would be a perception' if we lost: notice the anxious glance of the white man into the camera of the media and of public opinion. There would be a representation of us as impotent and as losers which we cannot risk. Control *this* representation, at the cost of the rights of women violated in pornographic representations.

One could say that this muddle of conventional political categories and of the concepts of what pornography is has the virtue of introducing, at last but clearly, the issue of gender. And the issue of gender does not principally reside in the pornographic scenario itself where the woman usually occupies the place of victim, the man the place of master. The gender issue here concerns the structures and functions of representations, the authors and the perceivers of pornography. For the feminist voter-against, for the liberals, for the Civil Liberties Union, and for the professionals of representation – the media (Newspaper Association) – women's civil rights are pitted against, are in competition with, human rights. The human rights protected here concern the freedom of expression, the freedom of the producers and purveyors of pornography (the white man behind the Instamatic), and the freedom of consumption of the pornographic clientele (the white man's guests). In the face of their claims, there is nothing to be done for the rights of the victim, who 'dies' in any case in the production of the representation. And if the victim has not died, an effort should be made to kill 'it', to silence the voice that might complain of the 'services' received. In the case of fact (murder in Namibia) as in the case of fiction (pornography) no overt connection is established between the particular individual who has fallen victim and a class of people who share the potential for victimization. In Switzerland, women took the military to court for allowing officers to use photographs of a woman as targets for shooting practice. The reply of the Swiss authorities was that only the particular woman, the model of the photographs, could sue. And she would be unlikely to, added a spokesman, since she had posed in the first place.[6] In other words, the victim was dead, on account of posing, for any subsequent role in the life and tribulations of the representation.

The attempts of women to introduce ordinances such as the one in Minneapolis, or to take the Swiss military to court on the basis that pornography and its use are degrading to women as a gender, constitute an attempt to establish the connection between the individual victim and a class of potential victims. The persistent denial of such a connection by courts, censorship commissions and media points to an implicit recognition of the far-reaching consequences that would ensue from the overt acknowledgement of this link. The denial comes from a consolidated establishment of powers that be, which bear the gender of the white male, despite the odd token woman who has erred into these institutions on her aspiration to be counted as 'human'. Women as a gender-class are in the anti-pornography lobby on the basis of their recognition that they and the particular victim are one.

A feminist critique of pornography therefore has to address this narrow literalism which particularizes the singular victim and detaches her or him from any class or race affiliation. We also need to challenge the literalism of the argument of fiction experts that the victimization in pornographic representations is only make-believe, and that in fact the woman model (usually) gets up unharmed after the photographic session, or does not really exist in the case of literature. We need to shift the discussion to an analysis of the role of representation in society, and to assert the civil rights of the victim in the scenario, to complement the rights of the master in the scenario and his guests. The human rights as they stand protect the rights of the author and the audience, but they do not protect the rights of the victim. We therefore need a cultural theory of representation, an analysis of power relations and the concepts of gender and race.

Representations are not just snapshots or texts, disembodied and innocuous. Take the photographs of the murder in Namibia. The victim is dead. Were it a pornographic picture, the victim would be paid and dismissed. What lives on, in either case, what has a continued existence and practice in society, is the structure of production and consumption represented by the two white men. The particular man behind the camera has opened up a dimension of viewing, has engendered a spectatorship, an audience of white men in general (a gender-race-class). And the white man in the picture is still at large, joins the viewers, is interchangeable with them.

There is collusion between the two white men of the picture. They look at each other. One is the host, the other his guest. There exists a structure of identification and solidarity, a common purpose, a shared understanding, a communicated pleasure between them. What is more, there are further white men: in the courts. Without the pictures, the court in all probability would have aquitted the murderer and his guests. But in this particular case the pictures are hard factual evidence. Yet 'despite the evidence of the pictures, the sentence was mild . . . van Rooyen was sentenced to just six years.'[7] And there are further white men still: manning the parole commission. 'The latest information from our Namibian sources is that van Rooyen actually was secretly freed on parole shortly after his prison sentence began.'[8] And there are further white men, in the police force, who occasionally make embarrassing blunders: 'The press would not have known of his release had he not been stopped for drunken driving.'[9] A case, no doubt, for the lobby for the freedom of expression and information, although there is no doubt as to who – what gender-race-class – has exercised its freedom of controlling information in the interests of itself. There might have been 'a perception', in the country at large, in the public eye, that we (justice and authority) had 'lost', that we couldn't or didn't do anything about racist murder. We are all concerned about racism and crime, but we don't think this is the way to go. Control this representation of us as 'impotent', or as not exercising our power, as 'losers' in the combat of racism and murder and as winners in the protection of white male privilege. Control this representation, at the cost of the rights and lives of the victims in the case.

The voices of black people, in the Namibian case (identifying with the victim as a race-class of potential victims), would have been outweighed by the voices of the white man and his guests. And the black people would sit neither in court nor on parole commissions, nor in the boardrooms of the media. The voices of women, speaking up on behalf of the woman as victim of pornographic representation, have so far been outweighed by the voices of pornographers and their clientele. 'So safe are the whites in their dominant position within the apartheid system', so safe are the men in their dominant position within the patriarchy, 'that, incredibly, the whole event was photographed at van Rooyen's request', that, incredibly, representations of the victimization of black people and of the victimization of women, are produced at the request of the white male.

Human rights rule. Women have not, until recently, sat on law commissions, censorship commissions, city councils; neither have they defined or interpreted 'human rights'. If a woman's voice is heard, is made to be heard, in single and particular cases such as those of Mary Whitehouse or Phyllis Schlaefli, or a woman member of the city council, it is because she speaks in the voice and language of the white man. She speaks the language of morality, man-made morality which covers up the immorality of women's oppression, subordination and violation. She speaks in the language of liberalism, protecting the liberties men take in their free self-expression at the expense of women's human rights. She speaks in the voice of conservatism, which conserves the privileges of white men. She speaks the language of experts, and it is the terms and premises of expert discourses that a feminist critique has to counter. The experts have already defined what pornography is and what it concerns and does not concern, and it is here that we must begin.

The powers that be – politicians, the law, the experts, the media – are not above the temptation to adduce the single token woman, Phyllis Schlaefli or Erica Jong or the female voter-against or a woman spectator of pornography, and make her stand for her gender-class. It is tokenism at its worst and most illogical, but it is of no great consequence as an argument of 'counter-examples'. A feminist analysis deals with patriarchy and male culture, the male gender on the one hand and the female gender on the other, and not with particular biological individuals. It challenges a culture which, on occasions of its own choice – in the courtroom in Namibia or in Switzerland – chooses to particularize the victim, treating each case as a singular case, refusing to recognize the structures of race and gender which not only typify the cases, but are at the very heart of its own social organization.

# Problem 3

# Obscenity and Censorship

Pornography is a feminist issue. It centrally concerns women, since women are the object of pornographic representation. Feminists have produced a substantial literature on the subject.

Pornography has again become a topic of public debate: space is given over to it in the media as it is not to other feminist issues. Many men, and many experts, seem to have a special stake in this issue and contribute to the debate with an eagerness not seen when the issue is domestic work. Pornography is a topic with media appeal.

Yet as a topic of public debate, pornography does not seem to have much to do with women. Women are defined out of the question of pornography as that question is being reframed as one of obscenity and censorship or of freedom of expression. The feminist contribution to the subject is either ignored or edited out of the debate, relegated to a safeguarding footnote or a catchy title.

In the arena of debate, 'public' debate is pitted against feminist debate, without any apparent contradiction, just as we have seen 'human' rights pitted against the civil rights of women. Whilst recognizing the opposition as gender-specific – *feminist* argument, the rights of *women* – the 'public' voice and the 'human' rights lobby do not identify themselves as gendered. Instead, they hide behind ostensibly gender-neutral categories like 'human' which we are told subsume, according to the grammarians and an 1850 Act of Parliament,[1] the gender of women. And perhaps subsume is nearly the right word, though 'subdue' would be more explicit.

However, conjoining 'feminism' and 'pornography' enhances the media appeal of the debate. Just as of late, we

are told, conjoining feminism and pornography enhances the
appeal of pornography.

> The February 1980 issue of *Hustler* carried a comic strip
> in which astronauts subdue, through their irresistible
> sex-techniques, a colony of uppity space-age Amazons
> who worship the goddess Steinem. *Penthouse*, that same
> month, carried a piece called 'Stand Up and Howl' (the
> coverline read: 'Women's Lib: the Male Strikes Back').
> Inside we find that ski instructor Clay Harris, for one,
> 'isn't affected by the feminist influence because he
> doesn't let it affect him. "I leave feminists right away,"
> he says, "because they're a problem. I move on." '[2]

Notice the two categories, 'astronauts' (gender neutral) and
'space-age Amazons', that is to say, women astronauts. The
space of the former is invaded by amazons. Like amazons,
feminists are seen to invade the space of public debate and the
turf of the experts, but the legitimate experts (no gender, nor
gender interests, of course) Stand Up and Howl. Pornography, as opposed to public debate, recognizes its own
gender and gender interests: the Male Strikes Back. Either
subdue by dazzling and irresistible technique, of sex rather
than astronautics; or don't let the feminist contribution to the
debate affect you. Because it's a problem. Move on.

Bernard Williams, chairman of the Williams *Report on
Obscenity and Film Censorship*,[3] contributes a piece to the
*London Review of Books*, called 'Pornography and
Feminism'.[4] He devotes two columns to the discussion of
pornography, reviewing John Sutherland's *Offensive Literature: Decensorship in Britain 1960–1982*, and one column to the
'misconceptions' of the issue by radical feminists. As his
source on feminism, Williams cites one publication, a review
of the film *Not a Love Story* by Susan Barrowclough, which,
according to the footnote, discusses the simplifications
committed by other feminisms. Neither Barrowclough's
own argument, nor that of the film, nor even their names or
titles actually make it into the main text.

More curious is the fact that Williams adds to Barrow-clough's name the name of her husband (a colleague of Williams's at King's College, Cambridge) in a double-barrelled formation of which no trace can be found in the original publication.[5] Is the husband's name meant to reassure us that this feminist is, after all, a wife and not an amazon, subdued already through sex if not through debate?

Williams reacts with some strength of feeling against the lack of concern by radical feminists for 'the question that preoccupies those who sit on the committees' reports – namely what should the law be?'.[6] Thus the concern of feminists has already successfully been made to vanish (we have left feminists right away) as we return once more to the committee's concern, set out at length in their report and liberally aired in the media following its publication. One can understand the perplexity at seeing the sweat of one's labour on committees and reports thus slighted by a colony of amazons, yet the sweat and ink of feminists fare no better at the hands of Williams. With his own concern so present to his mind he seems to suggest that everyone else's concern should be the same. Yet there is more to it than understandable personal preoccupation: Williams is engaged in the defence of the turf of his particular expertise. By his own admission, the radical feminists' concern is not (principally or exclusively) the law. Their concern is with pornography. Yet unless they talk about the law, he does not want to listen to what they have to say. For Williams, talking about pornography means talking about the law (and with this he goes further than most radical feminists in identifying pornography with the law). He is, in other words, fixing the terms and the domain of debate, and we know that within these bounds he is a virtually uncontested expert. What he seems to want to prevent is a re-staking of the ground of the discussion of pornography, and his expertise in the area of censorship seems to endow him with the authority to tell feminists what they should be concerned with. (Or is it his gender which provides the authority?) 'In face of the radical feminists, [Williams is] left also with a less wearily gradualist thought', namely why don't they go elsewhere? 'To go on about the particular nuisance of pornography is largely a diversion to a more traditional and much less significant target [than a general critique of culture]'.[7] In other words: leave pornography to us, and go talk about sexism in culture. (Move on.)

Feminists, in point of fact, are precisely talking about sexism in culture, but they are of the opinion that this analysis may be of some relevance to the experts sitting on law commissions. It might provide them with some other criteria than the old, tried and notoriously unsuccessful ones hitherto employed by the law, just as the feminists advising the Minneapolis City Council endeavoured to introduce new terms of reference for their ordinance, namely the civil rights of women. Feminists, to start with, are saying that pornography concerns women. But women, who are at the centre of pornographic representations, and who experience pornography not only as a nuisance, but as a direct assault upon their image, their dignity and their self-perception, are not part of the censorship committee's concern. The committee's concern is with the 'processes of law' in the 'bourgeois community',[8] that is to say, with the public image of our society rather than with the image of women in our society. Not once in his article does Williams seriously consider the viewpoint of a woman in a society which circulates pornography. Instead, we hear a great deal about 'environmental oppression', 'the question of nuisance, the obtrusive effect of publicly displayed pornography'.[9] And Williams proudly points out that in this respect, in the protection of the environment against oppression, the law has had some effect (the Indecent Display (Control) Act).

In the nineteenth century there was much similar concern about the nuisance and obtrusiveness of prostitution. The law-givers of the twentieth century seem to follow the measures adopted by their predecessors with respect to the contemporary nuisance of pornography: bringing in the 'planning powers', in order to lighten this 'urban plight', banishing the outside displays to the inside of premises, and then trying to banish the 'row upon row of shuttered shops all containing wares of matching uniform ugliness' – to some other area of town which has no hope of 'the urban renewal one would wish on central London'.[10] This reflects the mentality of the Neighbourhood Association, and precedents abound. A well-to-do neighbourhood in Cambridge has begun to lobby the City Council to shut down the shuttered sex shop in its area, but there is no stipulation that the Council take a stand on sex shops in general. It reminds me of the residents of Hampstead who successfully prevented the establishment of a MacDonald's hamburger bar in their district. There is no quarrel, in other words, with the institution of pornography, prostitution, or indeed fast-food chains, nor with the position of the law with regard to them. They should simply not be visible in 'nice' neighbourhoods, though preferably they should remain accessible elsewhere. They should not be part of the picture, the self-image of our 'bourgeois community', of Hampstead, of central London (where the tourists visit), but we may keep them available in some other area which does not form part of this self-image. Thus pornography today has staunch defenders amongst our good neighbours – the educated middle classes. The defence, however, is always indirect (e.g. freedom of expression), since it is the distinguishing characteristic of the middle-class establishment that it does not publicly wish to be seen to have any truck with pornography, which it asserts is the pleasure of some other (popular) class.

The public – bourgeois community, central London, etc. – sees itself in the picture, is casting an anxious glance at the camera of the wider public eye. The concern, as regards pornographic representations, is with the males and masters in the picture and their connection with the viewer; the intention is to dissociate from this structure and shove it on to East Londoners and the 'popular' classes. The women in the picture are left undisturbed, and handed over wholesale.

The concern with obscenity is a concern with the self-image of a society. But we know that such an image can never simply be a reflection, a match between represented object and object in the world. The society does not, as a homogeneous whole, image itself: different roles in the structure of representation are assumed by different sections of the society. Some section, in the position and with the power to do so, will produce the representation, and it is being produced for the benefit of a particular audience (the white man's guests). Some roles within the picture have no representation and voice outside it, no influence on the production of the image; they are objectified, they are pure objects. The question of obscenity confirms that the role of women, objectified in pornographic representations, shall remain that of object in the discussion of pornography as well. Even where the debate on pornography is ostensibly in response to feminism – the voice of women – it shifts the ground back to obscenity where women are not an issue.

In *The Guardian*, a public debate about pornography raged for over a month in the letters column. One reader points out in his letter to the editor that the debate has been bogged down by the impossibility of arriving at a viable definition of pornography. He suggests instead: 'Rather than comparing pornography with other issues such as racialism, it is more productive to compare it with the concept of "blasphemy", a term of similarly uncertain application.'[11] The charge of blasphemy could only hold if its originator and its critic (the white man and his guest) shared a frame of reference in which the concept of blasphemy was meaningful. 'The word "obscene", for example, may have . . . no meaning at all, as the accusation of blasphemy would have no force for the true atheist.'[12] And what, if not 'atheism' (metaphorically speaking) is the guiding principle and pride of the liberal cultural establishment when it comes to the question of 'sexual morality', censorship and pornography? Without further ado, pornography has been reduced to obscenity, the preoccupation of the bourgeois community with its self-image.

To find blasphemy offensive, you would have to believe in God. To find pornography offensive you would have to believe in women. But it is obvious that our cultural atheists do not share a frame of reference with the feminist critics in which the accusation that pornography is a 'blasphemy' of women would be meaningful. Worse still, they do share a frame of cultural reference in which it is acknowledged that there are still some believers about, a framework in which the myth of the existence of women is still culturally prevalent enough to add the spice of blasphemy to the debunking of the myth.

The comparison with blasphemy, the writer argues, is 'more productive': since we are all professed atheists, blasphemy/pornography is a non-issue and thus produces a wealth of unproblematical pornography. In particular, it removes the issue from a comparison between sexism and racism, the analysis argued for by white feminists. It little matters, apparently, that this removal is achieved by sheer fiat, without any supporting argument at all.

Implicit in the recognition of racism is the recognition of the full human existence of beings previously thought, by whites, to be less than human. Atheism, by contrast, involves the recognition of the non-existence of a being previously thought to exist. Dispense with the existence of women, and you have dispensed with the problem of pornography. In all three cases – racism, atheism, sexism – the systems of belief and their change involve a particular subject group of people – whites, believers, men – while the beliefs concern an object group who neither contribute to the value system nor are consulted in the matter – black people, God, women.

For Bernard Williams there still is a problem, however, even if it is the oppression of our neighbourhood rather than the oppression of women. The problem is the continuing difficulty of defining what is pornographic and, in the extended context of 'and feminism', how to place this ill-defined quality in relation to the feminist concept of sexism. Williams agrees that 'soft-core' pornography is very sexist. He also agrees that 'a lot of extreme pornography certainly expresses sadistic fantasies against women'.[13] But he maintains that the 'standard blue movie, too hard-core to collect a BBFC [British Board of Film Censors] "18" certificate, is usually less sexist, whatever else it may be, than the contents of *Playboy* or *Mayfair* or the unspeakable and endlessly popular *Emanuelle*'.[14] It would be interesting to know more precisely how the terms 'soft-core', 'extreme pornography' and 'standard blue movie' relate to each other and what are the values of his 'sexist', 'sadistic', and 'unspeakable'. His argument is that 'more hard-core' does not go together with 'more sexist'. He gets close to implying that extreme sadistic fantasy against women also does not necessarily (or usually?) mean 'more sexist'. And he is definitely saying that more hard-core, in fact hyper-hard-core (beyond BBFC '18') means less sexist than soft-core (*Playboy* et al.).

In fact, Williams gives a very good demonstration of why commissioners' concerns with the law are of so little relevance to feminists, and even to his own present argument. For it is, of course, precisely by censorship standards that *Playboy* & Co. are considered to be less 'whatever it may be', i.e. less hard-core, though more sexist. For the censors are concerned with 'whatever it may be' rather than with sexism. He argues, in fact, that censors allow the more sexist and censor the less sexist (the too hard-core). And he concludes from this that feminists are therefore on to the wrong thing. QED.

Feminist critique is concerned with sexism, not with indecency or obscenity. The values of 'obscene' and 'indecent' change with changing mores; in particular, they are middle-class values of proven duplicity. They are part of the make-up of the society's constructed self-image. The setters of standards *to whom* indecencies and obscenities are offensive do not seem to share the values of women to whom pornography is offensive. A feminist critique of pornography is not primarily concerned with censorship – the regulation and control of 'undesired' (by whom?) representations – but with the exposition of the pervasive presence of sexism and pornographic structures throughout our culture. It is concerned with the constitution of pornography itself, rather than with how a quality, 'whatever it may be', can or cannot be circulated in the bourgeois community. And the objective is potential change based on recognition and awareness of what is wrong with pornography, rather than the touching up of the social self-image.

At one point, Williams seems to have arrived at the same conclusion as feminists, namely that what needs to be questioned is sexism in the culture at large (rather than just the commissioners' particular object of censure). Only, he does not seem to be aware that this is what feminists are doing and have been doing for some time, and that they think that the law and censorship commissions are a part of this culture.

Yet beyond this apparent point of agreement, feminists and Williams part company again when it comes to the practice of a cultural critique. Williams clearly belongs to a particular cultural neighbourhood association who see their culture threatened by the unsavoury influence of a lesser neighbourhood: 'From the point of view of cultural criticism, when one is confronted with what is still the pervasive, lying and destructive sexism of almost all our popular culture, to go on about the particular nuisance of pornography is largely a diversion to a much less significant target.'[15] Perhaps so, if you take the nuisance to be to the environment. And we harken back, at this point, to Williams's earlier comment about the 'more sexist' soft-core scene, where he found *Emanuelle* both 'unspeakable' and 'endlessly popular', the wares in the shuttered sex shops all of a 'matching uniform ugliness'. Might the two factors, popular and unspeakable, uniform and ugly, have something in common? Williams holds that 'there is some truth, if only some, in the idea that mass-circulation soft-core pornography is sexist primarily because anything mass-circulated is sexist.'[16]

This is very interesting indeed. There is something 'sexist', certainly faintly (softly) pornographic in the idea of mass circulation. It makes MacDonald's hamburgers distinctly less palatable than those of some other restaurant. It means above all that private, individualistic pornography, in the privacy of your home or in the limited luxury edition of some publisher of taste, may be rescuable from the assignation to 'mass pornography' as a phenomenon of 'popular culture'. It gives us a principle for censorship: to curtail the manifestations of 'mass taste' (e.g. the endlessly popular sex shops), but to champion the freedom of expression in art and literature. The quality of 'obscenity' or the pornographic is thus not located in the representation itself, but in its distribution. 'Literature', as Williams notes, is often used to refer to written material in general, but he personally recognizes a work of Literature when he sees one, and thus knows that *Inside Linda Lovelace* (endlessly popular) is 'not itself a work of literature'.[17] He points out that 'the DDP seems to have given up on works consisting only of the printed word,' just as the Williams Report recommended that 'such works should not be restricted at all on grounds of obscenity,' in virtual recognition of the 'existing state of affairs'.[18] The existing state of affairs (apart from the law's alleged practical, though not legal, laxity) is, one infers, that the printed word on its own (unaccompanied by illustrations) is practically becoming, or is considered to be, a minority medium, replaced with the masses by the visual 'mass' media. It is also considered less 'immediate', and thus less harmful. Thus the Williams Report is most concerned with the visual display of pornography/obscenity (in the neighbourhood).[19] This might, of course, lead to attendant problems with the purely visual, were it not for some criterion of 'popular' versus 'high' culture which helps to remove paintings of potential obscenities by artists from the arena of debate.

Thus Williams is one step ahead of (or behind) the usual liberal argument for leaving pornography alone, namely that it would be so difficult to define exactly where art ceases and mass pornography begins, and that there would, in consequence, be a danger of throwing out the baby with the bathwater. Feminists, and cultural critics in general, have some interest in this concept of the baby and the bathwater, but not so much with a view to throwing out water, baby or both as they are so readily accused, as for the purpose of analysing the relations between the baby and the bathwater in which it lies. For a genuine analysis of culture, the prior division into 'high' culture (the baby) and 'popular' culture (the bathwater) not only does not serve, but obscures the very object of enquiry. If a connection is perceived between pornography, popular culture and the culture at large, if they are seen as merging at the boundaries, a sensible response would surely be to study this connection rather than argue, as do the liberal defenders of censor-free art and liteature, that pornography should not be rattled so as not to topple the high culture above, or as does Williams, that popular culture and its evils ('lying and destructive') should be the target of critique. The connection as feminists see it is that the scum on the bathwater has, after all, rubbed off from the baby.

The anxiety over a juxtaposition of art and pornography and the consequent defence of absolute boundaries between high culture and popular culture stem from an implicit recognition that the bare content of representations from either category might provide a match, just as a picture of 'fact' might be identical to a picture of 'fiction' (Namibia photographs). It is a tribute to the poverty of conception regarding representation with which the argument operates. The shift of focus from print to visual display, and from an elite culture to mass circulation is in fact an attempt to move out of the dead-lock conception of 'pornographic content' towards the structure of representation, through a consideration of the different media. The visual media, with their potential for display, contrast with the written medium in terms of the size of the audience. The experience of reading is, by custom, a private and individual experience (though this is a consequence of our particular cultural practice rather than of the medium's own potential): it is a communion between the white man and his guest. The visual, when displayed, is a party hosted by the white man for many white men. The concern of censorship is directed at keeping the party 'decent', and without causing offence to those not invited. Yet this shift in objective is neither systematic nor theorized, since the starting point still remains a conception of content.

Thus the concession made by the conventional conception of the problem of pornography to the fact of representation lies in a traditional notion of the private, also introduced from 'life' like the comparison of represented content with 'live' situations. It deals with the problem that what is 'done' in the scenario of a pornographic representation is published for viewing. Just as the marital bedroom is meant to be private, so the pornographic drama ought to be experienced in privacy. In the notion of a third party looking on lie both the voyeuristic titillation of the pornographic viewer and the bourgeois unease that our children might be watching too. (Hence for instance the notion of an '18' certificate).[20] The sense of the violation of privacy seems to increase with the size of the audience.

It is here that the law on obscenity place their concern and their protection: they mean to protect the spectator, and in two different ways. The present law's most crucial operative is the 'test' of whether pornography has a 'tendency to deprave and corrupt' the spectator.[21] This poses the question why he is watching in the first place. The Williams Report, which recommends the abolition of this test and redefines 'harms',[22] makes a distinction between a voluntary and an involuntary audience, relevant in particular to the display of visual pornography in our city streets which forces itself on a large involuntary audience.[23] But as concerns the voluntary spectator, there is as much eagerness to protect his freedom of consumption as there is to protect the pornographer's freedom of expression. Just as the latter shall express himself as freely as possible, so the voluntary consumer of pornography shall consume as freely as possible.[24] Only, we wish to save him from corruption and depravity, that is, from getting into trouble with the law, should such a cause-and-effect relationship be established. He is protected, in other words, for his own sake, and perhaps for the sake of the moral health of the nation, rather than for the sake of any identifiable potential victims. The suggestion that those potentially so corrupted and depraved might have a tendency to assault and degrade, let alone view a particular class of potential victims, that is, real women, along the lines of pornographic representation, is disregarded by committees, experts and lay men. The concept of gender, whether with regard to consumers or with regard to victims, is absent from the expert discussion.

The concern with the involuntary audience, on the other hand, is simply that no one, in our democratic society, should be forced to consume anything unless they choose to. Hence the choice for all is kept open, inside shuttered establishments, if necessary with warning signs,[25] while the threat of involuntary consumption has thus been removed. The involuntary audience is not defined in terms of gender either: it consists, we are told, of 'resonable people', and children.[26] They are, presumably, the representatives of our bourgeois community, minus their wayward sons – the voluntary consumers.

In his endeavour to relate the gender term 'sexist' to harder or softer core pornography in his piece on 'Pornography and Feminism', Williams also offers the following observation: 'Blue movies may exploit everyone, but they do not markedly more exploit the women involved in them than the men.'[27] 'Sexist' thus seems to have something to do with exploitation, but no further elucidation is provided. If Williams means (what some have argued) that the women actors involved in blue movies get equal pay to that of male actors, this hardly amounts to a relevant definition of exploitation, or indeed sexism, with regard to representation. Here the concept of sexism seems to be correlated with exploitation, yet not in a way which would mean that less exploitation entails less sexism, and vice versa. Rather, more exploitation, in Williams's scheme, may mean less 'sexism' if the exploitation is more equally distributed between the sexes, that is, if men get as much exploited as do women. This reveals a curious misconception of the concept of sexism, which Williams understands as a sort of 'tit-for-tat' argument grown out of the battle of the sexes. He seems to think that women would be happy to be exploited, misrepresented and to have violent fantasies projected at them, so long as 'their men' were equally exploited, misrepresented and abused − happy, since the concept of 'sexism' as Williams understands it would no longer apply. It remains to be asked who, under the circumstances, would be the perpetrators of the exploitation and the sadistic fantasies now so democratically directed at both men and women. Implied is a concept of 'equality' which in its very definition presupposes another inequality. We seem to have slipped back into the content of the picture, where now the role of victim may be taken by both men and women and both are being exploited by the white man and his guests.

Williams's notion of the production of pornographic representations does not refer to the structure of representation (and production) which our analysis has highlighted, and which is symbolized by the white men of the Namibia photographs. In the Williams Report, 'harmful material' is led back to a possible harm incurred by actors in the production of a representation, 'the exploitation of children and also of others where the infliction of physical harm was involved'.[28] In this case, the representation becomes a mirror reflection of an event that 'happened in actual fact', so that the actual fact ought to become liable to prosecution.[29] Hence the law is concerned with fact but not 'fiction', and with the literal victim only.

Williams does not make it clear whether 'everyone' who may be exploited refers only to the men and women involved in the production of the blue movie, that is, those acting in its content, or whether it may also extend to the spectators. If it was meant to include the spectator, Williams neither argues for this shift in theoretical perspective nor accounts for the kind of exploitation involved concerning the viewer. The spectator function, as we have seen, is crucial to the analysis of representation, and its omission from any further analysis of 'involvement' is critical. In particular, we know that the spectator function is not simply a democratically open choice of admission, but is structured by the very representation – structured in terms of gender. Pornography, like much other public imaging, is *constructed for male viewing*, framed by the white man for his guests. Whether any actual woman also looks on or not is irrelevant, just as a black person may or may not view the Namibia photograph without altering its structure of representation. Yet this structure, the construction of a male viewpoint on the axis of author to spectator, optionally via the generic male agent in the pornographic scenario, never forms part of the discussion by the experts, just as the consequent exploitation and objectification of women does not. Instead, the experts point to the great democracy of consumption, an invitation to join the viewing which, with the growing liberalization and the so-called 'sexual revolution', is now being extended to women as well – an invitation, in their case, to become a little more 'depraved' and 'corrupt', always within the (changing) legitimate bounds of the law. The pornography industry's major contemporary effort is to capture the women market.[30] It is twisting the involuntary audience's arm to become a voluntary audience.

The censorship commissions' shift to the mass audience of visual pornography and its display is largely a diversion. In terms of the structure of representation, the distinction between one spectator or reader and a whole 'mass' audience of viewers is irrelevant. The essential positions of author and spectator – the subject positions in the representation – and the objectified 'role' of the victim, are all present, whether you gaze at a pornographic image under your pillow or in the cinema, whether you read pornographic print or peep through the slot in a peep show. The 'privacy' of the pornographic scenario is violated in each case by the presence of the spectator or reader, the alter-ego of the author of the scenario. Here, in fact, we are moving closer to the crux of the matter.

Representations are not just a matter of certain objects – books, images, films etc. The structure of representation extends to 'perceptions' and self-images, the anxious pose of the bourgeois community in front of the camera of public opinion, the self-representation through 'high culture' of a dominant social minority. Representation is thus one of the most fundamental structures of conceptualization, centred on the subject. Just as fiction is not just a matter of stories in books, but of narrative conceptualization in general, whether of 'factual (historical or 'true') 'contents' or of imaginary ones, perception is the representation of something to oneself, a conflation of the author and the audience in one single subject. Perception externalized inserts itself into the structure of communication between different subjects: author and audience may be separate individuals. It will therefore be expedient to look at representation in the context of communication.

The public debate about obscenity and censorship is, in fact, a little internal quibble between sections of the bourgeois community. Those in charge of censorship follow the call to keep the community's self-image clean and decent. Those who argue for the total freedom of expression on the grounds of a modern atheism in sexual mores are telling us that today all forms of sexuality and representation of sexuality are clean enough, that the standards of cleanliness have advanced. For the cultured liberal the highest source of embarrassment is the suggestion, or perception, that he might be accused of Mary Whitehouse-ism, and he shares this with the leftist. This has in a large measure prevented even those from tackling an anlaysis of pornography who are convinced that it is essentially a question of mass culture (bad taste, poor values) and who, true to the nineteenth century Matthew Arnold, see themselves as the guardians of Culture against the onslaught of the 'philistinism' or the provinciality and vulgarity of 'popular culture'. This dilemma between the desire to guard Culture and regulate non-culture (popular culture) on the one hand and the fear of Mary Whitehouse-ism (the stake in 'atheism') on the other is negotiated by the liberal cultural establishment by a reinforcement and defence of the boundaries of high culture (the literary, the artistic) in preference over an outright attack on (censure of) the 'bad' culture. The assuredness with which Bernard Williams recognizes (declares) *Inside Linda Lovelace* as not a work of literature is an instance of boundary defence from the one side. We will have occasion to look at an example of boundary defence from the other side, that is, of the positive assertion of the 'literary'.

## Problem 4

# Porn vs Erotica

The women's movement, especially in the USA, but increasingly also in Britain, is beginning to split into two broad positions with respect to pornography. On the one hand there is the gut opposition to pornography, reflected in the activism of anti-porn groups and of groups against violence, rape, and wife battering who may subscribe to the rallying motto that 'Porn is the theory, rape is the practice'. On the other hand there is a new position gradually emerging out of theorized political debate which is summed up by Deirdre English in her article in *Mother Jones*, 'The Politics of Porn: Can Feminists Walk the Line?': 'many feminists, including myself, are coming to believe that in marshaling its resources against pornography, the women's movement is making a mistake, comparable to the error made by those 19th-century feminists who went to war against alcohol.'[1] This position is an important one, because it is the mature result of a long history of feminist experience and reflects important feelings of women in the movement. There is anxiety about wasting valuable energy, and there is recognition that the gut reaction against pornography is too blunt to be politically effective. In its authenticity, this position is thus very different from those with which, however, it is in effect identical: the position of liberal feminists who are too strongly anchored in the imperatives of a 'sexual revolution' to condemn anything to do with sexuality, a position largely shared with the reluctant left, and the position represented earlier by Bernard Williams's invitation to feminists to go elsewhere because pornography is 'largely a diversion'. The congruence of positions with such diverse, and diametrically opposed histories warrants a careful analysis. In fact, this new position furnishes the strongest proof that the feminist argument about pornography needs to shift its ground, since it is essentially an admission that the case of pornography, as it is defined, is unanswerable.

Deirdre English surveys the history of the feminist anti-porn movement and states that feminist theory has now, in general, advanced beyond the point of advocating prohibition, recognizing the dangers of aligning itself with censorship and the law. Much of that argument exhibits our problem 2 – the intersection of a feminist politics with conventional political categories: 'After all, it is usually the conservatives who sponsor censorship crusades,' and they are likely to lump our feminist books, such as *Our Bodies, Ourselves*, together with pornography.[2] Activist groups in the USA, as a consequence, continue to lobby against pornography, giving an outlet to 'so much pent-up anger about sexual abuse',[3] but without being able to formulate any clear political objectives. 'As a result, members of the movement allow themselves to be totally unclear about exactly what they are against,'[4] or what action, besides sheer protest, would be appropriate (a nod of recognition from those sitting on law commissions). The major difficulty, for English, is that this position 'fudges the difference between violent and nonviolent sexual material'.[5] 'As for the line between pornography and erotica, it is hopelessly blurred.'[6]

The crucial points of English's argument are the following: censorship is dangerous, and defining pornography (violent vs non-violent, pornography vs erotica) is hopelessly difficult. They are very familiar arguments, and they differ in nothing from those of the liberal and human-rights establishment except in their derivation: feminists have got there through their own experience and reflection. While thus the second feminist position, here represented by Deirdre English, is politically more astute than the gut opposition to pornography of activist groups, it is equally naive with regard to the question of representation. It is beginning to address the question of what feminist 'opposition' means, and it is beginning to move away from the idea that opposing pornography necessarily means prohibition or abolition by the law. It is an important point, which will have to be remembered. But English deals with it implicitly rather than explicitly. Her polemic is directed against the 'abolitionists': 'you can't just take fantasies away',[7] and 'taking men's porn away will not solve the problem',[8] while her implicit plea seems to be for some kind of 'education' instead of prohibition: '[Pornography] may not be programming anybody, but it isn't educating anybody either.'[9]

Curiously, the first to be educated are not, as you might have expected, the men who produce and consume and perpetuate violent fantasies, but women who over-react to them: 'we have to recognise that fantasies are not "brainwashing"; they are the expression of something profoundly real in the male psychology. It means that, as feminists, we face the difficult task of trying to figure out what that is.'[10] And English is making a start in re-educating us with respect to the male psyche: men's violent fantasies against women do not mean that men '*really* hate us',[11] rather, they are an expression of fear. 'Fantasies are often disguises . . . The fantasy of hurting a woman, for example, can mask the fear of something . . . much worse – like being hurt by a woman.'[12] 'We shouldn't be so naive as to accept men's fantasies at their face value.'[13] *We* should exert ourselves to comprehend the frailty and depth of the masculine psyche!

> It is well known, but often forgotten, that fantasies of aggression are a response to a perceived threat. It is an immature response; it may be an imagined threat. But the fear and the frustration are real . . . As women, we sometimes seem to get so paralyzed by our fear of men that we fail to see *their* weaknesses and fears.[14]

The womanly heart is beginning to melt. Pornography may be an 'immature response', but it is a *response* – and the cause is woman! By merely being, women constitute a threat, so far as men are concerned. The argument is not new; we have heard it, in many forms, from men. The knowledge with which English is re-educating us is male knowledge – a critique of behaviourism, psychology, Freud.

It is an attractive argument, attractive especially to men, who thus first of all divert the opposition to their fantasies into indulgent understanding of their psychological difficulties. Supposing men do fear women on such a profound scale, despite their social, economic and political supremacy: what degree of unspeakable violence would women, according to the same laws of 'human' psychology, have to fantasize against men, whom they have so much more reason, and so much more real reason, to fear? But, 'whether we love men or hate them, we – as feminists – have no task more necessary than understanding them.'[15]

Much male discourse about women ('What does woman want?' 'What is woman?') which has mushroomed since the nineteenth century, is couched in such language – 'understanding them', the mysterious creatures. Virginia Woolf asks: 'Have you any notion of how many books are written about women in the course of one year? Have you any notion how many are written by men? Are you aware that you are, perhaps, the most discussed animal in the universe?'[16] To quote a recent example, *The Working Woman: A Male Manager's View*: chapter two is called 'Understanding Women'; the subheadings are 'Penetrating [sic] the Feminine Mystique', 'Keys to Her Predictability', and 'Women Can Be Understood'.[17] The feminist psychological jargon is in danger of replicating this discourse in inverted form. 'They' are the other, a mysterious object for our understanding to 'penetrate'. No hint of a common humanity, a common culture and a shared form of communication which might bridge this mystique of the alien object. And if we consider how far off the mark men still are, in the latter half of the twentieth century, of understanding women – after so much ink and sweat – it is a singularly unpromising route to recommend to the precious energies of the women's movement.

At the root of the position taken by English is indeed a shared culture – a cultural understanding of knowledge, a cultural understanding of art – which prevents her from directing the logic of feminism at that cultural understanding itself. The knowledge is cited as authority, the form of the knowledge is taken over and replicated, the conception of art accepted unchallenged. For the second major point of her argument concerns the question of representation. It is posed in the very terms our law commissioners and our educated liberals have formulated it in their reports and their letters to the press: How do you define pornography? Where do you draw the line between fiction and the 'unspeakable', art and the gross, non-violent and violent 'sexual material', pornography and erotica?

The implicit assumption is still that some of it – the non-violent sexual material, the art, the legitimate fiction – has to be 'rescued', rescued it seems from abolition, but in fact from analysis and critique themselves. For, if we truly accepted what English advocates, namely that abolition is not the issue, but analysis and critique are, then the imperative of the rescue operation could recede, the defence of the arts and the legitimate relax. But English places her analysis unrescuably in the camp of the establishment, by presupposing moral, if not legal censorship, and by making pornography a question of 'sexual content'. Pornography, for her also, is a form of sexuality, a question of sexual material. Hence the problem of sorting out the good sex from the bad, the non-violent from the violent, the pornographic from the erotic. Women are nowhere in particular in this picture. Pornography is not a feminist issue.

'As for the line between pornography and erotica . . . what would feminists have thought about *The Dinner Party* by Judy Chicago if it had been created by a man – honouring 39 great women in history by making dinner plates of their vaginas?'[18] Quite. What *do* feminists make of this? Nothing, it appears, because they are too busy 'rescuing' a female artist. (Because being 'against' still means abolition, not analysis.) The overriding stumbling block here is art – to be rescued at all costs, and to be filled up, moreover, by a quota of women. The woman artist bears her credentials apparently in her genitals.[19]

Erotica, it is similarly taken for granted, is a 'positive' form of art and hence to be rescued, and it creates a positive problem for both anti-pornography activists and pro-erotica feminists like English: 'it's a difficult question. But it *is* at the heart of the issue. Without a reasonable effort to separate negative from positive sexual images, the movement will inevitably begin to see everything that is sexually suggestive as something that is tending towards rape.'[20] The reasonable effort, of course, has been made already by non-feminists, on behalf of reasonable people (by law commissions, censorship experts), and has been notoriously unsuccessful and will be so in the future, since this feminist position has nothing new to offer by way of criteria. What is worse, the real consequences of rejecting this reasonable effort are obscured by the caricature of a position already discussed and dismissed – that of confusing representation with rape. The real consequences of failing to separate negative from positive sexual images would be the obligation to recognize that there is no fundamental difference between erotica and pornography, art and 'bad taste mass culture', vaginas represented by men and vaginas represented by women – no way of attributing the scum exclusively to the bathwater.

On the one hand, English defends the fact/fiction boundary as assuredly as do the literati: 'The fact remains that no matter how disturbing violent fantasies are, so long as they stay within the world of pornography they are still only fantasies.'[21] Where exactly is the world of pornography if it is not part of this world? English assures us that 'The man masturbating in a theater showing a snuff film is still only watching a movie, not actually raping or murdering.'[22] Nobody says he is (though the censorship lobby ask if he will be). But he is watching a movie (English ignores the fact of it being a 'snuff' movie), in a theatre in this world, and he is not doing 'only' this, he is also masturbating, most definitely in this world (the cleaners can tell you). I will return to the significance of this point later on. What concerns us here is the blinkered vision produced by the given division into fact and fiction, reality and fantasy. English continues: 'I agree with those who say that what a man sees makes little difference in his behavior if he can distinguish between fantasy and reality.'[23]

Yet shortly afterwards we are told that the threat men perceive in the existence of women, whether real or 'imagined', is 'something profoundly real in the male psychology', as are the fear and frustration thus produced. This perception, in other words, this domain of fantasy in the male psyche, is something so real that women ought to undergo a re-education process instead of indulging their own fancies that they are being hated and perceived in pornographic fashion by men.

On the other hand, English, like Gloria Steinem in her piece 'Erotica and Pornography: A Clear and Present Difference',[24] slips easily from discussing sexuality to discussing sexuality represented, with scant attention to the medium of representation she so lightly jumps. Steinem writes: 'No wonder the concepts of "erotica" and "pornography" can be so crucially different, and yet so confused. Both assume that *sexuality* can be separated from conception, and therefore can be used to carry a personal message'[25] (My emphasis). Steinem discusses both erotica and pornography as forms of sexuality (and by 'conception' here she means biological conception and 'childbirth',[26] rather than conceptualization). Her criterion for differentiating pornography from erotica is the quality of sex, the tenderness and attitudes of the partners involved, extrapolated directly from real-life sex. 'Perhaps one could simply say that erotica is about sexuality, but pornography is about power and sex-as-weapon – in the same way we have come to understand that rape is about violence, not really about sexuality at all.'[27]

The expression 'is about' as an apparent concession to the fact of representation is also transposed into the real-life situation of rape, and hence loses its meaning as a consideration of representation: rape is similarly 'about' violence! And from here Steinem goes over seamlessly to noting how women have often been forced by violent families (are they 'about' violence, too?) to confuse love with pain, passes, in other words, directly to the discussion of sexual politics in reality. Henceforth, erotica is a quality of sex, and so is pornography: 'Our bodies have too rarely been enough our own to develop erotica in our own lives, much less in art and literature.'[28] One would have thought the term should be 'eroticism', but the distinction between representations of sex on the one hand and sexual practices on the other is deliberately blurred by Steinem, in an attempt to negotiate the difficult connection, required by the law enforcers, between sex on paper and sex in bed or in dark alleys: 'Until we untangle the lethal confusion of sex with violence, there will be more pornography and less erotica. There will be little murders in our beds – and very little love.'[29]

The connection, felt as a gut instinct, is forged rhetorically, not argued out carefully by establishing the cultural relations between representations, fantasies and behaviour. Deirdre English, on the other hand, skirts along a partial analysis of this connection, but only in terms offered to her by the male theory of psychology where suddenly, or momentarily, the realm of fantasy assumes the status of the real. But she fails to develop this argument consistently (it does not, for instance, extend to the 'fears' of women). When discussing the 'positive' sexual material of desirable erotica, English follows in the footsteps of Steinem. Her argument about the psychology of fantasies was that pornography serves a certain function: 'Fantasies are employed because they *work* . . . They offer temporary relief to some kind of recurrent fear or tension.'[30] But, she argues, 'the "problems" that porn "solves" (how to sexually dominate women) are those posed by a sexist society.'[31] 'So porn, for one thing, keeps men and women ignorant – ignorant, in fact, of erotica.'[32]

Again, the term should have been 'eroticism', since English goes on to discuss 'the complaint that most women have about sex as dominated by men': 'that it is too fast, too rough, and too phallic'.[33] The sex, one takes it, is in bed rather than on paper. And in order to get better sex in bed, 'we need nonsexist sexual images – a lot more of them.'[34] The underlying preoccupation, apart from sexual politics for the bedroom, is one with a possible feminist aesthetic –

guidelines for feminist artists. This in itself is to my mind a misguided project, but what is striking in this context is the near disappearance of the feminist issue of pornography. English opened her article with an emphasis on the monumental factor of the pornography *industry*, but while she dwelt on its size, its power, and the magnitude of the profits involved in the first part of her article, it has virtually receded into oblivion by the time she comes to what might be considered her 'solution' to the question. It resurfaces briefly on the last page, following the plea for more positive images quoted above: 'what we need even more than women against pornography are women pornographers – or eroticists, if that sounds better.'[35] Feminism should 'confront misogyny with new images'.[36] If this is a political rather than an aesthetic argument, it might be considered even more utopian than total abolition. There are no practical suggestions as to how women should stage this intervention in, or take-over of, a four-billion dollar industry 'already partly mob-controlled', as English herself points out.[37] The suggestion seems to be that if you cannot beat them, join them and reform from within, except that any sense that there is anything to 'beat' has apparently dissolved in the face of the recognition that abolition is no answer to pornography, and as pornography and erotica have become, finally, interchangeable. And there is an even more dangerous, or untenable, suggestion that a change in the genitals of the producers of pornography will result in 'positive' images and the extinction of the problem of pornography.

Already the example of Judy Chicago's *Dinner Party* raised rather than solved the question: Does the gender of the artist eliminate the entire problematic of a table full of vaginas? English's own suggestion for 'positive images' continues to raise this question: 'I can imagine some pretty intriguing scenes of older women with younger men, images of different body types, images of nonphallocentric lovemaking.'[38] The pornography industry with its unbounded invention has already served us with images of 'different body types', just as it has given us the 'positive images' of strong, independent, feminist women (remember 'The Male Strikes Back'). I would not be surprised if it had also thought of exploiting the intriguing image of 'the older woman', a cliché certainly of the soft literary genre. And as if to rub in that we have lost sight entirely of the question of representation, English gives us a real-life situation:

> One of the more erotic sights I ever saw was years ago at a feminist conference. It was a hot summer day in Pennsylvania, and during a break in the weekend-long conference we gathered at an outdoor swimming pool. There were no men around, so we all stripped and swam naked – dozens of women, most of them perfect strangers . . . The effect was incredibly beautiful.[39]

How does English imagine men 'see' feminist conferences, even when these are on a cold day and there is no swimming pool? How have men (pornographers) seen so many convents and girls' schools? And how would a representation of such a scene, produced by a woman eroticist, fare in the world of representations?

English in fact demonstrates, if she does not explain, the problematic of 'positive images'. It is significant that this 'image' is produced at some length, with the aid of existing narrative conventions. 'One of the more erotic sights I ever saw' sets the soft focus and the camera angle. The hot summer day warms up the setting for what, by now, we already see coming: the innocent Susannas in the bath, believing themselves unobserved – 'there were no men around'. Ah, but there are: there are the readers who join in this scene as pure voyeurs, the Elders rustling the pages and lurking behind the viewfinders. English no doubt felt that as a participant herself she was not guilty of voyeurism. But she has offered the intimacy and immediacy of the event to a public spectatorship by means of an aesthetic mediation, like the white man in the picture, inviting us to the party. And she has framed the position for us: though a participant, she has turned observer, appraised the scene, and snap goes the Instamatic: 'the effect was incredibly beautiful'! The experience may have been beautiful, and is no doubt part of what English would like to capture, but she captures its effect, its aesthetic effect, its effect on the non-participant onlooker.

The aesthetic and the beautiful have their own histories, as do the conventions of producing beautiful effects. We as women share in the cultural apprenticeship of perceiving the 'beautiful' in certain ways, and these ways are indebted to the male perspective of the viewer. In *Ways of Seeing*, John Berger writes:

> Men look at women. Women watch themselves being looked at. This determines not only most relations between men and women but also the relation of women to themselves. The surveyor of woman in herself is male: the surveyed female. Thus she turns herself into an object – and most particularly an object of vision: a sight.[40]

English here gives us an example of this apprenticeship: surveying the conference, she turns surveyor of women and thus 'male', turning the women she surveys into objects, objects of vision for us, and most particularly into a sight: 'One of the more erotic sights I ever saw . . .'

One of the founders of aesthetics as a branch of philosophy, Immanuel Kant, helps us understand the aesthetic in the following way:

> Of certain products which are expected, partly at least, to stand on the footing of fine art, we say that they are *soul*less . . . A poem may be pretty and elegant, but it is soulless. A narrative has precision and method, but it is soulless. A speech on some festive occasion may be good in substance and ornate withal, but may be soulless. Even of a woman we may well say, she is pretty, affable, and refined, but soulless.[41]

Note that a pretty woman figures among a range of *products*. What Kant means by 'soul' 'in an aesthetical sense', is the 'animating principle in the mind' of the perceiver, his faculty of 'creating a second nature [art] out of the material supplied to it by actual nature'.[42]

If we wish to discern whether something is beautiful or
not, we do not refer the representation of it to the
Object [in reality] by means of understanding with a
view to cognition, but by means of the imagination . . .
we refer the representation to the Subject and its feeling
of pleasure and displeasure.[43]

This leads Kant to a 'definition of the beautiful . . . as an
object of delight apart from any interest'.[44] In other words, it
is a precondition for Kant that the aesthetic sense be divorced
from any interest in (cognition or understanding of) the
object of representation, and that the aesthetic pleasure
derived stem entirely from the 'genius' of the imagination of
the perceiver who is representing the object to himself. And
the notion of women as objects of aesthetic perception,
soulless until animated by the genius of the perceiver, is
firmly grounded in the very definition of the aesthetic.

The scene English describes has a 'beauty' to offer which is
based on understanding (experiencing) it, and women with
an interest in feminist conferences and in women can
cognitively grasp it. But it is not aesthetic beauty. By
contrast, looking at the scene, surveying it with an aesthetic
eye which catches the sight and the effect, is premised on the
absence of cognitive interest: only then does the scene offer
the pleasure of the beautiful of pure imaginative representation, the sheer disinterested beauty. Looking at the scene,
framing it, taking a picture ensures this disinterestedness by
imposing the structure of representation on it, opening up
the positions of the white men and the Instamatic, engender-
ing a disinterested audience. The sense of outrage produced
in some of us by the pornographic abuse of convents or girls'
schools derives precisely from a recognition that our idea of a
convent, our cognitive understanding of it, has not been
respected, has been sacrificed to a 'disinterested' imaginative
contemplation of it. In just this way, the participants of the
feminist conference have been turned into a bunch of naked
women, offered up for aesthetic/erotic contemplation.

The firm association of women with 'certain products
which are expected, partly at least, to stand on the footing of

fine art' should, if nothing else does, alert us to the suspicion that something might be a little peculiar with our notion of 'fine art'. The fact that 'fine art' is one of the obstacles to a clear definition of pornography should help the suspicion along a little further.

English's notion of acceptable or feminist erotica, like Steinem's, like Mary Whitehouse's, is based on the selection of acceptable content. Replace the bad/too-explicit/violent/too-fast and too-rough/loveless sex with good (not too-explicit) sex. In order to guarantee the selection of sex acceptable to women put women in charge of the selection, in charge of the representations. While this last suggestion has a lot to recommend it in general cultural terms, it is applied by English in terms of the biology of singular individuals, at which point it becomes both blatantly absurd and blatantly false. It ignores the fact of women's cultural apprenticeship to the male point of view, the viewpoint of the surveyer of women. History is full of women who produced virulent anti-women discourse, representations, and politics. The genitals themselves are no guarantee for gender ideology: there are gender traitors as there are class traitors.

The fallacy of the genital-credential argument is, in fact, revealed by the example English herself offers: what would we make of a Judy Chicago *Dinner Table* authored by a man? 'Such intangibles as intention, experience and context are everything in this', argues English weakly.[45] She is telling us, in other words, that we would make one hell of a row if such a *Dinner Table* were presented to the museums by a man. But this is not playing by the rules of art and the museum, which themselves are professedly entirely object-oriented. If we want to elevate Judy Chicago's *Dinner Table* to the spheres of art, then we have to accept the *Dinner Table* as a work of art, whether or not we later discover that its author was a male imposter. As an aesthetic object, its merit is supposed to derive entirely from the disinterested contemplation by the spectator, who will be uninfluenced by the artist's intentions or genitals. (That this profession of pure disinterestedness is somewhat hypocritical in the art world and the art market is not the point here. Germaine Greer has demonstrated the duplicity of the standards of art in *The Obstacle Race*,[46] but this might simply be an argument for a purer and more honest practice. English here accepts the principle of the aesthetic in its pure form.)

English, it seems to me, wants to have her cake of art and eat it, as the pro-erotica feminists want to fight pornography and keep it (as erotica). To rely on good intentions (or is it genitals?) on the part of the artist for the validation of a representation creates more problems than it hopes to solve. Intentions are notoriously unverifiable; besides, most pornographers would hasten to assure us that their intentions are of the best. They will tell us that they are in the business because they *love* women – compare the film *The Man Who Loved Women*. In fact, it is what they have been telling us all along. The Marquis de Sade sees himself as the liberator of women: 'Charming sex, you will be free: just as men do, you shall enjoy all the pleasures that Nature makes your duty, do not withhold yourselves from one. Must the more divine half of mankind be kept in chains by the other? Ah, break those bonds: nature wills it.'[47] And they are telling us again, in the 1980s, as they are trying to capture the women market for the 'adult business' (the franchise at last): 'The new pornographers [bring] a kind of porn liberation spirit to their work.'[48]

## Problem 5

# Subjects, Objects, and Equal Opportunities

'I do a lot for feminism,' Gloria Leonard, publisher of the soft-core magazine *High Society*, told me. 'I show women, and men too, that it's all right to be a sex object. That's part of what being a whole person is all about.'[1]

Under the glorious banner of Equal Opportunities we are likely finally to lose sight of what the critique of patriarchy, of sexism, of the objectification of women in representation is about. Good sex vs bad sex does not alter the structure of representation, just as the increasing use of male victims/ objects does not. Bernard Williams invited us to settle for the opportunity of exploitation on equal terms with men. The feminist challenge to advertising – that it exploits, degrades and objectifies women – is in danger of seeing itself neutralized as an increasing number of inane males are smiling off the posters and pages, clutching bottles of *Brut*. Now Gloria Leonard of *High Society* (an Equal Opportunities Employer) is showing us that it's alright to be a sex object since, look, the men over there are learning to be sex objects too! In the midst of these waves of progress, it might be well to go back to the question of what it means to turn a person into an object. I shall continue to base my analysis on the model of the objectification of women – the generic object in our culture.

The objectification of women means the simultaneous subjectification of men. The relationship, however, is usually put the other way round, as Simone de Beauvoir notes: 'He is the Subject, he is the Absolute – she is the Other.'[2] Yet the exclusive talk of the 'object', as in the quotation above by

Leonard, omits to tell us who is assuming the role of subject, just as Bernard Williams omitted to tell us who is the profiteer and the perpetrator in the equal exploitation of men and women. The discussion of the objectification of women in our culture concerns the *gender* of women. When Williams, or Leonard, show us exploited and objectified men, they show us singularized individuals. In the objectification of women as a gender, the subject, the objectifier, the surveyor of women is the male gender. In the gender equality envisaged by the feminist critique of patriarchy, exploitation of and supremacy over one gender by the other would no longer be possible; it would mean, in other words, the end of exploitation, not 'equal exploitation'. But where the false equal-opportunities ticket is waved at women and men, there is always a third party involved behind the scenes, who will take over the exploiting, oppressing, objectifying from the once supreme male gender. This third party, proffering individual males for sacrifice and promoting individual women to the rank of sacrificers, sees itself as gender-free: it creates a new class, consisting of males and females, the object-class of another analysis. It is increasingly this other powerful subject, behind the objectification of 'men and women' in *High Society*, behind the equal exploitation of Bernard Williams's blue movies, that we have to inquire after in this heyday of equal opportunities. Yet the model of this subject is the male gender, the objectification it operates is modeled on the objectification of women.

The objectification of women is a result of the subjectification of man. He is a pure subject in relation to an object, which means that he is not engaging in exchange or communication with that objectified person who, by definition, cannot take the role of a subject. In the analysis of the role of representations in society, we have seen that the object class of women, or of black people in Namibia and South Africa, has no voice, no subject position in the society. Social relationships are relations between subjects: if there is exchange or communication, each partner is and remains a subject or agent of action, or a subject of speech and communication. The roles are reciprocal, the situation is one of intersubjectivity.

In the structure of representation, the two subjects are the author and the spectator/reader, the white man and his guests. The woman is the object of exchange. This is the dominant relationship, which remains constant across varying 'contents'. There is, further, a scenario of represented action, exchange or communication – in the case of pornography, usually 'sex'. It is this represented action scenario which has attracted analysis in the debate about pornography: the feminist observation that the 'sex' is always violent sex. There are, it is true, examples of pornography where the woman is represented as a 'sex object' for the man represented; but there are many other pornographic scenarios where this is not the case. The pornographic image may consist only of the display of a woman – 'no men present'. Just as Thomas Kasire 'poses' in one picture all by himself. Or else the pornographic image may represent the woman as a strong, or willing and delighted participant in the action – as an active subject in the represented scenario. The pornographic representation may show a domineering female abusing a male sex object. It may show two women, in a variety of roles of subject and object, or it may show men in the same variety of roles. Pornography has exhausted the whole gamut of possible commutations of roles within the represented scenario. This is why experts tell us that there is no generalizing as to the victimization of women in pornography. This is also why the rescue of feminist erotica gets hopelessly entangled in the middle of the pornographic spectrum of scenarios: the feminist conference, the convent, the loving lesbians are already spoken for. The scenario itself is the wrong focus for an exclusive analysis of pornography: the structure of representation must be taken into consideration.

As the Namibia photographs showed us, there is an optional place for the white master-author in the picture: he poses in one of them, holding his victim by the chain; but he is absent from the other one. The author has gracefully withdrawn from his composition. His place, however, remains virtual: his object, objectified, his victim, victimized, indicates the place of a subject, the perpetrator of torture, the subject of objectification. In the case of the Namibia photograph, this virtual presence of the absent master is symbolized by the white arm intruding into the picture, but the picture itself is the true icon of its author.

As a speaker, I am always present as the subject of my speech: I may represent myself by means of the pronoun 'I' within my utterance, or I may never say 'I' or 'me' at all, and yet I am implicitly present, the author of my speech, the speech the token of my presence. The pornographer is the speaking 'I' of the pornographic representation, and he may or may not represent himself as the subject/master in the scenario of the picture. He is in direct communication with another subject, the spectator or reader – the white man's guest. In the picture or out of it, he objectifies the woman/victim for the reader, the viewing subject who contemplates the object. If the pornographic scenario represents the male master-subject, the woman object is twice objectified: once as object of the action in the scenario, and once as object of the representation, the object of viewing. The former objectification is optional, the latter is always present: it is a structural feature of pornographic representation.

The philosopher with his penchant for abstract symmetry at the expense of social and political factors will tell me that the speaker or the composer of representations may be male or female, that the viewer/reader may be male or female, the subject male or female.[3] Such symmetry, however, is only a most philosophical possibility, which has failed to be realized in the history of culture. In the political realm of reality, very different values adhere to the positions of subject and object: the role of subject means power, action, freedom, the role of object powerlessness, domination, oppression. The two roles are not equally desirable. Hence the role of subject constitutes a site for a power struggle.

The history of representation is the history of the male

gender representing itself to itself – the power of naming is men's. Representation is not so much the means of representing an object through imitation (matching contents) as a means of self-representation through authorship: the expression of subjectivity. Culture, as we know it, is patriarchy's self-image.

We owe it to the cultural experts, the experts of the arts and of literature, that we are in the habit of contemplating cultural products – materpieces – as pure aesthetic objects under the banner of aesthetics, rather than as forms of self-expression. This has not always been so, as we will show later. Today, we have an overwhelming object-orientation in the field of art (and other cultural products), which deflects attention away from the importance of the role of the subject, the producer of art. Instead, the role of the producer has been abstracted to such an extent that the philosopher tells us it is gender-free, androgynous, democratically open to all those talented enough, and that the role of receiver (spectator, reader) is equally neutral. The focus is on the aesthetic object, the work of art, and its aesthetic quality, which derives directly from the concept of beauty.

Although the notion of the aesthetic, as it has been posited by Kant, makes the aesthetic explicitly a function of the subject, we talk of beauty and the beautiful as if they were part of the object, as if they were 'objective'. Let us see how Kant describes this connection. To repeat, aesthetic apprehension consists of

> being conscious of [the] representation with an accompanying sensation of delight. Here the representation is referred wholly to the Subject, and what is more, to its feeling of life – under the name of feeling of pleasure or displeasure – and this forms the basis of a quite separate faculty of discriminating and estimating, that contributes nothing to knowledge.[4]

From this, Kant argues, we can deduce a second principle, that 'the beautiful is that which, apart from concepts, is represented as the object of universal delight.'[5] This is so because, 'where any one is conscious that his delight in an object is with him independent of interest, it is inevitable that he should look on the object as one containing ground of delight for all men.'[6] Since his delight is not based on interest in the object represented, 'but the Subject feels himself completely *free* in respect of the liking he accords to the object' – his liking is without 'reason' and thus disinterested.

> He must regard [his delight] as resting on what he may also presuppose in every other person; and therefore he must believe that he has reason for demanding a similar delight from every one. Accordingly he will speak of the beautiful as if beauty were a quality of the object . . . although [the judgement] is only aesthetic . . . The result is that the judgement of taste, with its attendant consciousness of detachment from all interest, must involve a claim to validity for all men . . . i.e. there must be coupled with it a claim to subjective universality.[7]

Judgements of taste, of aesthetic quality, 'must have a subjective principle, and one which determines what pleases and what displeases, by means of feeling only and not through concepts, but yet with universal validity. Such a principle, however, could only be regarded as a *common sense*.'[8]

The claim to universality stems from the fact of the disinterestedness with which the subject regards the represented object. If you think the picture of your mother beautiful, you are excused because you have an obvious interest in and knowledge of the person represented, but your judgement is not aesthetic. If you like the picture of a total stranger, who means nothing to you personally, then your judgement is aesthetic. You may also claim universal validity for your judgement, and demand a similar liking from any other man, with whom you share a common sense – of pleasure and displeasure.

A pretty woman, as we have seen, is at the centre of the consideration of the aesthetic. She is, from the start, among the objects. The subjects, for Kant, quite naturally are 'all men' (explicit in the English translation). The position of subject, in principle, is open to all people, but in practice the principle of universal validity has been tested among a limited number of subjects, those in the business of art and literature and taste. Little would we know if some subject – a peasant, a woman – had come along and disputed the universal feeling of pleasure produced by a particular representation, the subjective principle which determines what pleases and what displeases. The very formulation of this principle turns taste into an imperative, where only the individual who disagrees can be at fault. No common sense, that's all.

It does not matter if the claim to universal validity has not actually been upheld by philosophers; but the notion of 'disinterestedness' has become a corner-stone among assumptions in the domain of the artistic. Although the aesthetic is grounded in the feeling of pleasure, the feeling of life of the subject, the axiom of disinterestedness allows us to underplay the function of the subject and especially his responsibility, and emphasize the objective. Thus Walter Pater, following Kant, gives us a glimpse of the political potential of this disinterestedness. He writes: 'Art . . . is thus always striving to be independent of the mere intelligence, to become a matter of pure perception, to get rid of its responsibilities to its subject [matter, i.e. its object] or material.'[9] And Roland Barthes, in the modern age, consolidates the claim of 'the irresponsibility of the text',[10] the irresponsibility, for both, having shifted, like the feeling of life, from the subject into the aesthetic object – art, the text.

With the twentieth century's professionalization and systematization of the study of the arts and literature – the carving out of expertises – being 'objective' or scientific in method and having a 'specific set of objects (the "texts")' has become an imperative.[11] The objects themselves, the works of art or the representations are firmly separated from any objects they might represent in the world, separated, that is, from reality, in a sphere of their own: the aesthetic, the artistic, the literary – fiction, fantasy, art. Feminist critique will have to get them out of there again and bring them back into this world for discussion and analysis. The focus on content observed in so many discussions of pornography is a tribute to this object-orientation: we never really ask what the pornographer is trying to 'say' – what, in other words, is his responsibility as an author of a particular communication. Instead, we discuss disembodied ('detached') texts, films or images. The pornographer finds shelter behind his cultured brother, the artist. Like the artist, he is striving to make his product become independent of the mere intelligence (of critique, of understanding), to make it a matter of pure perception, and to get rid of his responsibilities towards his subject matter, the woman 'material'.

There are many kinds of interest, and there are therefore more than one kind of disinterestedness. The interest Kant refers to and which has to be absent from aesthetic apprehension is the cognitive interest in and understanding of the object represented. The lack of any such interest gives rise to the feeling of life and of pleasure in the subject. The delight thus derived from representations becomes the interest in the pursuit of the aesthetic, itself understood as 'contributing nothing to knowledge', as having no direct correspondence with or relevance to any real objects in the world. The pursuit of the aesthetic is thus in a different sense far from disinterested: it is the pursuit of pure self-interest, the pursuit of the pleasure and the feeling of life of the subject.

Women, real and represented, are central to the range of products expected (by whom?) to stand on the footing of fine art. Representing to oneself a real woman, stranger though she may be, as aesthetically pleasing is regarding her as such a product, soulless until animated, is objectifying her. By definition the operation has nothing to do with the woman herself – that would be 'interest' – it has solely to do with the feeling of pleasure to be derived from contemplating her. Women are an inseparable part of our understanding of beauty, and they are ubiquitously represented in the fine arts. The fact that men do not in the same way form the core of beauty and do not themselves range among the products expected to stand on the footing of fine art – except in a growing male homosexual sub-culture – leads us to two observations. First, it is a symptom of the fact that men are the Subjects in question, are the cultural authors as well as the cultural audience; and secondly, this might lead us to inquire more deeply into the nature of the feeling of life, of delight and of pleasure that is the hallmark of the aesthetic. Might the disinterested aesthetic pleasure perchance be gendered? Might it even be a version of the sexual?

After Freud, and within the contemporary framework of the literary and artistic, this is by no means an outrageous suggestion, on the contrary, it is proudly and explicitly endorsed. What is missing, simply, is a conscious connection between this sexualized pleasure and the immunity of art from any critique which is asking after the subject and his place in the real world. What is needed is an explicit juxtaposition of aesthetic disinterestedness, or the irresponsibility of the text on the one hand, and the blatant sexual interest of desire on the other. Instead, art and literature are treated as sanctuaries – worlds apart – where we play according to other rules, valid in those worlds, where the subject is the subject of the text and has no dimension in the real world. The rules, needless to say, are man-made, although the spheres are so sublime.

Turning another human being, another subject, woman, into an object is robbing her of her own subjectivity. The systematic representation of women-objects is not a question of a single subject representing to himself another subject, who happens to be a pretty woman, as an object. In cultural historical terms, it is the male gender, unified by a common sense, who assumes the subject position: as the authors of culture, men assume the voice, compose the picture, write the story, for themselves and other men, and *about* women. The fact that women, as individual subjects, have inserted themselves into the cultural audience (not without a struggle), have apprenticed to the male viewpoint which surveys women as objects and as products of fine art, is itself one of the most fundamental sources of female alienation: women have integrated in themselves, have internalized, a permanent outpost of the other gender – the male surveyor. The male gender, in turn, has extended into the whole space of subjectivity and self-expression – the available 'human' right to freedom of expression. In a partriarchal society, men have spread into and usurped the available space for agency, for power and for action; patriarchal culture validates and replicates this expansion of the male gender into human space. '*Men act* and *women appear*', writes Berger: subjects and objects. The patriarchal subject constitutes himself through the discourse of culture.

Viewing and self-expression are themselves actions in the world, actions performed by the culture's legitimated subjects. In the structure of representation, the act of perception, of viewing and of self-expression, is predominant and overlays the represented action of a (potentially) represented agent. The (optional) agent in the scenario goes over into the roles of author and viewer: the place of the action-subject, the place of the hero, is the locus of identification for the viewer. Man the action-subject is identical with man the viewing subject. The ultimate symptom of this are the hundreds of thousands of men ejaculating into a bucket in their booths at the peep shows: subjectivity of viewing goes over seamlessly into agency in the world. The performative representation of the live peep show, like so many other cultural representations (like the one of the two photographs of Thomas Kasire), represents only the object. The plot, the action between the imaginary male and the represented woman-object spills over into the structure of representation: the viewer has to imagine himself into the plot vacancy, play the hero and represent the action to himself. He does so in his solitary booth with bucket. The so-called soft-porn, which does not depict any violent action (erotica for the feminists), which does not depict explicit sexual action (for the censorship lobby), follows an identical pattern: what is given, simply, is the object – the spread-eagled woman in the soft-core magazines, the smiling, inviting, sexy, erotic, beautiful, pretty (aesthetic) woman in the rest of our cultural products. The fantasy of porn is not fully depicted, it is not identical with the 'content' of representation, it is to be completed by the active subject, the viewer-hero of the representation. The zone of pornography-fantasy stretches from the viewing subject to the doing subject: what he is doing is watching, imagining, fantasizing, producing the feeling of life, delight and pleasure in himself, with masturbating as an optional extra.

It is not difficult to see why women fear that the doing might extend even further. It is not difficult to envisage a continuing process in the 'adult business' of live peep-shows to a point where instead of a bucket some other 'object' might be supplied. As it is, the viewing or peeping itself is already a mixed 'doing': from behind their metal slots, the viewers may view with their eyes, their hands and their tongues.[12]

It is possible, however, to surmise that the current development of the 'adult business' is not tending towards a live 'doing' of a sexual scenario with real women, coming full circle back to ordinary prostitution (or rape for their clientele who want to have it gratis). Rather, the fingering and tonguing in the peep-show are part of the peeping, aids of the medium, like cinema-scope and stereo sound, improved 'reality effects' the better to stimulate the imagination. The goal, under this perspective, is not 'live sex', with real women; the goal is the feeling of life, the pleasure of the subject. The pleasure is more fully realizable under the sole control of the subject, through the total objectification of the 'object'. Real-life women, as we know, have a nasty tendency to assert their own subjectivity at the most inopportune moments, disturbing and interrupting the pleasure of the subject. Fantasy, that is, the unadulterated pleasure of the subject, is a great deal more popular than the (troublesome) interaction with another subject. It is, culturally, in the process of superseding intersubjective action.

Patronizing the subject position, refusing to grant subjectivity to another subject in interaction, is the fundamental egotism and the fundamental solipsism of the male culture. As Andrea Dworkin notes: 'The power of men is first a metaphysical assertion of self, an *I am* that exists a priori, bedrock, absolute, no embellishment or apology required, indifferent to denial or challenge.'[13] It does not, of course, exist a priori: it is made to look a priori with the help of the cultural self-image, the culture of mankind. It does quite evidently require apology, for why else this repeated apology and self-justification which is the discourse of culture, a culture which, in its careful construction, has the permanent job of editing out, suppressing and silencing any denial and challenge offered to it through the contribution of women? The excavation operation conducted by contemporary feminist scholars reveals not only that such a challenge, such a contribution by women, has existed through most of the history of culture, but that the male producers of the cultural self-image have systematically controlled this contribution through their economic, social and political power, their position of supremacy in the 'public' organization of society which permits them to silence the cultural voice of women. Dale Spender's *Women of Ideas (And What Men Have Done to Them)*, Joanna Russ's *How to Suppress Women's Writing* and Tillie Olsen's *Silences* are only a beginning.[14]

The censorship experts are asking for proof that men who have looked at pornography will go and do something similar (to the 'content') in the world. So long as we see sexual crime as the (sole) reality and pornography (exclusively) as pornographic content, we will never find a satisfactory description of the relationship between 'fantasy' and 'reality'. 'So long as [the violent fantasies] stay within the world of pornography they are still only fantasies,' argues Deirdre English; 'what a man sees makes little difference in his behaviour, if he can distinguish between fantasy and reality.' What the men are doing in the world is continuing to *see* – to see women as objects of their pleasure and their feeling of life. It is quite enough 'behaviour' in my opinion. What the man is doing is watching pornography, seeing, fantasizing, and he is doing this already in the world. And he continues to view in the real, without any difference: in fact, he sees nothing at all except what he represents to himself. Under his aesthetic gaze any woman, known or unknown, turns into the 'stranger', that object of no interest except for its capacity to stimulate the subject's feeling of life.

The fundamental problem at the root of men's behaviour in the world, including sexual assault, rape, wife battering, sexual harassment, keeping women in the home and in unequal opportunities and conditions, treating them as objects for conquest and protection – the root problem behind the reality of men's relations with women, is the way men see women, is Seeing.

The censorship experts are asking for proof that men who consume pornography will go and behave 'pornographically' in the world. What further proof do we need of man's behaviour in the world than his cultural self-representation – the culture from high to low, from hard to soft to aesthetic? The image is made in the image of its maker, after his likeness, and not the other way round.

As usual, the pornographer himself is more honest and more astute about pornography than are the cultural experts engaged in defending it. Ron Martin, producer of a live sex show in New York, is asked by his interviewer if he does not think that he degrades women for profit. His reply: 'I know I do. So does *The New York Times*. I have one girl who felt degraded every time she stepped outside. She came here because she was constantly getting hit up by men anyway, so why not get paid? Is working here any more degrading than walking down the street?'[15]

In the newspaper we read of the murder of a four-year old girl by a 45-year-old man, who 'was well-known to . . . police as a compulsive child sex offender'.[16] He had previously sexually assaulted two girls, and 'was charged and acquitted, although indecent photographs of the girls were found in his flat later'.[17] Producing pornography was a part of his sexual assault on the girls, part of his action in the world. If there is any chronology between his criminal behaviour and the representation of it, the behaviour comes first, the desire to represent it after. The look through the camera, prefiguring the look at the picture, creating a 'world of fantasy' out of the real, or creating, in Kant's words, 'a second nature out of the material supplied to it by actual nature'. Reality is but the raw 'material' for another, 'higher' reality, the reality of the subject. Or are the 'indecent pictures' any less pornographic because they are 'fact' rather than 'fiction', according to the fiction experts?

In the business of pornographic representation, the objectified and represented woman victim seems to be the only element pertaining unambiguously to 'fiction'. If we consider the men in the live peep shows, their fantasizing, their viewing, are real, their involvement in the 'represented action' or the plot is real, as viewing that extends to doing, fingering, tonguing. The only make-believe aspect of the whole show is the woman–object, behaving according to a fantasy scenario authored by the producing institution and its clientele together. In the case of Pat Cowan, an actress who presented herself for a role at the theatre, she was the only one who thought that the theatre was engaged in make-believe. 'As she acted out an argument scene . . . the black male playwright picked up a sledgehammer and bludgeoned her to death from behind.'[18] The man: author of the 'play', *metteur-en-scène* of the 'acting out' of a real murder, master-actor in his own scenario.

The male gender's project of constituting male subjectivity is a serious business that has nothing to do with fictional and playful fantasy. It is the means by which the male subject convinces himself that he is real, his necessary production of a feeling of life. He feels the more real, the less real the Other, the less of a subject the Other, the less alive the Other. And the reality he creates for himself through his cultural self-representation is the Authorized Version of reality, the dominant reality for all of us, the common sense which determines what pleases and what displeases.

# Why Look at Women?

John Berger has done much to illuminate our ways of seeing in his book, *Ways of Seeing* (1972).[1] His later book, *About Looking* (1980), contains an essay, 'Why Look at Animals?' It is well worth reading in its own right. In the present context, however, it has an additional uncanny dimension: re-reading his essay while substituting 'women' for 'animals' gives us as sobering an account of the implications of the representation of women as the original gives us of animal imaging.

Berger takes nineteenth- and twentieth-century attitudes towards animals and tries to understand how these came about.

> The 19th century, in western Europe and North America, saw the beginning of a process, today being completed by 20th century corporate capitalism, by which every tradition which has previously mediated between man and nature was broken. Before this rupture, animals constituted the first circle of what surrounded man . . . They were the man at the centre of his world. Such centrality was of course economic and productive. Whatever the changes in productive means and social organisation, men depended upon animals for food, work, transport, clothing.
>
> Yet to suppose that animals first entered the human imagination as meat or leather or horn is to project a 19th century attitude backwards across the millenia.[2]

Re-read this passage, substituting 'women' for 'animals', and considering the four-billion-dollar corporate capitalism of the pornography industry which makes us think that women had always entered male consciousness in the form of meat in want of a hiding. For 'transport' put 'reproduction'.

Berger then goes on to consider earlier attitudes to animals, the projection of 'magical functions, sometimes oracular, sometimes sacrificial' on to them (p. 2). Similar functions, of course, have been projected into women, so that we can read on, with our substitution of 'women' for 'animals':

> [Women] are born, are sentient and are mortal. In these things they resemble man. In their superficial anatomy – less in their deep anatomy – in their habits, in their time, in their physical capacities, they differ from man. They are both like and unlike. (p. 2)

The basis of every argument on gender differences, from Aristotle to Arianna Stassinopoulos or the Government White Paper *Equality for Women*,[3] is the superficial anatomy, which renders women 'unlike' men, and which, until today, has far outweighed whatever might render them 'like'. 'Unlike' is the basic presupposition, 'like' is then what fascinates man and appears to him uncanny.

> The eyes of a [woman] when they consider a man are attentive and wary . . . [S]he does not reserve a special look for man. But by no other species except man will the [woman's] look be recognised as familiar . . . Man becomes aware of himself returning the look.
>
> The [woman] scrutinises him across a narrow abyss of non-comprehension. This is why the man can surprise the [woman]. Yet the [woman] – even if domesticated – can also surprise the man. The man too is looking across a similar, but not identical, abyss of non-comprehension. And this is so wherever he looks. He is always looking across ignorance and fear. And so, when he is *being seen* by the [woman], he is being seen as his surroundings are seen by him. His recognition of this is what makes the look of the [woman] familiar. And yet the [woman] is distinct, and can [must] never be confused with man. Thus a power is ascribed to [woman], comparable with human power but never coinciding with it . . .

The relationship may become clearer by comparing the look of [a woman] with the look of another man. Between two men the two abysses are, in principle, bridged by language. Even if the encounter is hostile and no words are used (even if the two speak different languages), the *existence* of language allows that at least one of them, if not both mutually, is confirmed by the other. Language allows men to reckon with each other as with themselves. (pp. 2–3)

Woman, in the history of culture, has occupied a place on a par with animals. She has been recognized as similar but different: in her look man recognizes himself. In her look, however, he experiences fear and ignorance: he does not like *being seen*, abrogating the subjectivity of his own look and becoming the object of another's look. The subject function of looking must be preserved and reserved for him.

In the history of culture, woman has been denied the function of speech. Language, the potential for bridging the abysses between individuals, the bridge to intersubjectivity, must be reserved for men, so that they can mutually recognize, mutually confirm each other. If men allowed women their voice, they would have to reckon with them as with themselves. The bonding between two men, even if they are 'hostile', is stronger than any bond between a man and a woman; the recognition between men, even if hostile, is that of belonging to a common species.

No [woman] confirms man, either positively or negatively. The [woman] can be killed and eaten [metaphorically speaking] so that [her] energy is added to that which the hunter already possesses. The [woman] can be tamed so that [she] supplies and works for the peasant. But always [her] lack of common language, [her] silence, guarantees [her] distance, [her] distinctness, [her] exclusion, from and of man. (pp. 3–4)

No neater account of the history of patriarchy, of men's absorption of women's energy. Compare the *United Nations Report* 1980:

Women constitute half the world's population, perform nearly two thirds of its work hours, receive one tenth of the world's income and own less than one-hundredth of the world's property.[4]

'The greatest virtue of a woman is her silence,' claims a Sicilian proverb, 'Nothing is so unnatural as a talkative woman,' goes a Scottish saying. 'Silence gives the proper grace to women,' writes Sophocles in *Ajax*.[5] The silence of women, ordained by men, guarantees women's distinctness.

> Just because of this distinctness, however, a [woman's] life, never to be confused with a man's, can be seen to run parallel to his . . . With their parallel lives, [women] offer man a companionship which is different from any offered by human exchange. Different because it is a companionship offered to the loneliness of man as a species. (p. 4)

What better description of that patriarchal institution, marriage, for most of its historical existence such an 'unspeaking companionship', 'offered' to the loneliness of the male species without thereby affecting his species-specific malaise, without bridging the abyss of his self-inflicted solipsism, since he deems himself alone master of language. The connection between women's and animals' relationship to man in fact resides exactly here, as Berger shows, quoting from Lévi-Strauss:

> We know what animals do and what beaver and bears and salmon and other creatures need, because once our men were married to them and they acquired this knowledge from their animal wives. (Hawaiian Indians quoted by Lévi-Strauss in *The Savage Mind*.) (p. 2).

Marriage, the 'unspeaking companionship', fundamentally different from any offered by human exchange.

> Such unspeaking companionship was felt to be so equal that often one finds the conviction that it was man who lacked the capacity to speak with [women]. (p. 4)

A dawning suspicion, yet never strong enough to challenge the received assumption of women's silence and man's capacity to use language. On the contrary, the belief in woman's distinctness becomes imperative: while woman 'can never be confused with man', now a woman's life *is* '*never to be* confused with a man's'.

Berger argues that man's fascination with the silent species centres around the 'animals as an *intercession* between man and his origin' (p. 4). It is not difficult to see how this applies *a fortiori* to man's anxious fascination with the silent sex, an intercession indeed between him and his origin.

> An animal's blood flowed like human blood, but its species was undying and each lion was Lion, each ox was Ox. (pp. 4–5)

Woman, too, has been seen as timeless, unchanging, Nature. Her blood flows like human blood, but the 'eternal feminine' is undying, and every woman is Woman.

> This – maybe the first existential dualism – was reflected in the treatment of [women]. They were subjected *and* worshipped, bred *and* sacrificed. (p. 5)

Oppressed and put on a pedestal, endowed with magical and oracular power and burnt as witches.

> Today the vestiges of this dualism remain among those who live intimately with, and depend upon [women]. A peasant becomes fond of his pig and is glad to salt away his pork. (p. 5)

A man may become fond of his wife and is glad to make her his maid and housewife. A man may love women and is glad to consume them in pornography.

> What is significant, and is so difficult for the urban stranger to understand, is that the two statements in that sentence are connected by an *and* and not by a *but*. (p. 5)

The feminist critic, alienated as an urban stranger from her pig existence, does not find this peasant logic of *and* not *but* difficult to understand, so much as why it goes by the name of love. Perhaps it is neither 'and' nor 'but', but *because*.

Berger now goes over to representation:

> The parallelism of their similar/dissimilar lives allowed animals [and women] to provoke some of the first questions and offer answers. The first subject matter for painting was animal. (p. 5)

Not long after, it was followed, and certainly superseded, by woman.

> In his book on totemism, Lévi-Strauss comments on Rousseau's reasoning: 'It is because man originally felt himself identical to all those like him (among which, Rousseau explicitly says, we must include animals [and among which, I insist, we must include women]) that he came to acquire the capacity to distinguish *himself* as he distinguishes *them*' . . . Animals were seen in eight out of twelve signs of the zodiac. Among the Greeks, the sign of each of the twelve hours of day was an animal . . . The examples are endless. Everywhere animals offered explanations, or more precisely, lent their name or character to a quality, which, like all qualities, was, in its essence, mysterious. (pp. 6–7)

Think of all the female personifications, especially of qualities, from virtue to justice, the Muses, countries and ships.

> What distinguished man from [women] was the human capacity for symbolic thought. (p. 7)

What distinguishes man from woman is his access to representation, to cultural symbolization, the power of naming, in which he uses women, along with all the other silent animals, as symbols, as objects for representation.

Berger uses the generic word 'man' advisedly in his essay. It does, in all instances, mean man and male, never 'human' in the sense of men and women. His use of 'human' occasionally, in distinction from 'animal', goes with the general use of 'human' as in 'human rights', applying in the overwhelming majority of cases to men and men only. The essay reads entirely plausibly with the substitution of 'women' for 'animals'. It would read entirely implausibly with the substitution of 'women and men' for 'man'. Woman, in the cultural perspective, is much closer to the animal Other than to the hu-man subject.

However, Berger's analysis then goes over to the 'feminization' of a class of men when he traces the process he set out to study, namely the reduction of the animal to an industrial commodity.

> In the first stages of the industrial revolution, animals were used as machines. As also were children. (p. 11)

As also were women.

> Later, in the so-called post-industrial societies, they are treated as raw material. Animals required for food are processed like manufactured commodities . . . This reduction of the animal, which has a theoretical as well as economic history, is part of the same process as that by which men have been reduced to isolated productive and consuming units. Indeed, during this period an approach to animals often prefigured an approach to man. (p. 11)

While the anthropological subject of culture, the subject of representation, is the male gender – in Berger's analysis 'man' – there is another subject emerging here in the economic analysis. The analysis of species – man/animal – and the analysis of gender – male/female – is going over into another analysis of exploitation: that by producers of consumer/workers. The gender of the economic subject is still male, is modeled on and arises out of the supreme male gender, but it is no longer identical with the whole of the male gender as we enter a class analysis.

As the work of feminists has shown, class analysis does not simply apply to 'human' society, but has been carried out predominantly in terms of the male gender and needs the correction of the gender–class analysis supplied by feminist critique.[6] Gender, however, lends a powerful cultural metaphor to oppression, as the working class becomes the object to the economic subject, becomes objectified, 'feminized', animalized, commodified.

> F. W. Taylor who developed the 'Taylorism' of the time-motion studies and 'scientific' management of industry proposed that work must be 'so stupid' and so phlegmatic that he (the worker) 'more nearly resembles in his mental make-up the ox than any other type'. (p. 11)

And Berger points to the close connection between social conditioning and animal experiments. Yet animals, instead of disappearing under the pressure of the industrial process, multiply.

> Never have there been so many household pets as are to be found today in the cities of the richest countries . . . In the past, families of all classes kept domestic animals [women] because they served a useful purpose – guard dogs, hunting dogs, mice-killing cats, and so on. (p. 12)

In the past, domestic women – wives, daughters, unmarried sisters and so on – were kept by 'families' of all classes because they served a useful purpose: they were part of the household economy.

> The practice of keeping animals [women] regardless of their usefulness, the keeping, exactly, of *pets* . . . is a modern innovation, and, on the social scale on which it exists today, is unique. It is part of that universal but personal withdrawal into the private small family unit, decorated or furnished with mementoes from the outside world, which is such a distinguishing feature of consumer societies. (p. 12)

The practice of keeping women as pets, regardless of their (economic) usefulness, is a modern innovation, a result of the industrial revolution and the rise of the bourgeoisie – at least to the extent to which it exists today, especially in the cities of the richest countries, and in the richest families of the poorest countries as well. With the growing use of the mass of women as the cheapest, sub-standard labour force, the keeping of an individual woman pet in the private home has become the dominant fashion. As the angel in the house, a status symbol of the man who does not need a working wife, she is one of those decorations and furnishings of the bourgeois home of the consumer society. As Nora says in Ibsen's *A Doll's House*: 'Our home has been nothing but a playroom. I have been your dollwife, just as at home I was Papa's doll.'[7] And here, a perfect description of the languid salon female of the nineteenth-century bourgeois household:[8]

> The small family living unit lacks space, earth, other animals, seasons, natural temperatures, and so on. The pet [the lady of the house] is either sterilised or sexually isolated, extremely limited in [her] exercise, deprived of almost all other animal [woman] contact, and fed with artificial foods. This is the material process which lies behind the truism that pets come to resemble their masters . . . They are the creatures of their owner's way of life. (p. 12)

In the case of the female pet, she is the creature of the life-style her owner imposes on her and her lap dog. The owner himself, of course, has access to the space beyond the limited family unit: he exercises in the world, known as the 'public' domain. Berger goes on to examine the pet's owner:

> Equally important is the way the average owner regards his pet [woman]. (Children are, briefly, somewhat different.) The pet [woman] *completes* him, offering responses to aspects of his character which would otherwise remain unconfirmed. He can be to his pet what he is not to anybody or anything else. Further-more the pet [woman] can be conditioned to react as though [she], too, recognises this. The pet offers [her] owner a mirror to a part that is otherwise never

reflected. But since in this relationship the autonomy of both parties has been lost (the owner has become the-special-man-he-is-only-to-his-pet, and the [woman] has become dependent on [her] owner for every physical need), the parallelism of their separate lives has been destroyed. (pp. 12–13)

This describes the dominant romantic conception of 'love marriage', the sentimental marriage that supersedes economic union. It is widely regarded as an improvement on, a progress in civilization from the earlier economic marriage, both by the western world and by the bourgeois parts of the developing world who aspire to western industrialization and feed on imported western values.

And consider the implications of polygamy, an additional potential for status symbolization, through the acquisition not of a single pet, but of a whole little zoo of them:

When they were founded . . . [zoos] brought considerable prestige to the national capitals. The prestige was not so different from that which had accrued to the private royal menageries. These menageries, along with gold plate, architecture, orchestras, players, furnishings, dwarfs, acrobats, uniforms, horses, art and food, had been demonstrations of an emperor's or king's power and wealth. (p. 19)

The bourgeois king of the family does things just on a smaller scale, but his ménage – pets, architecture, furnishings, gold plate, food etc. – is just as much a source of prestige to him as the extended menagerie is to the emperor. And in certain circles the keeping of a rare, imported exotic pet or wife adds a similar prestige as does the acquisition of a somewhat more exotic animal pet than the common indigenous variety.

Now Berger comes to representation proper:

The cultural marginalisation of [women] is, of course, a more complex process than their physical marginalisation. The [women] of the mind cannot be so easily dispersed. Sayings, dreams, games, stories, superstitions, the language itself, recall them. The [women] of the mind, instead of being dispersed, have been co-opted into other categories so that the category [*woman*] has lost its central importance. Mostly they have been co-opted into the *family* and into the *spectacle*.

Those co-opted into the family somewhat resemble pets. But having no physical needs or limitations as pets do, they can be totally transformed into human puppets. (p. 13)

Berger cites the drawings of Beatrix Potter or the productions of the Walt Disney industry as animal examples. The bourgeois novel and the industry of romantic fiction would be a counterpart for the construction of domestic 'mind women'.

The animals transformed into spectacle have disappeared in another way. In the windows of bookshops at Christmas, a third of the volumes on display are animal picture books. (p. 14)

There is no shortage of women picture books, especially in the photography departments of the bookshops.

Baby owls or giraffes [baby dolls or long lean models], the camera fixes them in a domain which, although entirely visible to the camera, will never be entered by the spectator. All [women] appear like fish seen through the plate glass of an aquarium. The reasons for this are both technical and ideological: Technically, the devices used to obtain ever more arresting images – hidden cameras, telescopic lenses, flashlights, remote controls and so on – combine to produce pictures which carry with them numerous indications of their normal *invisibility*. (p. 14)

The Susannas in the bath must think themselves alone, or look as if they did: soft-core erotica representations of women often simulate the intimacy of privacy, of the women's domain, a domain normally closed to the male eye but made accessible to it by the 'hidden camera' – through artificial composition and posing – giving a peep through the key-hole into the boudoir, the girls' school, the bathroom, the convent, or simply upon a woman 'alone'.

> In the accompanying ideology, [women] are always the observed. The fact that they can observe us has lost all significance. They are the objects of our ever-extending knowledge. What we know about them is an index of our power, and thus an index of what separates us from them. The more we know, the further away they are. (p. 14)

It is what feminists have been saying for a long time. (Remember all those shelves in the library full of books about women by men, so much ever-extending knowledge.) The fact that women can observe men has lost all significance. Their contribution to knowledge has been declined, thank you; for it does not enhance 'our' knowledge, and 'our' power, to be the object of analysis and observation. Knowledge about men and produced by women would not only reduce the power of men, but also the distance which separates women from men.

> Yet in the same ideology, as Lukács points out in his *History and Class Consciousness*, nature is also a value concept . . . 'Nature . . . can be understood as that aspect of human inwardness which has remained natural, or at least tends or longs to become natural again'. (p. 15)

In the same ideology, Woman is equated with Nature and the values of the natural.

> According to this view of nature, the life of a wild animal becomes an ideal, an ideal internalised as a feeling surrounding a repressed desire. The image of a wild animal becomes the starting point of a day-dream: a point from which the day-dreamer departs with his back turned. (p. 15)

Alongside the domestication of women household pets, the institutionalization of the sterilized, desexualized self-sacrificial angel in the house, there arises a day-dream of the wild animal-woman, the sexual beast, an image which is becoming ever more pressing today after a long suppression of desire. An example from the music scene is Vanity's LP *Wild Animal* (RCA). A French magazine reviews it as follows: 'She rubs herself, rears like a horse (*se cabre*), she hesitates, this girl is a rare animal. Prince had exploited her sexy bestiality with the group "Vanity 6" . . . When Vanity murmurs her sweetnesses, one glides into the sensuality of one of the coming great singers of America.'[9] The cover shows Vanity, the singer, with the 'eyes of a tiger' and the 'mane of a lion', clutching fur to her bosom.

Berger thinks there is confusion in this dream. He quotes a news story about a woman who won a 'grant-a-wish' charity competition, and who expressed the wish to cuddle and kiss a lion. She was taken to the lions' compound of a safari park, but

> as she bent forward to stroke the lioness, Suki, it pounced and dragged her to the ground. Wardens later said: 'We seem to have made a bad error of judgement. We have always regarded the lioness as perfectly safe'. (p. 15)

A cautionary tale, perhaps, for those men who day-dream of kissing and cuddling the wild woman beast; and for the wardens whose 'knowledge' of women and beasts may lead to grave errors of judgement.

Berger's discussion of zoos makes interesting comparison with the more recent but mushrooming peep-show, the woman-zoo.

> Public zoos came into existence at the beginning of the period which was to see the disappearance of animals from daily life. The zoo to which people go to meet animals [women], to observe them, to see them, is, in fact, a monument to the impossibility of such encoun-

ters. Modern zoos are an epitaph to a relationship which was as old as man. They are not seen as such because the wrong questions have been addressed to zoos. (p. 19)

Peep-shows signal a period where women are disappearing from daily life, where the category of woman 'has lost its central importance' and man-made mind concepts of women have been co-opted into other categories; where the fact that women can observe 'us' has lost all significance, and where the concept of women as *subjects* has lost all meaning. The daily life in question, of course, is the daily life of man, and the mind in which woman has been recategorized is the mind of the male gender. It little matters that there are still as many women as ever – about 50 per cent – and more of them actually visible in public life, just as it little matters that there exist as many animals as ever (though fewer species). The absorption of individual women into public life means the distancing of these women from the category of 'women' and granting them (surrogate) 'human' status – viz the denial of many professional women of their gender identity and their assertion of their 'human' and professional qualities. The ever-growing achievements of individual women have been singularly ineffective in the rehabilitation of the category of 'women'. Hence the existence which counts (ideologically, culturally) is not absolute existence, but existence which impinges on man, his daily life, his consciousness. And from these, animals and women, as significant categories, are disappearing fast. They reappear as meat on his plate and in his leisure magazines, in ever-increasing abundance.

The peep-show, as I have analysed it in problem 5, does not in fact develop in a movement from represented woman towards real woman: it is, on the contrary, a monument to the impossibility of any encounter between man and woman, an epitaph to a relationship which was as old as man. The 'people' who go there to 'meet' women go there to observe them, to see them, but not to encounter them.

In the 19th century, public zoos were an endorsement of

modern colonial power. The capturing of the animals was a symbolic representation of the conquest of all distant and exotic lands. (p. 19)

Peep-shows and the pornography industry in the twentieth century are an endorsement of the modern colonial power of the male gender over the female gender. Colonial power has always included a double colonization of the female gender and expressed itself especially through this double conquest, viz the rape of the Sabines, the taking of women slaves and concubines from conquered tribes, and the ritual rape of women by conquering soldiers into the modern age. Similarly, the reaction to colonial power, the rebellion of colonized males, is 'symbolized' through the conquest and rape by the excolonized man of the colonizers' women.[10]

A look at representations specifically geared to children gives us a further idea of the recategorization of 'mind-animals' and 'mind-women'. Berger notes that children in the industrialized world are swamped with animal imagery – toys, cartoons etc. – but that in the preceding centuries there had been but few animal toys' 'and these did not pretend to realism, but were symbolic' (p. 20).

The difference was that between a traditional hobby horse and a rocking horse: the first was merely a stick with a rudimentary head which children rode like a broom handle: the second was an elaborate 'reproduction' of a horse, painted realistically, with real reins of leather, a real mane of hair, and designed movement to resemble that of a horse galloping. The rocking horse was a 19th century invention. (p. 20)

Without necessarily claiming a complete parallelism between animal toys and 'human' toys in terms of their proportions, a similar development certainly took place with regard to dolls. Earlier, a rag doll would symbolize a doll-child but, increasingly, realistic reproductions of 'humans' were being produced, and the nineteenth century is famous for them. Porcelain heads and extremely elaborate dress simulated proper little Victorian girls.

> This new demand for verisimilitude in animal toys led
> to different methods of manufacture. The first stuffed
> animals were produced, and the most expensive were
> covered with real animal skin . . . the manufacture of
> realistic animal toys coincides, more or less, with the
> establishment of public zoos. (p. 21)

The demand for verisimilitude in dolls also led to the
manufacture of dolls with real rather than artificial hair, to
dolls with orifices and with moving eyelids, and finally to the
speaking doll. What is more, dolls are no longer toy children
with round lumpy bodies, but they are either realistic babies,
often life-size, or else they are 'young ladies', full-breasted,
well curved and pouting, preferably blond. The American
doll 'Barbie' has captured an international market, diffusing
the western stereotype of the secretary-wife, and she comes
complete with domestic outfits, the bourgeois home in a
packet. For boys, the counterpart stereotype 'Action-man' is
similarly internationally pervasive, and he too comes complete with action-loaded environments, mostly wars of every
kind.

Thus the large-scale manufacture of people toys corres-
ponds with an increased ideological diffusion of gender
stereotypes – 'mind people' – the process of the recategorization of woman leading the way, but now being followed by
a recategorization of man. It appears that an approach to
animals preceded an approach to women which eventually
leads to the same approach to men. Experiments are being
made of male strip-shows for a female audience: the
establishment of women-zoos prefigures a possible introduction of men-zoos, if the 'adult business' has its way. The
driving motivation behind this process is the distillation of
power: from the establishment of 'human' supremacy over
the animal kingdom (always the metaphor is feudal), to the
supremacy of the male over the female gender, to the
formation of a capitalist elite of economic and ideological
subjects. Meanwhile the zoo at Miami exhibits a specimen of
'Urban Man' in an ill-conceived jocularity which bespeaks a

confusion over the implications of zoos and 'man's' relationship to them.[11]

> Zoos, realistic animal toys and the widespread commercial diffusion of animal imagery, all began as animals started to be withdrawn from daily life. One could suppose that such innovations were compensatory. Yet in reality the innovations themselves belonged to the same remorseless movement as was dispersing the animals. The zoos, with their theatrical decor for display, were in fact demonstrations of how animals had been rendered absolutely marginal. (p. 24)

The remorseless diffusion of gender stereotypes, of ready-made and imperative life-styles, of regulated uniform 'relationships' – the ideological diffusion of 'mind images' of humans – through the remorseless diffusion of their material basis – consumer goods – renders human subjects increasingly marginal. The techniques for conditioning began with animals and were perfected on women, and they are in the process of extending to men. Within human culture, woman has been the generic object, marginalized for centuries, stereotyped more effectively and remorselessly since the industrial revolution. Both the cultural output, predicated upon the aestheticization and objectification of woman, and the representational side of the consumer-goods industry – advertising – testify to this. But we find ourselves now at the juncture where men are drawn into the same process too, in the era of equal opportunities.

> The reproduction of animals in images . . . was competitively forced to make animals ever more exotic and remote. (p. 24)

The reproduction of women in images makes woman-images ever more exotic and remote – remote from any real experience of women. Women starve themselves to death in an attempt to force their bodies to correspond to the surreal body-shapes designed by the fashion designers. They kill their own experience in an attempt to conform to existences imaged for them. The images and ideals are getting ever more 'exotic' and remote.

The sex-object woman envelops herself in animal skins – the rarer the animal species, the more prestigious the woman who wears it and the man who buys it. The woman-image in the woman-zoo peep-show wallows on fake tiger skins, surrounded by exotic and theatrical props remote from any woman's real life environment.

> The zoo cannot but disappoint. The public purpose of zoos is to offer visitors the opportunity of looking at animals. (p. 26)

The purpose of peep shows is to give men visitors the opportunity of looking at women.

> Yet nowhere in a zoo can a stranger encounter the look of an animal. At the most the animal's gaze flickers and passes on. They look sideways. They look blindly beyond. They scan mechanically. They have been immunised to encounter. (p. 26)

The clientele milling around Soho or Times Square Show World are not known for their happy, joyous or satisfied expressions. The visit to the woman-zoo cannot but disappoint. And of course, nowhere in the zoo can a man find the look of a woman, the sign of an encounter (not that he is actually looking for one). The women's gaze flickers and passes on; they look sideways, blindly beyond, scan mechanically. They have been immunized to encounter. Henry Schipper's visit to Show World reported in *Mother Jones* yielded the following observations:

> On the tiny stage, one dancer carries on a loud conversation with a dancer who is leaving. 'Tell that son of a bitch I'll kick his ass if he comes here again,' she shouts . . . Another pretends the dollar bills in her hand are a gun. She welcomes each new face with a quick-draw blast.[12]

Passing a row of glass booths with a woman sitting in each,

he notes their fake look of 'come-hither eyes' as they compete for his patronage. But

> by-passed, the eyes turn off, the tongues recede. The masks dissolve, disclosing underlying expressions of boredom, irritability, or stupor-like sadness.[13]

And Berger observes:

> Therein lies the ultimate consequence of their marginalisation. That look between [woman] and man, which may have played a crucial role in the development of human society . . . has been extinguished. Looking at each [woman], the unaccompanied zoo visitor is alone. (p. 26)

The look between man and woman – both looking as active subjects – has been extinguished. The woman zoo extends beyond the metal slots and shutters of the peep-show. The cultural space of women, captured and framed in images, is one big Show World. There remains but one kind of look: looking *at*. Man gazing at woman, one-way.

# Art and Pornography

Bernard Williams, as a member of the Committee on Obscenity and Film Censorship, asks a French official how to define a 'film's being pornographic'.[1] The Frenchman, dismissive of the philosopher's problem, replies: 'Everyone knows what a pornographic film is. There are no characters, there is nothing but sexual activity, and it is not made by anyone one has heard of.'[2] Williams insists: 'But . . . what if these criteria diverged? What if a film of nothing but sex were made by, say, Fellini?'[3] According to the Frenchman's criteria the case is clear: the film is (would be) made by someone one has heard of, hence not all of the defining criteria (would) have been fulfilled. The film would not be pornography.

What Williams is in fact asking is how we distinguish between pornography and art when there is a match of content: nothing but sex in both. A good question, considering that the commonsense definition of pornography rests on 'nothing but sex' in the content. We already had the problem of a match between a picture of fact and a picture of fiction. Earlier we saw Williams trying to distinguish between 'high' culture and 'mass circulation' culture by having recourse to the size of the audience, since his feeling was that anything mass-circulated was faintly pornographic – or at least sexist. With the medium of cinema, however, we are beyond a doubt in the presence of a mass medium, and a distinction is now to be made within this mass circulation medium between pornography and something more acceptable or even belonging to art. With this new problem, it is no longer the presence of 'pornographic material' – nothing but sex, no characters – that is the distinguishing characteristic of pornography (since this would not allow us to distinguish between pornography and art), but rather the context within which the work is produced and sold. To determine this context, the status of the producer is decisive. If 'one' has heard of him already as an artist, then the work is a work of art. If he is unknown, he is bound to be a producer of popular art or pornography.

While the British film censors may not be as happy to enshrine this criterion in law, it is precisely the criterion of the literary establishment, the liberal cultural elite, and emulated moreover by cultured feminists. It does not matter if the work is a table full of vaginas – great women represented through/as their genitals – if the creator is an artist, and in this case, if she is a woman. Leaving aside the fact that there is extensive room for argument over 'nothing but sex' (at what point does a character cease to be a character, or sexual acivity cease to be/have plot), there have been films which pose precisely this dilemma, amongst them Pasolini's *Salo* and Oshima's *Empire of the Senses*. Film censors in different countries have responded with different measures, but the cultural establishment has, by and large, firmly adhered to its tradition of recognizing, and defending, its artists. The motive for defence is the recognition of the artist, but the argument of defence is then carried out in terms of seeing the artistic, literary, aesthetic and even profoundly true in the 'nothing but sex', some qualities of aesthetic execution which prevent us from seeing 'just sex' in the work. Yet there is trouble ahead for the critics, or at least for the more inclusive definition of a film's being porno-graphic, since the pornography industry, close at their heels, has decided to upgrade its products aesthetically and to develop a New Porn style: 'The old-time, 16mm cheapies (boy meets girl, 15 seconds later they're in the sack, again and again and again) were replaced by costlier, 35mm 'quality' films (better sound and colour reproductions, and some semblance of plot around the porn).'[4]

All the more reason for adhering to the 'someone one has heard of' criterion. The French censors' solution responded to this factor, for they did not banish *Salo* to the blue-movie houses with a 'P' certificate, but confined it by special decree to two art movie houses in Paris,[5] where, one presumes, it met only with a responsible metropolitan audience who appreciate the artistic Pasolini and where it was safe from abuse by the masses and the provincials. But the pornography industry is edging in this direction too: '"The next big moneymaker," film director Chuck Vincent predicts, "will be celebrity porn. There won't be any more block busters like *Deep Throat* and *The Devil in Miss Jones*. No, the next big hit will star Farrah Fawcett, nothing less . . . That is the porn everyone is waiting for. Everyone."'[6] Except among the film buffs, the someones one has heard of in cinema are more likely than not the stars rather than the directors. And the reason why 'everyone' is waiting for this kind of pornography is that the quality actor will ratify the film as alright, just as for the more cultured the director (Fellini) ratifies the film as not only alright, but as art. So the industry, one might say, is going in the right direction.

The definition or categorization of something as 'literary' or artistic relies crucially, and in the end circularly, on the successful association of it with something else already classified as literary, and the identity of the author provides the easiest such association (never mind the lack of logic). The hypothetical case of Fellini pornography, and the actual cases of *Salo* and *Empire of the Senses* obligingly illustrate the point. Critics will of course expend much energy and effort in arguing the literary or artistic qualities of the works in question; but the decision of the critic to put himself thus on the line and defend the daringly pornographic, has been reached (a) beforehand, and (b) in the safe knowledge that Fellini, Pasolini, Oshima, *mean* 'literary', 'artistic', 'of quality'.

D. M. Thomas' *The White Hotel* is a similar case in point, and an excellent example for the study of the interaction between the literary and the pornographic, since it explicitly, 'daringly', places itself on the boundary between 'literature' and 'pornography' through the use of blatantly 'pornographic material'. This is nothing new in itself in the domain of literature, since the twentieth century has known a tradition of what is conventionally seen as an increasing liberalization of respectable art and literature. Thomas' novel is a more refined example, however, than the work of, say, Norman Mailer or Henry Miller, with a particular set of artistic and intellectual pretensions guaranteed to trigger the 'literary' responses from the cultured elite. I will examine the novel in the extended context of its critical acclaim, since we need for our analysis not only a text classified as literary, but all the attendant buttressing of literary critical appraisal which, more than the text itself, indicates the points of defence: the felt points of daringness which push the boundary, the points at which the category of the literary is invoked in order to salvage the pornographic, where the literary is said to neutralize or redeem the pornographic.

While Thomas may not have been quite as assuredly known as, say, Fellini, he nonetheless already belonged to, and participated in the domain of the literary as a poet, translator of literature and novelist before the publication of *The White Hotel*. The publication of this novel by Victor Gollancz and as a King Penguin (Penguin's answer to Picador, the specialists in the 'contemporary literary'), and its presentation to the Booker Prize and the Cheltenham Prize (1981) are all indicators of its claim to the literary. The piquancy of the case, however, rests on its obvious, its 'daring' pornography. In fact, the British reception was somewhat hesitant at first, and the proper boom in this country started only after the book's stormy reception in the USA. Since then, it has been widely discussed in the media and prominently displayed and promoted by publishers and booksellers, and its rising sales figures quickly put it on the bestseller lists. While the novel did not, in fact, win the Booker Prize competition, held before the American success (rumour has it, owing to objection from women on the panel), it is now advertised as the book which 'narrowly missed the 1981 Booker Prize',[7] and as 'soon to be a major film' on the back of the Penguin edition. (Note that the future film is already rated as 'major' on account of its association with a known author.)

My argument is that it is due to the conjuncture of the pornographic with the literary that the novel enjoys such insistent acclaim, and that the arguments for its literariness 'in spite' of its pornographic qualities reveal the fundamental investment the literary has in the pornographic. The pornographic structure, however, extends far beyond the overtly 'obscene' 'sexual material' of its content and pervades the literary practice of author and critical reception alike. The literary arguments address only the changing quality of the obscene, the increasing explicitness and growing violence of the 'sex' represented, in accordance with the dominant view of pornography as a question of sexual content. But they are in fundamental agreement with the pornographic structure of representation, which is not only not criticized, but also replicated in the critical arguments.

I do not need to prove the conventionally pornographic presence in *The White Hotel*, as there seems to be general agreement that it is there, notably in the first two chapters, '*Don Giovanni*' and 'The Gastein Journal', and the Babi Yar section towards the end. The literary argument runs from there,[8] namely that it depends on what Thomas 'does' with the pornographic element, what literary use he makes of it that moves it beyond 'nothing but sex' and gives it that 'meaning' which Susan Sontag finds in the 'meaninglessness' of *The Story of O*.[9] The expression 'nothing but sex' connotes gratuitousness and meaninglessness. The literary provides a frame in which this element, which otherwise might appear gratuitous and meaningless, may be anchored; it provides artistic purpose.

Interestingly, the novel's conception follows this plot of the provision of artistic purpose: on the acknowledgements page, Thomas states that 'Section I of "*Don Giovanni*" was first published as a self-contained poem.'[10] *The White Hotel* was subsequently provided to accommodate it. And in an interview, asked how he constructed the novel, in what order he wrote it, and whether he actually first wrote the poem and then elaborated it, Thomas answers:

> Yes. And when I wrote the poem I had no idea that it was going to become a novel . . . I wrote a poem called

'The Woman to Sigmund Freud', which was actually the first of the poetic pieces [i.e. section I of '*Don Giovanni*'] in the novel. It was an open-ended poem, that I was quite pleased with in itself, but it didn't seem to lead anywhere. I wrote three more sections and it still didn't seem to finish . . . So it was the poem first, quite independent of any idea that it fitted into a novel.[11]

In other words, the poem was gratuitous ('in itself', 'independent'). It was open-ended, leading nowhere, it could have gone on and on for ever – nothing but sex, no plot. No characters either, just 'The Woman', the woman to Sigmund Freud, Subject. But it was a poem the author was 'quite pleased with', it gave him the feeling of life according to the common sense which determines what pleases and what displeases. Thomas seems surprised that it 'fitted into a novel', unaware, apparently, that he provided a novel specifically to fit it. Let us see how he found the novel:

It was only when I read Kuznetsov's *Babi Yar* that it clicked and I suddenly realised that the poems were, in fact, beginning a novel which would end in *Babi Yar* . . . Well, that seemed to be a very exciting idea . . . So, from the poem I then wrote the prose expansion, taking each part of it and re-framing it as narrative. Then it went into realism.[12]

It was only when he read the account of one of history's most violent and sadistic massacres, abounding in gratuitous brutality, that he saw an 'end' to which his pornographic poems could lead. It was an 'exciting idea to work on'.

I shall now briefly examine the true extent to which the acknowledged pornographic parts of the novel are pornographic in the feminist sense of the term: not just whether they are 'obscene', whether there is 'too much sex', or sex too explicit, but what structure of sexuality, what sexual politics are represented and what structure of representation, what subject–object relationships, are employed.

It is above all the two parts of the novel purporting to be the writings of Lisa Erdman which are overtly pornographic (in the usual sense): they are in the received mould of conventional pornographic literature, a picture of male-defined sexuality, not to mention a picture of male-defined female sexual hysteria – a more refined minority genre. They are about fucking. Violence is an integral part. 'She' is the passive recipient of the fucking, suffering what is done to her and how and when it is done to her. She is the object in the represented action-syntagm, objectified in the scenario. The penis, or its various substitutes, or the man – all paradigmatic alternatives – are the only agents, the true subjects, of this almost plotless action:

> Two, then three fingers he jammed into me . . . his thrumming fingers filled me; then he rammed in again . . . that night he almost burst my cunt apart . . . Beneath our rug your son's right hand was jammed up to the wrist inside me . . . driving like a piston in and out . . . your son impaled me . . . I think something inside me had been torn . . . I was impaled upon a swordfish . . . Then gradually it was the ice itself that cut into me . . . a breast was sheared away . . . the blizzard tore my womb clean out . . . he came behind and rammed up into me . . . he took my hand and slid my fingers up behind him there . . . Your son crashed through my modesty . . . my rump taking his thrust.[13]

Agency, as is clear from these extracts, means violent action. Apart from being the passive, receiving, suffering counterpart to this aggressive and violent actor and his action, the woman-object is further characterized by a lack of control even where she is, linguistically, the grammatical subject:

> I could not stop myself I was in flames from the first spreading of my thighs, no shame could make me push my dress down, thrust his hand away . . . juices ran down my thighs . . . I was split open by your son . . . his finger hurt me jammed up right up my arsehole . . . it makes me blush . . . weakly I tried to push away his hand . . . pulling me upon him without warning . . . I couldn't sleep that night, I was so sore . . . I couldn't tell

which hole it was . . . by the second night my breasts
were bursting . . . I opened up my dress, and my ache
shot a gush out even before his mouth had closed upon
my nipple, and I let the old kind priest . . . take out the
other . . . I've never known my nipples grow so quickly
. . . my face lay buried in the pillow . . . I didn't mind
which one of them was in . . . it was good to feel part of
me was someone else, no one was selfish in the white
hotel.[14]

Where she is not overpowered by him, 'your son' (address-
ing Freud), and occasionally by substitute blizzards and ice,
she is overcome by involuntary bodily reactions, mostly of
pain, while anything else she might undertake is rendered as a
failed attempt – I could not, I tried, I couldn't tell, I've never
known – characterized by impotence and ignorance, her
fragmented body beyond her control, its parts acting
autonomously, and the only successful 'act' on her part being
that of letting others do things to her.

No one was selfish in the white hotel: this is the same
'meaning' that Susan Sontag finds in the meaninglessness of
*The Story of O*, where 'O progresses simultaneously towards
her own extinction as a human being and her fulfilment as a
sexual being.'[15] And here is what 'sexual being' means: 'O
does not simply become identical with her sexual availability,
but wants to reach the perfection of becoming an object.'[16]
'It's alright to be a sex object,' or rather, it is 'perfection' to
lose one's self, one's subjectivity, to be extinct, and progress
to the status of someone else's object, someone obviously
still very much a subject. Selflessness: the definition of
perfect femininity, the goal of virtue for wife and mother, for
womanhood – today the double-bind of every mother in the
country. Virtue: the prerogative of 'women', men being
content with less than sainthood for themselves. Encourag-
ing women to find their salvation in the extinction of self, the
evaporation of selfhood, the 'transcendence of personality',[17]
the loss of subjectivity, taking upon themselves the risk of a
slower salvation in the hereafter and the privilege of a selfish
existence in the here and now: the assertion of self, the

egotism of *I am*, the exclusive right to subjectivity. This spiritual altruism, this material egotism, preaches to woman that 'her own extinction as a human being' means her fulfilment as a 'woman' in the nineteenth century: the angel in the house; her fulfilment as a 'sexual being', as 'sexual object' in the twentieth: the angel in the bed.

No one was selfish in the white hotel. This one is woman, rapidly becoming a no one herself. Everyone else, in the white hotel, is very selfish: they all want to fuck her, have her. They assert their subjectivity by means of her object-body and her evacuated humanity.

The assumption of the female point of view and narrative voice – the assumption of linguistic and narrative female 'subjectivity' – in no way lessens the pornographic structure, the fundamental elision of the woman as subject. On the contrary, it goes one step further in the total objectification of woman. It is indeed one of the well-tried pornographic devices to fake the female's, the victim's, point of view and many pornographic books are published under a female author-pseudonym. It is the narrative equivalent of Berger's 'hidden camera', giving access to 'a domain which, although entirely visible to the camera, will never be entered by the spectator' (viz *Inside Linda Lovelace*). The so-called female point of view is a male construction of the passive victim in his own scenario, the necessary counterpart to his active aggressor: whether 'she' resists her own violation, whether she enjoys it in involuntary bodily response and against her will, or whether she is voluntarily and infinitely available to his impositions – all available alternatives serve to enhance the pornographic pleasure, the active subjectivity of the male, his feeling of life. The options are strictly defined within the one imperative that it *will* happen to her; 'she' can choose an attitude. As Roland Barthes defines it with characteristic oblique strokes:

> The scream is the victim's mark; she makes herself a victim because she chooses to scream; if, under the same vexation she were to ejaculate (sic), she would cease to be a victim, would be transformed into a libertine: *to*

*scream/to discharge*, this paradigm is the beginning of choice, i.e. Sadian meaning.[18]

Note how suddenly the passive female sufferer becomes an apparently active agent: *she makes herself* a victim because she *chooses* to scream. Note how 'the same vexation' she is under is beyond any choice, beyond alteration. The text, the scenario, is given, 'she' can choose to mark it. While the simple objectification, the straightforward victimization, annihilates the woman's subjectivity, denies, ignores and elides it, this second 'option' appropriates and fakes her subjectivity: her male master constructs and projects a man-made subjectivity on to the empty object vessel.

We have the whole spectrum of the victim's 'choices' in the pieces quoted from *The White Hotel*: from the resisting victim, who suffers pain from the struggle; through her involuntary 'pleasure' in spite of herself – 'his thrumming fingers filled me with a great gape of wanting', 'it was so sweet I screamed' – to her total conversion to his intentions: 'I said, Please fuck me, please.'[19] The female gape of wanting, the void to be filled, the great emptiness waiting for the male stuffing, is one of the favourite male myths, tallying with the male obsession with the size of members and the male fear that 'the bigger, the better'.[20]

I do not wish to reproduce Thomas' text any further, and take this as sufficient illustration of the pornographic structure, of the sexism, of the sexual politics embodied in this female character's writings. I shall now look at one critic's response to, and reproduction of, the pornographic structure, the wholesale objectification of woman, the elision of female subjectivity. George Levine in his review of the novel in the high literary *The New York Review of Books* certainly recognizes the 'obscene' passages as conventionally pornographic: 'her first violent and pornographic "phantasy" is written in a loose blank verse.'[21] But he is safe in the knowledge that he will proceed to prove the novel's literary qualities, the desired remedy which salvages the pornographic from being pornography. Susan Sontag, in what remains one of the most influential apologias of literary pornography, her article 'The Pornographic Imagination', tells us that 'What makes a work of pornography part of the history of art rather than of trash is . . . the originality, thoroughness, authenticity, and power . . . incarnated in a work.'[22] These are not terms of very great precision, but we will find them echoed. 'Thoroughness', moreover, we might have thought to be a characteristic of pornography: 'nothing but sex', 'again and again and again'. 'Originality', on the other hand, is a key term of literary evaluation, and 'authenticity' a romantic inheritance.

The feminist critic, like the literary critic who looks beyond the overtly pornographic passages to identify literary originality and authenticity, is worried about more than the 'obscenity' of Lisa Erdman's 'writing'. Looking at the larger structure of the novel, she will find in Thomas' use of the holocaust further proof of his bad faith. It may have seemed implausible already that a contemporary novelist should be unaware of the conventions of narrative and representation to the extent of thinking that he could 'speak through a woman', of believing that 'you are involving the feminine aspect of yourself in poetry', or that in creating a female character he would be writing 'from the point of view of a woman'.[23] It is inconceivable, however, that he should believe that linking sexual violence with the holocaust was a profound, original artistic achievement. Nazi sadism is a stock in trade of pornography, and one of the most marketable ones at that. Let us see what a literary man makes of this devastating conjunction.

George Levine finds *The White Hotel* 'a novel of immense ambition and virtuosity [what Thomas does with it]. With the strength [power] of its precise and risky use of language, it moves us from the self into history.'[24] Whose self? Whose history? Whom 'us'? Levine notes that the novel begins with Freud (and Jung) and 'ends somewhere beyond history . . . Between these extremes, we follow the life of a fictional woman, Elisabeth Erdman.'[25] Lisa Erdman, alias Anna G. is, we noted, at the centre of the pornographic experience related in the two parts purported to be her writings, i.e. in the two pieces of acknowledged hard-core pornography; and she is at the centre of the experience of the sado-horrors of the holocaust narrative. For these narratives to be salvaged from the realm of the pornographic *per se*, the culture's rubbish bin, into the sanctuary of the literary, would require something major to be 'done' by the rest of the novel, would require audacity as well as ambition, originality as well as power, to follow the literary argument. (Although in practice, we know that nothing more needs to be 'done' than that it is written by someone one has heard of). Levine senses the enormity of the task: 'The audacity of Thomas's achievement can be felt most immediately in its ambition.'[26] He obviously feels that the ambition has been fulfilled, the task accomplished. And how does he see it accomplished? Already in terms of the novel's structure he sees Lisa Erdman's life as the mere transition between the historic self (Freud) and the 'beyond history' of the holocaust. The focus, the point of attraction, is the self, the subject: 'Freud is one of the major characters, both investigating the experience and participating in it, speaking the reticent and revelatory language of his obsessive pursuit of scientific truth.'[27]

An affinity is obviously felt between the writer/reader and this major character Freud, and their joint project of 'investigating the experience' of horror, torture and sexual assault of Lisa Erdman; participating in her experience in the voyeuristic relation of the analyst/fictionalizer, participating vicariously in the experience of another by 'speaking the reticent and revelatory language' of representing her as an object, the one in his obsessive pursuit of scientific truth, the other in his obsessive pursuit of the (marketable) literary. The mutual glance of recognition between the white man and his guest, between author and reader, has been established, through the axis of identification with their represented representative, Freud, the major character. That this 'reticent and revelatory' relationship of language, of representation, to the particular 'experience' in question might be problematical, indeed is the problematic which might justify the task, seems hardly to dawn as a suspicion. The author, in his only narrative intervention that might represent an attempt to salvage the audacity of his endeavour, blithely calls Lisa Erdman's experiences (and those of all the other victims) in the Babi Yar massacre 'amazing experiences'.[28] His awareness of the problematic of his relationship to it finds expression in the triteness of 'Nor can the living ever speak for the dead.'[29] Yet speak he does.

Levine's assertion that 'neither Freud nor Babi Yar is cheapened or exploited by the fictionalizing, and [that] neither diminishes the fictional heroine, Elisabeth, who becomes a case study . . . and a victim of the slaughter,'[30] is a claim which goes without any proof or evidence and seems to me to betray a pointed unease. Already, from the centre of experience we have moved to the priority of Freud and Babi Yar, man and history, in our quick glance to check that neither has been cheapened; the 'fictional heroine' (no longer even 'woman') enters as an afterthought, and she enters in the conventional form of diminished identity, the feminine first name. 'Freud is one of the major characters . . . Elisabeth enters the book almost as an aside . . . in a letter . . . by Freud to his friend and disciple Hanns Sachs.'[31] Among this pantheon of historic men, Lisa Erdman is Elisabeth *tout court*, the fictional heroine, a mention in a letter, a case study, a victim of the slaughter, an aside, and if Levine cannot see any diminishment in this, it is because he cannot conceive of any stature for a woman in history. The critic's glance and the novel's structure in an harmonious homology.

After a quote from the letter, Levine continues: 'The images here (which will recur throughout the book) seem almost more important than the patient' (that is, Lisa Erdman).[32] The projects of 'Freud' (fictionalized) and of the writer/reader remain closely linked: in the one Lisa Erdman becomes a patient and a case study (no diminishment), in the other a fictional heroine of minor importance, subordinate to the imagery of the author and clearly distinguished from 'the subject of the novel' as established by Levine, that is Freud: 'these [letters] are often by Freud, and all of them imply that he is the subject of the novel.'[33] Moreover, the fictional heroine, in Levine's opinion, remains a 'mystery' despite her writings. However, 'her "writings" . . . alone (though they leave their author a mystery) are enough to justify the admiration this novel has already evoked from critics.'[34] (Remember that we set out to justify the 'writings' by the literary novel into which they were integrated.) 'Her' fantasy, represented by the dazzling 'virtuosity' and 'cleverness' of Thomas, becomes the delighted focus of this critic's obsessive pursuit of the literary, just as it does for the fictionalized Freud: 'a prose elaboration of her verse, carefully repeating images, developing them . . . The language of the poem and the letter ranges from the merely vulgar, or banal, to a lush, romantic intensity, with a remarkable precision of imagery. Her writing is full of dislocation and surprise; it is seductive, frightening, and beautifully alive.'[35] It is in fact full of pain, violence and violation: 'whatever else the book is, it is a pleasure to read.'[36]

After a quote ending in 'I jerked and jerked until his prick released/its cool soft flood. Charred bodies hung from the trees,' Levine comments: 'Such language immediately establishes the mysterious "Anna G." as a powerful presence.'[37] I do not know whether Levine is conscious of what he is saying here, as for once I can agree with him. Remember that he said that Lisa Erdman remains a mystery despite her writings, her alleged self-expression. The presence of woman is not easily established through the means of representation, through the power of naming which has been men's for and in recorded history. The presence established here is that of 'Anna G.', who is the construction of 'Freud', who is the construction of Thomas. The experience of Lisa Erdman is still nowhere, for all Thomas's speaking 'through a woman'.

But we have noticed already that Levine's interest in the novel lies elsewhere, that he reads the presented novel like the usual consumer of pornography, with the interest of the male experience to be got from it ('her' writing is 'seductive'); the woman in the piece reduced to object, means to a certain end, vehicle for his pleasure. His worry about the novel is not how the salaciousness of the pornography and the holocaust titillation might be justified: his worry is whether Thomas might stoop to discredit Freud. With a sigh of relief he observes: 'Discrediting Freud is neither a particularly interesting narrative enterprise, nor Thomas's true purpose. Thomas's Freud is both vulnerable and heroic, ambivalently confirmed in his unscientific guesses, made touchingly human in his reading of the death instinct into history.'[38] Lisa Erdman is both vulnerable and heroic, unambiguously condemned beyond the touchingly human in her experience of the death instinct manifested through Babi Yar. But Levine is immune to this side of the story. Freud, on the basis of his own persuasion, has become the uncontested hero of his reading ('But Freud is not merely a background figure here'); Freud 'is a hero of the quest for a world that makes sense, and he is himself a victim.'[39] Freud is the hero of this novel beginning with gratuitous pornographic exploitation, ending in gratuitous violence and horror laced with sexual sadism, whose plot, we understand, consists of the heroic quest for scientific truth, the vagaries of unscientific guesses, the touching vulnerability of the genius who explores 'virgin' territory of knowledge. The depth of the romantic intensity, of the emotional scope of this drama, lies in the reduction of the hero–genius to 'victim'. A most moving, stirring drama of humanity.

'Moving', incidentally, is how Levine describes Babi Yar, moving, because the intrusion by the narrator concerning the 'amazing' experiences of its victims, is 'something other than a mockery of Freud's work'.[40] The humanity of the author lies in his not mocking his fallen hero. And as this critic penetrates beneath the facts of this novel to the drama of its hero, its reader and its writer, so the hero Freud 'penetrates beneath the facts, forces the patient out from behind her firmly willed deceptions'.[41] No change of register is needed from the pornographic to the literary (critical): penetration continues, the patient continues to be forced, forced out from behind her firmly willed masquerading as a woman, a subject, an agent. She is patient, it will be done to her; she has the choice between resisting (clinging to her firm deceptions) and welcoming it, marking the text (it is already written) with the'marks of 'her choice': the scream of the victim or the discharge of the libertine. She does, like every pornographic victim, do both: she protests and marks the text with a footnote and a postscript (the text remains), as she literally marks and postscripts Freud's case history 'Anna G.', and she is grateful to the wise professor, her master, to boot. And the other text remains; whichever choice she makes, sadean meaning results: it is a pleasure to read, her 'writings' alone are enough to justify the admiration this novel has already evoked.

And the true purpose of Thomas's novel (no, thank goodness not the denigration of Freud) emerges clearly: 'it is not simply in the ideas, in the criticism of Freud or in the dramatic confirmation of him, that this novel achieves its power and significance.'[42] Although the '"death instinct" is everywhere in the novel', Levine is convinced that 'the forces on the side of life [are] more powerful still' in the final balance of the work: 'In the proximity of actual death (of Freud's mother and child, and even of his sisters in the Holocaust) to a theory that explains it, we sense the pressure of life is close as well.'[43] In the face of death made actual perhaps through kinship, the proximity of a theory that explains it may well be cheering to the surviving observer and insinuate the closeness of the forces of life. Freud's capacity to theorize the death of others (as it happens, women, and women defined in relation to him, rather than by their own names), like Thomas' capacity to fictionalize, makes them sense the pressure of life, the feeling of life that is the boon of the subject. Likewise, Levine is fascinated with the death instinct:

> Thanatos exists in the energy of Eros, or so Freud thought. Elisabeth's fantasies provide evidence for this view, and it is true that the effectiveness of the pornography in her writing makes the inevitably accompanying fantasies of disaster the more frightening. When, for example, one of the mother figures, in her second fantasy falls to her death from a cable car, there is an almost serene sexuality.[44]

Not much serene sexuality, presumably, for the mother figure, but for those looking on and reading on, and who do not seem very frightened by the disaster. Pornography exists in the symbiosis of Thanatos and Eros. Elisabeth's, Thomas's, Levine's fantasies provide evidence for this view. And it is true, rather, that the frightening disasters inevitably accompanying their sexual fantasies make the pornography more effective. It is the more 'beautifully alive' and 'serene', the more dead the victim and sexual object.

Lisa Erdman is dead many times over. Almost killed through the sexual violations by 'Freud's son' (Thomas's fantasy), mutilated through 'Freud's' forcing of her into the case study 'Anna G.', and dying a multiple death at the hands of her torturers at Babi Yar, she is buried once more by the literary reader Levine, who relegates her out of the novel, out of the plot, tossing her back at the hero Freud as a toy, an object, a means of stimulation for his fantasies. At best, the woman, Lisa Erdman, 'the neurotic "Anna G."', in successive stages of fictionalization at the hands of her fictionalizers, 'provides a moment of potential healing for Freud himself'.[45] The great hero, in his untiring fantasies, is 'vulnerable and heroic' in his supremacy, 'ambivalently confirmed in his unscientific guesses' about women, made touchingly human in his reading of the death instinct into history, in his projection of sex and violence, the pornographic axiom, into the history of humanity, the culture of mankind.

Thomas, with his 'precise and inventive prose', 'his cleverness in mixing fiction with history,'[46] which makes him join the pornographic fantasies with the atrocities of the history of Babi Yar, has become the snuff artist of the cultural establishment: he understands that Lisa Erdman is not just the fantasized victim of his narrative, the fantasized construction of Freud's case history, but for true literary consummation has to be the real victim of authentic history. She must be a true woman and she must be truly dead to trigger the literary climax. He knows, because he has one as he writes:

Writing is also a surrogate sexual pleasure, a sublimation of the sexual instinct. And what *does* happen is that you find yourself writing something which you're enjoying sexually. Then you look back on it and say 'I enjoyed that, but it doesn't work in terms of the book' . . . It was only when I read Kuznetsov's *Babi Yar* that it clicked . . . So, from the poem I then wrote the prose expansion, taking each part of it and re-framing it as narrative. Then it went into realism.[47]

Writing is a surrogate sexual pleasure. It gives the feeling of life. Is it surprising, then, that this literary art is a reflection, a mirror image, of the conventional male-defined sexual act, the sexual assault on the sex object? 'My editor says my novels are like explosions, and I think that's right. It [sic] may go off like a damp squib, or it may make a nice bang, but it's not going to be one of those long drawn-out . . . [sic] I can't work that way.'[48] What did the women say: 'that it is too fast, too rough, too phallic'. And as regards the reciprocity of that sex act, look at what happens to Thomas's 'partner': 'It's got . . . to have . . . impact, so that the reader is left shaken by it . . . but over very quickly, or else it's just not going to interest me . . . The idea of writing a five-hundred, eight-hundred page novel would be inconceivable.'[49] I am quite sure.

The male literary reader, identifying with his hero Freud and his hero writer, turns on to this, responds to Thomas's realism and mistakes it for reality: 'Thomas suggests a reality at once vital and deadly, and more accessible than we – protected behind our documents and books – might care to know.'[50] And in his enjoyment he has 'no reservations' about this great work of art, 'its strengths remain.'[51] 'It's title suggests that life can be seen either as a matter of peace or of violence.'[52] Perhaps it depends on your point of view. Levine, at any rate, feels at peace, feels secure and protected in the literary sanctuary.

The feminist reader, by contrast, can find no place to take up in this literary romance. Hers would be the designated place of the victim, but if the truth be known: she does not wish for Thomas' impact, she has no desire for his big bang (however quickly it is over). This kind of reading, pornographic reading, is 'for men only'. For the woman reader has no part in Levine's 'we': *she* finds no protection behind his ('our') documents and books, the literary is no sanctuary to her. And she has every reason to 'care to know': how easily accessible this reality is, how easily accessible she is to this reality – deadly to her, but so vital to the patriarchs, our literary men.

*Problem 8*

# The Literary and the Production of Value

As we have seen, the disagreement between feminist critic and literary critic or defender of pornography is not about whether or not the pornographic is pornographic. The dispute is at the level of the literary argument which claims that the literary pornographic is not pornographic literature because of what the literary 'makes' of the pornographic, what it 'does' with it. What it does with it, as we have seen, is ratify it. Caught unawares, the literary critic can be seen to accept the pornographic elements on their own, without the literary framework which 'makes' of them more than pornography: 'her "writings", and these alone . . . are enough to justify the admiration this novel has already evoked from critics.' We hear of 'virtuosity', 'cleverness' and 'remarkable precision of imagery', but we are nowhere told of what these consist, or how exactly imagery is 'precise'.

Originally, feminists thought that their task was to prove that pornography degrades women; they thought that showing in stark irrefutable ways the mechanics and structures of the pornographic plot would speak for itself, would make their case for them. The pornographic would be revealed, exposed, there for all the world to see. But their opponents concur that they see perfectly: they know that they degrade women, 'I know I do. So does *The New York Times*'.

The dispute, in other words, is finally about whether or not there is anything wrong with that, whether there is anything wrong with the systematic degradation of women, the wholesale cultural objectification of women, the usurpation of women's subjectivity by the male gender. In this dispute, however, the feminist critic, the feminist objector to pornography, is a lonely voice without any other ally, for the professed objectors to pornography do not object to the degradation of women in pornography, but to the presence of a particular kind of 'sex' in pornographic representations. The literary critic may object to a lack of 'originality', 'cleverness' or precision of imagery in the mass-produced works of unheard-of authors, but he does not object to the presence of pornography in literary works, much less to the degradation of women in them. With her claim that there is something wrong with the systematic degradation of women the feminist critic, therefore, finds herself arguing not only with the pornographer, but with the established experts of cultural representation. In the face of the *feminist* objection to pornography, the pornographer, rather than defending himself, takes shelter behind the general cultural practice of representation, which condones the degradation of women, and the free market economy, which underpins the freedom of expression. For in terms of representation, and with respect to the objectification of the female gender, the pornographer only reproduces, on a less elevated level and within a less exclusive circulation, what the artist does in the esoteric fields of high culture; and he derives from it more profit in return for reduced prestige.

Women waking up from, or to, their cultural education, their apprenticeship to the common sense of what pleases and what displeases and the perspective of the male subject, may well ask how this is possible, how this degradation of women is tolerated by a culture that represents 'the highest achievement of humanity',[1] 'the noble aspiration to leave the world better and happier than we found it',[2] a culture which Matthew Arnold felt is 'properly described . . . as having its origin in the love of perfection'.[3] Women ought seriously to ask themselves where they are in this project of perfection of humanity – whose perfection exactly is being striven for and at whose expense? For, whilst the subjects of culture ('humanity') are perfecting themselves as subjects, women have the dubious cultural benefit of progressing towards their extinction as human beings (of being erased from the membership list of 'humanity') and reaching the 'perfection of becoming an object'. It looks as if the highest achievement of humanity consists of an elaborate justification and rationalization of the social, political and economic organization which already embodies this extinction of women as subjects with 'human' rights.

What women find objectionable in pornography, they have learnt to accept in products of 'high' art and literature. What feminist analysis identifies as the pornographic structure of representation – not the presence of a variable quality of 'sex', but the systematic objectification of women in the interest of the exclusive subjectification of men – is a common place of art and literature as well as of conventional pornography. It is in the expert domains of cultural representation and the critical discourses which support them that the attitudes to representation, the 'acceptable' structures of representation, are developed and institutionalized. And it is on their concepts of expression, and their understanding of the role of representation, that the law bases itself in its endeavour to protect the freedom of expression. We should therefore turn to these expert attitudes to representation and to the value systems of high art to see how the objectification of women is construed as an acceptable feature of the perfection of (male) humanity. We should investigate more closely the nature of these values, so elevated and noble as to warrant the sacrifice of the female half of humanity to the perfection and happiness of the male half.

We have seen the writer, D. M. Thomas, as well as the literary critic, George Levine, produce and reproduce the pornographic structure in which the male subject imposes a scenario of violence upon the female subject which eliminates the latter and reduces her to object status. The represented scenario featuring Freud, Freud's son, and Nazis in the role of subject, Lisa Erdman in the role of object, is carried over into the structure of representation. Writer and reader bond in the exercise of usurping female subjectivity and experience, moving into the whole available space of writing and of reading which thus become activities predicated upon the male gender, yielding the pleasure of the feeling of life at the cost of the death of female subjectivity.

The pornographic scenario is but a stark representation of the cultural position of the male gender *vis-à-vis* the female gender. It is extremely limited in scope, revolving around the sadistic act of sex/violence, which accounts for the literary experts' feeling that there is almost no plot, just sex, again and again and again. Yet there is a plot: the cultural archeplot of power. There is power on the side of the agent (hero), and there is powerlessness incarnated in the victim-object. The archeplot has the structure Subject-verb-object, and the verb is transitive, always. But we also need to include the structure of representation in order to understand this modern folktale in its entirety, where the hero, through his act of bravery – agression and dominance – wins his prize, his princess. Where once we had Bluebeard, dragon or witch as the opponents for the hero to overcome, we now have woman, the 'cause' of the perceived threat to the male psyche. The princess, the prize the hero wins besides the kingdom of his absolute supremacy in culture and society, is his pleasure, the feeling of life which every renewed assertion of his supremacy, subjectivity and dominance yields for him. He starts out as hero (powerful), and ends up as king, spawning through the consummation of his pleasure a succession of little heroes, a patrilinear descension of aspiring cultural subjects, ready to become heroes themselves. While in the traditional folktale the hero overpowers the father, the witch, the dragon or breaks down the fortress which bars his access to the female (not herself, even in the folktale, an agent or subject, but a prize of exchange),[4] the modern cultural hero battles against woman who stands in the way of his consummate experience of pleasure, the experience of total, supreme and exclusive subjectivity.

As with the traditional folktale, it need not worry us that there occur minor variations of plot: these are firmly contained within the structure and 'morphology' of the pornographic scenario, reducible to it.[5] Within the patriarchal culture whose product it is, the hero is male, the victim female. The few inversions of gender roles within the represented scenario are, precisely, *inversions*, a familiar transformation of the archeplot and dependent on it, just as there are occasional folktales (edited out of the 'corpus' mainly during the nineteenth century, which found even inversion a threat to the archetype), where the youngest of three *daughters* is sent out to do battles and deeds.[6]

As we have seen, there are two dominant variations in the plot concerning the object–victim. She is either unwilling, or willing object; victim she remains. She has a 'choice' of attitude to the event, but she has no choice of action in the event. The imperative of the plot is strict: it will happen to her, whatever her attitude. The fundamental structure of the transitive plot, which assigns her object status, remains the same. It is a paradigm of domination, of coercion and of the degradation of the Other to object status. The plot, the choice of action-verb, admits only transitive verbs, those requiring a subject and an object.

There is no need for feminists to lay bare this basic structure and expose it for what it is, for a startled world to recognize. There has, rather, been a need for the early feminist movement to discover the universality of this basic cultural plot, for a gender who only recently began to participate fully in the reading of cultural representations across the board to recognize the cultural archeplot for what it is. The male gender, the cultural subject, already knows it, can see it perfectly. The question that feminist critique wants to raise now concerns the *responsibility* for this archeplot of subjugation. And responsibility for the dominant modes of representation, as we have already begun to see, needs to be sought in 'responsible' art and 'high' culture, rather than in its waste products.

We have seen the literary critic assist in laying bare the structure of Thomas's novel, assist in the relegation of any inquiry after the subjectivity of the woman at the centre of the plot out of his reading. The critic's job, as he sees it, as the literary critical practice defines it for him, is to lay bare and assist, not to ask any critical questions. In particular, he is to lay bare the great work within its own artistic domain, and not to ask any questions that point beyond its boundaries and towards 'the real', to the continued functions of representations in culture, to the distribution of representational roles in society or to the position of a representational victim-class in society. For, in the great carving up of domains of expertise, art and literature have been designated as a separate domain, a realm apart from reality.

The experts of culture are in charge of a special domain of brain products which explicitly 'contribute nothing to knowledge'. The aesthetic is the purest expression of man's playful thought, thought produced in play, as play, for the sake of play and pleasure. It stands in contrast to 'work'. Its products are leisure products. Leisure, from Latin *licere*: to allow or permit. This permission, granted by the expert authorities, this permissiveness of the aesthetic, is a first clue in our quest for the responsibility of culture.

Those in charge of the aesthetic domain discuss it in most peculiar terms. First of all, the products of writing, painting, music, cinema and so on are called 'works'. Works of art being the purest expression of man's brain power and creative spirit, they are treated with the awe and respect due to the Creation itself. The works *are*; they have come into being. They are man's answer to the Lord's creation. Like those in charge of the Lord's creation, the cultural experts set to the study of the works of art posing as the 'cultural scientists'. They study, describe and classify works, continuing to admire the spirit which created them; they accept them like another gift from the gods. They call it, in the case of literature, literary criticism. This literary criticism has its roots in the criticism of the Scriptures, the word of God; it is the criticism of the modern scriptures, the word of man. The word is to be studied, researched and admired, but it is not to be put into fundamental question. It is sacred, the pure manifestation of spirit. And in particular, its author and creator, the Artist, is beyond doubt, beyond question, beyond criticism. What an Artist produces is by necessity

Art, even if it is pornography, as we saw in the cases of Fellini, Oshima, Pasolini and Thomas.

Modern literary criticism, as indeed much of the modern study of texts, is scriptural in an essential way. It hoists the text on to a pedestal, the better to admire it from below. Modern scriptures, for instance, include Marx, Freud, or the established canon of literature. A great deal of work may be done, say, on Freud or on Shakespeare, a great deal of textual criticism and analysis, but it is done mostly within the fundamental and a priori acceptance of those texts, as an elaboration on the texts. Textual criticism embodies the principles of scriptural criticism. The word 'criticism' is most inappropriate. What critic of Shakespeare would ever seriously criticize Shakespeare – criticize in a sense which might shake the fundamental faith in the sacredness of the shakespearean text? And if he does, once in a while, he is an aberration, one of those who have failed to learn the principles of taste, of detachment, of disinterested aesthetic contemplation which guarantee the literary criticism. It is indeed one of the tacit (tactful) assumptions of literary etiquette that critics work on works they revere: it is considered in bad taste to criticize with critical intentions.

Critics of contemporary literary productions are a special case: they are confronted with an amorphous body of un-canonized productions which it is their task to sort into scripture and ephemera (the 'history of art' and 'trash'). Hence they might be expected to 'criticize' and to reject some of the products they review and evaluate. Yet even in this field it is the exception rather than the rule, and the tacit principle of positive reviewing also applies. That is to say, negative reviewing and rejection of a work is achieved mainly by non-reviewing, by tacitly leaving it out of consideration. There is a conspicuous absence of any formulated connection between the two critical activities, the literary criticism of the canon and the reviewing criticism of new work. Many critics of canonized literature in fact abstain from reviewing the modern and leave it to journalists and reviewers, thus implicitly admitting the impossibility of doing it with their own critical methods. If an argument is invoked to justify this practice, it is usually that *history* will make a judgement, which is the converse of the argument that the canon comprises those works which have (already) passed the test of time. A curious abrogation of responsibility in the Synod, one might think, until one investigates the motives for this modesty.

For reasons best known to himself, man likes having power, but does not like to be seen taking it. It is a touching display of sensitivity, considering the power he has taken. But the distribution of power among men themselves is also a serious problem, and man has developed a considerable body of knowledge, ethics and justifications concerning this issue. Among these ethical values there is one which deems the desire for power ignoble. Power, it says, is a grave responsibility and duty (handed down by the highest power, God or Nature) and reserved for the best among men. The sheer desire for power for the sake of power is, as man knows to his cost, a great danger to all the others who have the same desire. There is therefore, among the noblest of brothers, very little talk and even less open display of power – and literature belongs among the noblest of men's pursuits, with its absence of any claim to power in 'reality'.

In the literary establishment we therefore only see the executive – also called the servants of art (like the servants of God) – at work; the legislative is hidden. In the apprenticeship to the service of art, we are trained to approach great literature with the questions of how and why it is great and to learn to elaborate its greatness. We are not meant to ask why it is there, or who put it there, and what would have been the alternatives. The selection of the canon – the canonization of the great – precedes our apprenticeship: it is beyond our question and our criticism. When we ask nevertheless, we are told that *history* put it there: the great works passed the test of time. And history, as everyone knows, is not made by men: it is a natural disaster like any other. The fact that the works passed the test of time proves that they were among the fittest. We are, as literary students, helping to prove it over and over again, following our precedessors who proved it before us.

As students of literature we hear next to nothing about the economic infrastructure which underpins the literary establishment. We do not subject works to an analysis of labour and production within the economy; we learn to talk only of values: moral values, aesthetic values, imaginative values, complex values, technical values, innovative values, textual values. We are not taught what we thereby validate. We are taught to see literature in terms of mental constructs, expressions of the creative spirit; we are not encouraged to expend much energy on the study of the production of the economic entities in the world we call books. Even though we are taught to cite the publishers of books in our references and footnotes, we are to see these publishers as in the service of literature, rather than see literature as in the service of their business. We think they publish books out of the goodness of their hearts, out of their recognition of the values, out of their genuine enthusiasm for literary culture. We give little attention to the way in which our literary values mesh with their market values.

Feminist criticism, some marxist criticism, and cultural studies have cut a huge breach into this seamless construct of the literary by recovering the rejects of literary history and thus throwing light on the processes of selection and rejection which have led to the literary canon. The question of who is responsible for the choice of works to be included in the canon or excluded from it can no longer be shelved, can, above all, no longer be attributed to the higher agency of history. It is clear that people (men) have been actively involved in this process, reviewing books and choosing them, attributing values to them, or not reviewing them and thus leaving them unvalued, unevaluated. And that there were people (men) involved in decisions of choice even at an earlier stage, deciding what to print in the first place and what to reject for publication. People involved again at a later stage, deciding on reselection for reprinting and inclusion in anthologies, on making work available or not available, thus administering the test of time and bestowing further value on the chosen works. So many white men helping the work along in its life in reality as a physical, economic and cultural object.

Editors, critics and reviewers, who make these decisions, are usually first trained, then influenced and guided by the professional critics of literature, but they are also guided and influenced by the values of the business of producing and marketing books which is their livelihood. Literary critics in the academy have some influence over the values which help determine market values; they are part of the marketing department. (Their direct influence is difficult to measure, as are the effects of other marketing processes such as advertising and sales promotion.) But the present-day division into publishing business on the one hand and the academy on the other encourages the continuation of the myth of the ivory tower (apart from reality), where literary values are pursued disinterestedly and for their own sake.

Literary criticism in its purest, that is to say, in its academic form, remains curiously unaffected by these discoveries and arguments. It continues to use a methodology premissed on the scriptural; it continues to discuss literary productions in terms of Texts that are given as rocks are given by nature. It is not for the literary critic to question the *raison d'être* of a book, to ask why it is there, or how its existence affects the world. There is no responsibility acknowledged in the existence of a literary work or a work of art, in the sense that there is acknowledged responsibility in the existence of a particular political institution; no question is asked after the author's authorship. In the contemporary conception of art there is no author behind the work in terms of a social and political being, as there is apparently no process of production behind its publication in terms of social and commercial decisions. There is only 'creative spirit' or 'genius', 'imagination', 'innovation' and 'literary quality' to be admired in every renewed manifestation of the literary. The author of literary scripture exists only in such a rarified sense as God exists behind his Scripture: In the beginning was the Word – I am the word. The author is the word incarnate. As Barthes puts it in 'The Death of the Author': 'Writing is the destruction of every voice, of every point of origin.'[7] Despite – or on closer inspection in harmony with – the long tradition of author celebration in literary criticism, which preceded the present text celebration, there are only Authors, Artists, but no authors, originators of their works. There are, it seems, new literary productions in the world as there is ever renewing rain coming out of the sky, an inexorable law of Nature, a natural law of Culture and History. Most individual practitioners of the literary know full well that more than creativity goes into the making of a literary work (let alone the making of an Author); yet this personal knowledge (their own position as practitioners is determined by such practical political factors) does not find its way into their practice, their methodology, their theory. As critics they wish to share with the author that non-responsibility of the manifest scripture; like authors, they wish to be part of the law of Nature. Why?

It is not difficult to see why *authors* want their works to be there as if by law of nature: implicit is the myth of the survival of the best as in nature's survival of the fittest. The social beings who are also authors are fond of dissociating themselves from any willed authorship and frequently describe their books as 'writing themselves', beyond their conscious control, impelled only by the madness of inspiration that will out. As concerns the second process, that of production and promotion, it is also better passed over and replaced by the myth of the test of time, the myth of the public and historical consensus which declares the work a work of art. This myth of public and historical consensus upholds a literary class system as the myth of meritocracy upholds the class system in our educational and all other promotional fields: those who are there are there because they are the best. There are experts along the way judging and examining them, giving rationalizations of the fact that they are the best. It is thus easy to see why the critics, the experts, are equally wedded to the myth: their own quality, their own existence qua experts, rest on the same system of ratification: they, too, are there in their expert places because they are the best. It is the great myth of democracy, which to this day survives unblemished, when the processes of promotion and marketing, the commercial dictates of consumerism, are so ubiquitous as to be impossible to overlook. And within this myth, there are the component myths of equal access and equal opportunity, and the myth of free choice, without consideration of the factors of production – material production as well as the production of merit, of opinion and the production of values.

Even among the so-called ideology-critical brand of literary criticism, critique does not necessarily go beyond the boundaries of the literary. The critic committed to a left-wing political ideology will discuss ideological content and even form in works of art, perhaps criticize the author's political ideology as revealed through the work. But he will accept the work as a work of art,[8] and he has a special technique for avoiding critique of the literary *per se*, since he still needs the work to do his criticism. The most notorious methodological ruse exonerating both artist and critic is the technique of 'showing up' or laying bare, derived apparently from the secular notion of realism, but going back to the medieval understanding of art as 'showing forth God's creation'. Frank Kermode, giving testimony during the obscenity trial of *Lady Chatterley's Lover*, made allusion to a tradition of realism, 'the tradition which uses novels not as forms of entertainment so much as ways of examining – not for propaganda purposes – but simply *examining and laying before the reader* a picture of contemporary moral reality'[9] (my emphasis).

Similarly, the repetitious bourgeois sexual dramas of film director Roehmer, for instance, are hailed as showing up the repetitious bourgeois sexual dramas of modern society, for all the world to see. The increasingly violent tales of modern cinema are exonerated as revealing the increasingly violent tendencies in modern life. Under the imperative of realism it seems natural that representations reflect the salient features of reality, and in the face of the natural existence of works of art, no question is asked why we should want such representations or reflections, no question is asked why someone produces them, and least of all, how these works themselves are engaged in shaping the reality they are said to reflect. Artists as well as critics are there to show up the realities of reality, in the separate realm of art.

Werner Herzog, celebrated cineast of the cultured avant-garde, produces *Fitzcarraldo*, a film about the massive mega-ego of a colonialist who wants to build an operahouse in the middle of the Peruvian jungle and who, in order to carry out his plan, makes a crowd of native Indians carry a steam boat over a hill. The left-wing critic is satisfied: the film exposes (shows up) the massive arrogance of a latterday colonialist industrialist. No mention of the fact that the massively inflated mega-ego of a western cineast repeats this self-same act of colonial imperialism and arrogance, carrying the production of his film into the jungle like the opera of Fitzcarraldo, and making, in the process of his venture, a crowd of native Indians carry a steam boat over the self-same hill, impervious to the effect of his own intervention in the economic and cultural situation of the native population. The justification for the repetition of this ego-drama is that it is all in the interest of a great work of art, while nothing is said about the fact that this great work of art is all in the interest of a great artist-ego of the western literary and cinematic establishment, to say nothing of the financial interests of the producers. Herzog, a great artist, sets out to prove himself and returns a great artist. The commitment to the individual-ism of great art and the artistic ego is so strong as to silence even most of the marxist critics, who are supposed to disapprove of inflated ego-individualism. It is difficult not to suspect that the awed critic would have loved to make the film himself.

The art film highlights the inflation of the artist ego to gigantic proportions. Unlike his poor brother, the writer, the cineast can no longer cultivate the image of the Bohemian who scribbles in an unheated attic with the stump of a pencil.

This artist needs a few million dollars and a crew of subordinate technicians to express the madness of his inspiration, to inscribe his subjectivity on the cultural screen. The critic is all the more impressed, apparently by the proportion of the inspiration, the magnitude of creativity. The stylization of this mass medium, cinema – which neither can be handled by a single man, nor is designed for a single reader – into an art form on the model of the artistic already developed, shows a choice. The choice is in keeping with the culture's celebration of artist-egos, with the culture's creation of individual star artists. The medium itself would more readily have yielded to a conception of collaborative creation, the collective authorship of a team who all contribute, and are all necessary to the production of the work. Instead, tradition has led us to select one member of the team and single him out as the giant creator and artist, to be celebrated and fêted like our other artists. And despite the conspicuous features of production, their obvious embeddedness in industry and commerce, the art critic once again creates an artistic sanctuary around the work, discussing it as text, as work of art, miraculously come into being.

The literary critic with his attitude to literary works as to rocks of nature connives in the author's non-responsibility for good reason. It provides him with work, with a *raison d'être*. There is an apparent division of labour, which makes the author abdicate his critical responsibility in order to create a job for the critic. The critic, grateful for the share in such a noble task, a share in the great Creativity, will show himself worthy: he will refrain from criticism in return for the reflection of the glory of art. The critic, admiring the great display of the imagination of the author, will spend his time applauding the range of imagination displayed. Were he to question the immaculate conception of literary works, he would question himself out of a job; worse, he would question himself out of a position among the cultural elite. The literary guild depends upon there being Authors, Writers, Artists as well as the attendant crew of critics, editors and reviewers. Otherwise, there would just be people writing, which might mean all people write, and then there would be a real task in evaluating who writes 'best' (if best needs to be established) and what are the criteria for evaluation. There would be real dialogue instead of a hierarchical division of labour, there would be debate as one reader would write in response to someone else's writing. But the literary establishment, for all its stake in the production of value, shies away from any explicit formulation of values, from any criticism that criticizes the values of the literary. 'Literary and art critics have been renowned for the ease, if not arrogance, with which they have presumed definitely to rank works of art or individual artists in levels of greatness,' writes Michèle Barrett, who, significantly, is a sociologist rather than a literary critic or art critic.[10] Ease, because evaluation with reference to anything beyond the self-referential 'literary' or 'artistic' or 'great' hardly occurs. Arrogance, since nothing more than the authority of the speaking critic – the expert – is needed for the affirmation of the 'great'. Instead of true evaluation according to acknowledged criteria, we have a continuous celebration of the literary, a self-affirmation of 'creativity', in an endlessly circular motion. By celebrating, the critic shows that he is worthy of the company of the creative Authors.

Let us take an example, the construction of the literary by Picador, a publisher specialized in the contemporary literary. This is not just an example of commercial book promotion, since the latter goes hand in hand with literary expertise. The contemporary literary, as noted, offers a particularly interesting example since it is at the juncture where present literary production is turned into the historical canon.

The term 'literary' is a word like 'tasteful', that is to say, not descriptive, but discriminating in terms of a scale of values, containing value judgement. Related to 'quality' – like 'taste' an ellipsis of good quality, good taste – 'literary' means good literary quality, literary merit. Thus concepts like 'taste', 'literary', 'quality' do not directly denote what they mean, but allude to a set of rules made elsewhere. The judges of the Observer-Virago Short Story Competition in

1981 regretted the 'poor quality of the writing' in most contributions, without telling us what high quality consists of.[11] Those who have taste, precisely, know what it 'means', what it consists of; not to have it means to be ignorant of that definition (rather than not following its precepts). Having and not having it – taste and no taste: these terms are turned into a binary opposition rather than a difference. In the terms of the determiners of taste, there is no different taste, only no taste (also called bad taste, or poor taste). 'Literary' is another such exclusive category: things either are literary, or they are not. In *Keywords*, Raymond Williams cites as the apparently 'natural' question to ask with respect to literature 'whether all books and writing are literature (and if they are not, which kinds *are excluded* and by what criteria)',[12] and one could add 'by whom?'. Taste – having it and knowing what it is – defines a group and its membership, a taste elite, and the clan itself in turn implicitly defines taste by having it. The value of taste is highest to those within that self-defined group, just as lack of it seems gravest to them, but not necessarily grave at all to those who do not 'have' it. (This is a significant difference between this kind of 'having' and material having.) Recognizing the literary requires literary taste, which recognizes literary quality. Let us see how, by what means, such quality is recognized.

Picador starts out with lists of unassigned works; it picks up where the tradition of literary history has left off, roughly fifty years ago with the already classified 'modernism' of Joyce, Faulkner, Beckett etc. Picador's marketing is aimed at defining the new literary; the overall object is to promote inclusion in that desirable category of the works offered by its company. Its arguments are made through the blurbs on covers and advertisements in the back of books.

There are two major ways for a new book to become a member of the new literary: to be chosen or valued by an authority, an already adjudged member of the literary elite (who therefore knows – see taste), or by being similar to or like an already accredited member, another literary work (arrogance or ease). Best of all, of course, is a combination of the two. In either case, we have a transfer of the quality of the literary through association – with someone one has heard of, or with some book one has heard of. The quality itself, the inherent literary values, need neither be stated, nor analysed or demonstrated.

Thomas Pynchon's *Gravity's Rainbow* carries the following blurb on its back cover: '*Moby Dick* and *Ulysses* come to mind most often as one reads . . . *Gravity's Rainbow* marks an advance beyond either.' What constitutes an advance beyond *Moby Dick*, beyond *Ulysses*? Advance in what respect? And further: '"The compendiousness of a Thomas Wolfe, the density of a Faulkner, the learning of a John Barth" *New Society*.' The qualities apparently stated are not of course themselves either necessary or sufficient for guaranteeing the literary. It is the compendiousness associated with the literary Thomas Wolfe that becomes a literary quality through association, not the compendiousness of the British encyclopaedia, the density of a Faulkner, not of a legal document, the learnedness of a John Barth, not of an academic pedant. Hence the definition of so-called qualities is an illusion: what has been stated is 'literary quality' by association with the literary.

Amongst the authorities who say so – the someones one has heard of – are both well-known individuals and institutions, i.e. reputable authoritative journals and newspapers which have some claim to membership among the literary. *Gravity's Rainbow* has mostly authorities of the second type speaking up for it: *The New York Times*, *Saturday Review*, *Time*, *The Listener*, *Newsweek*, *The New Statesman*, *The Sunday Telegraph*, *New Society*. Pynchon's *The Crying of Lot 49* can boast both the first type of authority: '"The best American novel I have read since the war" Frank Kermode', and a hybrid of the first and second: Norman Shrapnel of *The Guardian*, where there seems to be some question as to who/which carries the more (literary) weight. Additional authority may be invoked through literary prizes: 'Nobel Prizewinner' (Beckett), or 'Winner of the Somerset Maugham Award' (Ian McEwan).

With the second authority invoked on behalf of *Gravity's Rainbow* we can see the division into newspaper reviewers ('hacks') and 'pure' literary personalities from the academy evidenced: the former are usually subsumed under the name of the paper they work for, the latter stand under their own well-known names: Frank Kermode, Adrian Mitchell, Pritchett, Gore Vidal, Canetti, Toynbee and so on. Occasionally the problem comes up, as in the case of *The Crying of Lot 49*: are Norman Shrapnel or Peter Lewis personalities themselves or hacks of *The Guardian* and the *Daily Mail* respectively? And the question, perhaps, is also: are *The Guardian* and the *Daily Mail* prestigious enough in *literary* terms to count as literary authorities without their respective critic's name?

The second way of becoming a work of the new literary is through association with already established literary works, which may be cited by title or by the name of the author. James Joyce is one of Picador's most frequently invoked authors, for instance with regard to *Gentlemen Prefer Blondes*, or on behalf of Flann O'Brien's *The Third Policeman*: '"Even with *Ulysses* and *Finnegan's Wake* behind him, James Joyce might have been envious" *Observer*.' The implication, again, is that O'Brien's novel is on the one hand 'like' *Ulysses* and *Finnegan's Wake*, and on the other an 'advance beyond either'.

Concerning Beckett's *Murphy*, the blurb invokes the trope of history: 'Historically, *Murphy* forms a bridge between the novels of James Joyce and the new literature of the post-war world in which Beckett's work occupies such a prominent place.' Circularity indeed: Beckett forms a bridge between Joyce and Beckett, a bridge between the modernist literature and the new literature, which thus must be literary through linking, as well as through the association of *Murphy* with Beckett. With similar circularity, Borges is invoked to give a recommendation for the work of Borges; he becomes the authority in the blurb for his own *A Personal Anthology*: 'South America's major prose writer makes his own selection of the pieces on which he would like his reputation to rest.' Borges, at the end of Borges, creates his own oeuvre in historical terms, makes his own posthumous reputation. And concerning Borges's *The Aleph and Other Stories*, Picador announces: 'Most comprehensive collection available in English. It contains a long specially written auto-biographical essay as well as a brilliant selection of fiction.' Not only critic, editor and historian of Borges, Borges is also his own biographer. And as to his editing of his work, note that it is the selection which is brilliant rather than the fiction. Borges manning the whole literary institution single-handed.

The tropes employed in the praise of new work constantly make allusion to the *becoming of literature* according to the classical model: becoming literature through historical permanence, through reputation, through assessment by authorities of the literary. Thus Brautigan is said to be 'established as one of the major writers of our time', his establishment having happened elsewhere. We have to take it on trust, on the authority of this assertion, rather than being persuaded through argument. He is no longer said to be great by one or another literary authority, he is said to have been established, presumably through the unnamed consensus which witnesses the becoming of history of *our time*, the next period of literary history. There is frequent reference to this period-in-the-making (though not to who makes it or how): 'One of the greatest prose writers of this century' (re Beckett), or Frank Kermode's 'The Best American novel I have read since the war'; Philip Toynbee with respect to Musil: 'One of the very few great comic writers of this century'. History selects, the consensus of the literati distils, the few rare masterpieces. Toynbee's emphasis is on 'One of the very few', Cannetti's estimate of Musil that he is 'The only writer in any language as exciting as Proust', where Proust serves as reference point of the very rarest, the unique. 'If I were banished to the moon tomorrow and could take *only five* books, this [*Gravity's Rainbow*] would be one of them,' says the critic of *The New York Times* (my emphasis). 'Only a few novels change people's lives. This is one of them,' claims the blurb on the back of Gabriel Garcia Marquez's *One Hundred Years of Solitude*.

The quality or qualities which make of these works literary masterpieces are self-referential qualities: greatness, artisticness, masterliness: 'One of the great works', 'one of this century's greatest', 'a comic masterpiece', 'a masterpiece', 'a shamelessly original work of art', 'a contemporary American classic', 'a little masterpiece of appalling fascination', 'just about perfect', 'a major contemporary work of literature . . . the Latin American *Don Quixote* . . . a classic'. All the questions remain: What is greatness, what a classic, what original or perfect in a work of literature, what a work, what a masterpiece, what a work of literature? The highest praise accorded to a work is that it is a work of literature; the most striking fact in this construction of the new literary is that it is circular, self-referential. We establish through the established, through assertion of 'similarity', and through the paradoxical combination of opposites: likeness and utter unlikeness – originality. No comparison in analytical terms, no demonstration of likeness, but asserted likeness in greatness, in masterpiece-ness, in literari-ness. Those who judge can judge because they are already literary; they do not need to say what makes them value a text, they just need to say that *they* do. 'The best . . . *I* have read', If *I* were asked', 'If *I* were banished to the moon' (my emphasis).

The narrow circularity of Picador works like a microcosm of a demi-mode: some of the authorities who are quoted on behalf of other works are themselves published by Picador, have, in other words, been 'established' and made 'literary' through Picador, e.g. Cannetti (before the Nobel Prize), Kafka, Borges etc. Finally, these Picador authors can almost stand on their own – the Picador Pantheon – as they are collected in an anthology called *The Naked I*: 'included are Kafka, Borges, Nabokov, Coover, Ken Kesey'. The beginning of the blurb: 'In this age of no fixed values . . .'

Nor is this just a case of commercial sleight of hand; as we have seen, the publishers work closely with the experts of the arts and the academy, and the Picador Pantheon closely resembles the modern literature curriculum of English departments. In the 'purer' academic spheres we can see the same principles at work. The anthology *The American Tradition in Literature*, edited by professors of renowned English departments in the USA, deals in similar fashion with modern poets – the contemporary literary. Elizabeth Bishop gets a recommendation from her contemporary Randall Jarrell, himself already 'established' in the period before the immediate contemporary as a poet of the 'mid-century', and she is also said to show 'similarity to her long-time friend Marianne Moore' (established poet of the early century).[13] 'Literariness' transferred from a literary authority and through similarity with some other literature.

By far the most frequently invoked reference point for the literary (the James Joyce of poetry) is Robert Lowell, also of the mid-century establishment, who has already 'won serious critical attention'.[14] He is said to have 'power and originality' (remember Susan Sontag), and his greatness is further evidenced by a much longer biographical entry than those of any of his contemporaries, and which includes many 'proofs' (through association) of his membership among the literary. Randall Jarrell again wrote a review of his poetry, which the editors say is particularly interesting because 'Lowell approved it, in lieu of his own introduction, for publication with a selection of his poetry.'[15] Who is proving whom great and literary? The critic is supposed to evaluate the poet's work, but the sacred authority of the poet himself is invoked to approve and to prove that the critic is right (cf. Borges). Although 'likeness' is also required: Lowell 'shares with Pound' the inclination to recreate in translation the poems of other serious poets, such as Homer, Rilke and Pasternak. For good measure, three further critics are named and quoted. Thus established beyond doubt as a member of the literary, Lowell is then invoked to validate the talents of less certain poets, such as Anne Sexton, who 'studied poetry with Robert Lowell at Boston University' and must thus have acquired some literariness through proximity.[16] Or Adrienne Rich, whose verse 'Robert Lowell . . . sees as "a poised and intact completion," deeply reminiscent of "old poets . . . and still more . . . of our prose writers – Hawthorne above all" '.[17] Or Sylvia Plath, who in *Ariel* 'reached what Robert Lowell has called "appalling and permanent fulfilment" '.[18]

It might be considered conspicuous that Lowell's testimony is adduced for the benefit of three out of four women poets represented in this section of 'poets at three-quarter century', while no named authority is cited on behalf of the twelve male poets, who 'received honours', 'won recognition', 'literary prizes', 'a following' all by themselves and are themselves quoted as authorities on their work.[19] The fourth woman poet, Denise Levertov, is an American only by marriage, and a poet apparently also through marriage: 'She married an American author, Mitchell Goodman, and through him became interested in the American experimental poetry.'[20]

In this way do the editors of *The American Tradition in Literature* fulfil their task of sorting contemporary production into the 'titans' and the 'writers of lesser stature whose works endure'.[21] They are helping them endure by titanic association and by inclusion in the anthology. But they would have us believe that these works 'endure' all by themselves, out of their own strength, due to their fitness, passing the difficult spiritual test of time and approbation, winning the consensus of disinterested spectators. In the very book object for which I have paid so many pounds sterling I indulge in the illusion that such 'endurance' is happening elsewhere, out there in the sanctuary of Value, whilst this physical object and this critical and editorial enterprise are the very determining factors in the works' renewed enduring. To say nothing of the contribution of the anthology to the oblivion of works not included in it.

# The Book Business

It should be clear by now that a separation of the literary academy from the book business is illusory, since they both need each other to exist, depend on each other and mesh harmoniously. Critics become company advertisers, academics are hired to review books in journals, professors train future publishers, publishers publish books and teachers put them on the curriculum. Yet popular mythology keeps them sharply distinguished: just as the myth of artistic disinterestedness defines an isolated sanctuary for art and literature, so the myth of the disinterested pursuit of truth together with the myth of pure meritocracy draw a firm boundary around the academy which apparently separates it from the world of business and commerce.

Thus the concept of the commercial and productive side of the literary – the production of literary books – poses some problems for the popular mythology. The marriage between the virgin in the ivory tower and the businessman in the market place makes us predict some tensions. As we have seen, the high literary is concerned with the production of an elite – an elite of great works and an elite of literati. The principal concern of the literary is exclusion: exclusion of the masses of writings and of authors which fall beyond its rigid though ill-defined standards. The high literary is like the high society of the community of verbal representations; reading its journals and magazines is like reading the gossip columns of ordinary newspapers. Names are being dropped of someones one has heard of, and they are usually dropped by someones one increasingly hears of.

By contrast, publishers are in business rather than in drawing rooms. Their overriding concern is inclusion: including the masses of consumers among their clientele, including products among marketable commodities. One might predict some marital conflict. Yet the two – business and the literary – do get along rather well; let us see how they do it.

Picador, we have seen, is a publisher apparently devoted to the interests of the literary, at the forefront of the difficult task of electing the future elite from among the younger generation. They are the organizers of a *débutants* ball. The publishers pander to the concerns of the established literary by signaling 'literary' and 'exclusiveness' by different means. Penguin, for instance, uses different categories: black for dead classics, grey for classics in the making, orange for the somewhat undecided modern literary of general interest, and latterly a different format, King Penguin, to intimate, through like format and cover quality, a likeness to Picador and Virago progressiveness. But publishers at the same time wink at the not-so-literary customers that they are not really excluded, enticing them with cover pictures of a less exclusive genre. Favourites are pictures from films made of the books (e.g. D. H. Lawrence, Kate Chopin, Henry James, John Fowles), or unconnected photographs which look as if they could be from a movie, or off the cover of women's magazines or soft-core magazines (e.g. Edna O'Brien's, Muriel Spark's, Iris Murdoch's novels in Penguin, or the soft focus, soft-core sub-Hamilton photos on the covers of Picador's Ian McEwan). The mass media of film and photography increasingly replace reproductions from the more exclusive genre of 'high art' painting.

The verbal blurbs continue to promote the literary myth of exclusiveness, of unique masterpiece, of one in a thousand, as we have so many novels hailed as 'the *Ulysses* of the latter half of the twentieth century', each more unique than the other. Critics and reviewers involved in the literary connive in this multiplication of the few for more than one reason: the first, of course, is that no critic or reviewer can live on one masterpiece per half century, the second is the fear of being made a fool of by (literary) history. We all still remember the fools who rejected *Ulysses* or D. H. Lawrence in their days, and we would not like to follow in their footsteps. It is thus wise to put your bet down frequently in hailing a master-piece, the more often, the better the odds. For the same reason it does not pay to speak up *against* a new work: history will forgive those who said nothing (they cannot be quoted), but will ridicule those who exposed themselves unwisely. But the critic or editor who has to make such a difficult decision is never really out there alone: there is guarantee already in the fact of the work's having been published, and published by a particular publisher and perhaps in a particular category, to help the critic along. Similarly, the editor deciding whether to publish or not relies on critics and other literati ('readers' or lectors) to share the responsibility of decision. If you can publish with a famous critic's 'The best $x$ I have read since $y$' you are fairly safe. But it is easiest of all for those who have to judge a work by someone one has already heard of.

In her recent experiment of publishing a novel under a pseudonym, Doris Lessing has neatly put publishers' and critics' ability to recognize 'literary quality' to test. Pub-lishers, it emerges, fare slightly better than do critics, with the exception of Lessing's two usual British publishers, who declined the manuscript of the unknown 'Jane Somers'. A third, Michael Joseph, bought the novel because it 'reminded him of the young Doris Lessing'.[1] European publishers also bought the manuscript, the German publisher because he has a rare policy of publishing young and unknown (*un*heard-of) authors. The French publisher also bought the manuscript, the astute editor spotting a similarity of style and suspecting that Lessing had helped the unknown 'Jane Somers'. Once the book was published under the pseudonym of 'Jane Somers', it was sent to 'all the eminent critics who have been analysing my work for a long time, all those who have written theses and entire works on Doris Lessing, those who said I was better in my realist phase [rather than in her later 'space fiction' phase]. There wasn't one among them who wrote a single line.'[2] The critics, in other words, chose to reject by non-consideration. Their famous analysis of likeness and similarity, of recognition of 'literary quality', so safe in the knowledge of Lessing's authorship, had miserably failed them without that knowledge. And if it did not fail the critic, it failed the editors of renowned literary magazines or journals:

> No 'serious' journal chronicled my book. *The New York Times Book Review* sent my novel to a free-lance journalist [a lesser hack than the fully employed critic or reviewer]. She wrote an enthusiastic review but they didn't publish it.[3]

And further:

> The only articles that were published were published in provincial papers. Women journalists had read on the cover that the author was a famous British journalist disguised by a pseudonym.[4]

It looks as if the less literary prestige there is – provincial rather than metropolitan paper, free-lance rather than fully employed critic, journalist rather than critic, woman rather than man – the more chance there is that a serious effort of study and analysis will be made, the less chance that the already accumulated capital of literary prestige (authority) will be made to stand in for bona fide judgement. And the best chance there is obviously where a maximum of inferior credentials coincide – in the woman journalist of a provincial newspaper, unless here we have a new factor in professional solidarity, as Lessing seems to intimate.

Critics in the USA were also quite explicit about their marketing criteria and how these override literary judgement: 'two excellent literary critics rang their editor to tell him that they liked the book very much but that they couldn't push it: no photograph, no biography. Today, if one wants to promote a book, one has to have a personality to sell.'[5] If there is not already an author one has heard of, promoters can engage in the process of making one, in creating a personality out of the author's looks and the curiosities of biography. Never mind the 'qualities' of the literary work. Personality, the very dimension that is played down by the literary values of pure disinterestedness, is the best capital for the promotion of the literary product. The highest literary quality, the most reliable and the most relied upon, is the literary prestige of 'someone one has already heard of' that is manufactured in the world, in the commercial reality, and not in the pure and separate domain of the literary and its abstracted text, the word, the spirit incarnate. One fix of the cultural capital accumulated in the commodity of Doris Lessing's name would suffice to ensure the commercial success of anything published under her name; no amount of injection of the literary quality of a Doris Lessing's writing will ensure the same success. The competitive spirit of the free market does anything to avoid any real and open competition.

The value of author prestige is the literary value *par excellence*: it not only signals 'literary' through previous association with something/someone already literary, but it indicates the highest value of the elite system, exclusiveness and uniqueness. Other qualities such as 'compendiousness', 'originality', 'style', 'literariness' and so on may be incarnated variously; Doris Lessingness, Beckettness, Joyceness, are absolutely unique, the ultimate guarantee of exclusiveness. If the Lessingness cannot be defined and pinned down in Lessing's writing, it can be derived from the uniqueness of her person, her biography as author. The star status of individual authors embodies the epitome of the elite quality, the singular one-and-only, and is the direct opposite of what belongs to the mass, the mass media, the masses, the common man and woman (remember that mass circulation was softly pronographic, the opposite of the artistic). The implicit tendency within the elite culture of the high literary is to establish an ultimate hierarchy of *the* greatest, the highest, the only one, the unique.

But since even the high literary has its feet on the economic ground, the full consequences of its elite tendency are never absolutely drawn, exclusion is never pushed to the final extreme, and hence we have the peaceful co-existence of many of these greatest, these unique, these original and solitary manifestations of the literary, an artistocracy without its king. We thus have a semblance of democracy among the elite: the democracy of consumerism, of choice on the shelves of the literary trading station. The marriage of the elitism of the high literary with the principle of consumerism yields the necessary class system within the system, exemplifying the selection of the 'best', the ratification of the rulers, without thereby losing the lesser members for commercial exploitation. It is a necessary part of the manufacture of the class system, of the values of class, classics and quality. The literary stands at the top of the production of verbal culture, producing and perpetuating the myths and values of disinterested meritocracy, of irresponsible authorship, of historical and audience-produced consensus, which enable and protect the production of pornography as mass product on a lower scale. In economic terms, the production of this literary book nobility is sustained by the production of 'mass circulation' literature. In terms of value, if there is a 'high', there must needs be a 'low'; if there is a star, a unique individual, there must needs be a mass from which he or she is distinguished.

At the lower end of the spectrum we have the production of mass culture, a mass of commodities for a mass audience. Here, the principle of inclusion rules supreme, preferring the buck in hand over the two bucks in the bush of the more complicated production of prestige. Neither the product need distinguish itself from other products, nor the author and reader from the mass of producers and consumers. In the circles of the high literary, as we have seen, the uniqueness of the author is valued by the reader and critic because the glamour of the former reflects on the latter who recognizes it. Just as the mass of consumers who buy the exclusive Chanel no. 5 perfume advertised by the star Catherine Deneuve are encouraged to feel as unique and star-like as she,[6] so the considerable mass of the literary minority who read star authors are encouraged to feel uniquely literary and artistic with a share in the elite. Mass production, by contrast, simply does not hide its consumerist objective and aims at an audience of consumers who do not care if they are excluded from a taste elite. The product itself is a simple consumer product, which will be consumed in the process of consuming (it is 'ephemeral' rather than 'enduring' literature). The literary product, by contrast, is also an investment opportunity for the production and reproduction of literary capital. What is lost in terms of a wider circulation is gained in terms of reinvestable capital: the product – book or author – can be used for transferring literariness on to another product in future.

Despite these differences, mass production and literary elite production share in important features of production, which have bearings on the question of representation. They share the principle of meritocracy and the irresponsibility of authorship, of production itself. The chief value of consumerism is what the majority swallow. Consumers are said to swallow of their own free will and to swallow in a consensus. The producers assume no responsibility for the product: the majority have selected and ratified it as 'good enough' (rather than 'the best') by swallowing it. The product has passed the test of consumption. That there is preselection of what is offered to the great swallowing is commonly underplayed, and that there is advice for the consumer as to what to consume (offered by the producers) has become such a fact of life as to appear 'natural' and hence beyond question and criticism. The consumers, after all, may choose what to swallow, may choose between Kellogg's cornflakes and Kellogg's sugarpuffs, Kellogg's wheatabix and Kellogg's ricecrispies. Swallow they must. There is no choice not to swallow, according to the consumerist scenario. The very trade marks of consumerism are that the market is free and that there is choice for the consumer (remember Soviet Russia, where consumers are coerced to choose government monopoly cereals). The available range of goods exists as if by natural law: the goods are, they have come into being, they are there for the consumer to evaluate. The fact of supply, of production, of authorship is put under the shadow of demand: the demand by the consuming public. Just as the literary consensus of the reading public is said to ratify the offered production of artistic goods, so the public demand, the consensus swallowing, is said to ratify the offer of produced consumer goods. The consensus witnesses the test of time in the case of art, or of competition in the case of general consumer goods, for the selection of the best or the fittest or those most in demand. The public's wants, demands and desires are treated as if they were the manifestation of an authentic and unadulterated instinct, the instinct to secure what is necessary for survival, a kind of biological urge. In the rhetoric of the free-market economy, demand becomes a 'natural' law, while little is said about the creation of demands and of the values and aspirations produced through the very production of goods, through the range of choice and the canonization of available consumer goods.

The most ubiquitous argument of pornography producers and of the mass media is that they serve and supply what is in demand. They agree in face-to-face communication with their critics that what the public want is shameful or in bad taste but – it's a free world and a free market. As individuals they align themselves with a minority of taste and values and dissociate themselves from that mass public. Raymond Williams quotes a former head of the *Mirror* group: 'Of course you have to give the public what it wants, otherwise you go out of business . . . it is only the people who conduct newspapers and similar organizations who have any idea quite how indifferent, quite how stupid, quite how uninterested in education of any kind the great bulk of the British public are.'[7] The responsibility for production has thus been shoved off, apparently on to the shoulders of the consumers, while the authority, the authorship of production has been made to disappear from view. The responsibility of authorship and production, in the pure literary as well as in business, is denied by the producers and attributed to, in one case, the literary, educated, history-making minority reading public, in the other, the incredibily stupid 'bulk' of the rest of the public masses. The responsibility of the producers, as they see it, is towards their business – making the literary and making profit – rather than towards the product or the consumer. The cultural responsibility which the feminist critic is looking for – responsibility of the author towards the cultural output; responsibility towards the 'subject matter' of the work of art instead of irresponsibility – does not seem to exist, does not seem to fit into the scheme of things in the production of the literary and in the book business.

The literary itself is a productive system grafted upon the business of publishing, influenced and controlled by industrial interests and its accompanying ideology. As a culturally 'high' domain it is involved in producing the values of the literary and the artistic, the class values of elitism, in the interest of which it needs to hide the processes of production and promotion which would reveal these as self-interested and far from ideologically 'pure' and disinterested. Works of art are therefore treated as if they had come into being by law of nature, and their continued survival as ratified by consumer consensus of the minority audience which itself aspires to membership among the elite. Under the principle of clannishness where the new literary is produced on the basis of family resemblance with the old literary, a very limited range of creativity actually finds expression or acceptance and it is characterized by certain features of sameness underneath the trademark of originality. Under the pressure of business, the 'unique' literary is multiplied, enhancing the impression of sameness. The 'modern American novel', now also produced in England, is an example. The mass market of pornography is only the extreme of the literary's business aspect realized. What is more, the pornographic element of mass culture, characterized by eternal sameness, adds an element of uniqueness when featuring in the pure literary. As the Russian Formalists noted, the literary, in order to renew itself, in order to replace forms which have lost their avant-garde quality of originality, draws on 'sub-literary' genres, such as for instance pornography.[8] The modern literary critic has decided to play in the given scenario, to match the producers' lack of responsibility with his own, for the treat of being allowed to play, to take part in the glamorous world of art, the showbiz of the upper classes, the Hollywood of the educated.

The pornographer knows that he has nothing to fear from any literary critic. The literary establishment sanctions the display of creativity, values the expression of fantasy as the product of the unconscious which constitutes the source of truth, of nature, in the domain of culture, the great given of humanity. It values them all because it values itself, because it has no criteria, no position, no connection to political reality which could serve as a reference point. It thus welcomes 'all' excretions of the mind (produced under its licence), values them for the fact that they have been created, a marvel in the eyes of man (or a hang-up on creativity, a case of womb envy?). Within its pluralist unity, it invokes values of this kind or that – compendiousness, density, originality, power, perfection – but the literary itself is beyond value, is Value itself.

# Playing in the Literary Sanctuary

The conception of art and literature as aesthetic domains, disconnected from reality through a boundary between fiction and fact, has also led to the arbitrary cutting off of the author from reality. The scriptural attitude towards works of art sees in the artist not a member of the human community, but the ideal of the Subject: incarnated in the word, finding full expression in the medium. 'Writing is that neutral, composite, oblique space where our subject slips away, the negative where all identity is lost,' writes Roland Barthes.[1] The 'subject' which slips away is the subject of social identity; writing is the space of the Subject, of living subjectivity, where subjectivity is liberated from social, economic, gender, class and all other intersubjective constraints and the subject constitutes and loses itself in language, in signification, in the infinity of meaning. This aesthetic stance towards this metaphysical space has become so naturalized that we see nothing wrong with it. The critic accepts the boundaries, leaps within, and continues to show up and lay bare what the artist has shown up and laid bare before him, for him. What they lay bare is, if not 'reflected reality', the attainment of full subjectivity, of fulfilment in expression, of the play with meaning and the consummation of the feeling of delight by the privileged cultural subject.

Thus Angela Carter as literary critic can claim Sade as a virtual 'forerunner' of feminist critics: he has said, shown, enumerated and laid bare the mechanisms and mechanics of the pornographic scenario, of the degradation of women, before them and for them. They need only enumerate after him. Carter writes:

Sade remains a monstrous and daunting cultural edifice; yet I would like to think that he put pornography in the service of women, or, perhaps, allowed it to be invaded by an ideology not inimical to women. And give the old monster his due; let us introduce him with an exhilarating burst of rhetoric: 'Charming sex, you will be free: just as men do, you shall enjoy all the pleasures that Nature makes your duty, do not withhold yourselves from one. Must the more divine half of mankind be kept in chains by the other? Ah, break those bonds: nature wills it.'[2]

Here Carter, the potential feminist critic, has withdrawn into the literary sanctuary, has become literary critic: 'Sade' is no longer the man she so carefully researched, the multiple rapist and murderer, but as writer, as pornographer, deserves a literary critical response that treats him as artist and writing subject. Like good modern literary critics, we move from the author/writer to the *oeuvre*/text which by literary convention bears his name: Sade is a Cultural Edifice (a rock of culture). A literary artefact, removed by convention of the literary beyond the reach of political, of feminist critique. Sade's pornographic assault on one particular patriarchal representation of woman – the Mother – renders him, in the eyes of Carter, a provider of a service to women. His murderous 'misanthropy' (sic), she argues, 'has bred a hatred of the mothering function that led him to demystify the most sanctified aspects of women and if he invented women who suffered, he also invented women who caused suffering'.[3] Women, of course, neither produced nor sanctified the mothering aspect of their patriarchal representation, but it is doubtful whether they would thank Sade for replacing the myth of the Mother with that of the victim or the inverted pornographic sadist. Besides falling into the trap of the literary sanctuary, Carter here lapses into the fallacy of equal opportunities: following her provider, she seems eager to take up the opportunity he invents for her: to cause suffering, 'just as men do'.

But Sade is more subtle than Carter gives him credit for.

He does not rattle her chains in order for her to escape them, and she should suspect his 'liberating' spirit bred from hatred. But dazzled by the offer of equal opportunities, she misreads him. While his options are strictly binary – to suffer or to cause suffering, to belong to one half of 'mankind' or the other – these are not for her to choose from: they are gender specific. What he offers her – as Barthes is to offer later on – is to choose an attitude to her preordained role: 'break those bonds', 'be free' – embrace your chains with ecstasy. 'You shall enjoy . . . your duty'. Freedom and enjoyment are ordered with the authority of a direct imperative, they are a strict duty. Sade, with the flourish of his magician's hat, emerges from this extraordinary edifice of rhetoric to bow with a smile: Nature Himself! For, these pleasures of women (chains, rape and murder), Nature makes their duty, Nature wills. Carter, still lolling in the literary sanctuary, applauds this creation and sees an 'ideology not inimical to women' in this 'exhilarating burst of rhetoric'. Since it all happens in the realm of the literary, it cannot possibly be 'inimical' to women in the real world, and the literary in turn is far beyond the reach of feminist or moral terms such as 'inimical'. Barthes thus has no news for us in his reformulation:

> The scream is the victim's mark; she makes herself a victim because she chooses to scream; if, under the same vexation she were to ejaculate, she would cease to be a victim [would be free to enjoy], would be transformed into a libertine [would cause suffering rather than suffer]: *to scream/to discharge*, this paradigm is the beginning of choice, i.e. of Sadeian meaning.[4]

The trick is achieved by means of rhetoric: both Sade and Barthes, accustomed to the authority of naming, decree that the discharging victim shall no longer be called 'victim'. Her role under the vexation – the imperative of the pornographic plot – remains unchanged, still she is victim of the vexation inflicted upon her, but the subtle connoisseur distinguishes between the victim's reactions ('attitudes'): scream – expression of pain and resistance; discharge – bodily response of pleasure. The former the expression of a will, mingled with the direct expression of the body; the latter the expression of the body that imposes itself on the will.

Once again, there is no disagreement between the pornographer and his critic, Barthes or Carter. They are both showing up, analysing, laying bare and reformulating what they have so carefully noted. But the feminist critic disagrees, and disagrees as much with the literary critic. The feminist critic (of pornography, of the literary) argues that the pornographic, the porno-writerly, is not beyond the reach of a feminist critique. She develops her critique from within the realm of representation; her argument is not simply sociological (and hence dismissible by the literary critic), and not simply 'moral' according to the morality of the censorship lobby. Her argument is literary political, a political critique of the literary, a critique of the politics of the literary and of representation. Her argument is that writing is political, a political act in the real world. Her argument is also that the tradition of the literary, of the critical discipline, is itself political, ideologically weighted, and that the conception of the literary as separate, as aesthetic, as non-political sanctuary, as the pure field of desire, is a political conception, an ideological cornerstone of patriarchal culture. The pornographic is protected by virtue of its participation in the literary as the 'low' to the literary's 'high', and it is protected by the literary connivance in the pornographic, in the irresponsibility of authorship.

The contemporary conception of the literary is undergoing a transformation which is structurally homologous with the plot transformation plotted by Sade. Already we have noticed a mutual approximation between the 'low' pornographic and the 'high' literary, as pornography upgrades its literary qualities of aesthetic execution, plot, character and originality, and literature incorporates ever more conventionally pornographic elements. But the homology exists on a deeper level. The division of an earlier, conventional conception of the literary into Literature on the one hand and

Literary Criticism on the other is disappearing, as writing approximates writing, becomes *écriture*, ecriture sharing the most important structural feature with pornography. We can trace this development either in terms of 'creative literature' or in terms of 'literary criticism', since the two interact dialectically, criticism feeding on literature, literature evolving out of evolving critical theory, theory forming out of literary practice, the two merging, becoming the same: writing, fictions, political acts.

A certain genre of 'modern American fiction' may serve as a reference point for the development in literature (though it is no longer bound by national frontiers): Miller, Mailer, Boukowsky, Roth, Heller, Styron, Bellow, Pynchon, McEwan, Sinclair, Jong, etc.; a certain type of literary critique hallmarked by the surrealist project, Bataille, Sartre, Lacan, Barthes, Foucault, Sontag may sketch the critical project. The common theme of both: the pursuit of pleasure (all marked by Sade), the play of desire. Naturally, this is not just a thematic concern, but a formal, a structural one. That pleasure, that desire, is explored and defined through sex/sexuality, is explored and defined in writing. The common structure is that of scenario no. 2, the common evolution a transformation from scenario no. 1 to scenario no. 2. Scenario no. 1, remember, is the one where the victim objects to the vexation and cries out in pain; scenario no. 2 the one where she 'chooses to ejaculate or discharge', transforms herself into libertine, enjoys herself and her vexation. The hero, in both scenarios, remains the same: the Hero, now also called anti-hero or the common man in the street in the plots of the modern 'American novel'.

Henry Miller and Norman Mailer are still firmly within the 'sadistic' tradition (sadistic having come to stand for scenario no. 1 with the reluctant and suffering victim). The modern American hero is in pursuit of his sexuality, the novel, as usual, takes the form of a quest. In the earlier version represented by Miller, the hero pursues his pleasure with brutality, inflicts pain, regardless. It is expected that the victim cry out. The evolving hero, however, undergoes a transformation: for his pleasure, for his sexuality, he must have the pleasure of the woman, the 'emancipated' woman, the liberated woman, the one liberated by Sade's imperative: you shall enjoy (your duty, your pleasure), do not withhold yourself. The hero no longer enjoys his rapes and murders as did Miller's and Mailer's hero: he wills his woman's lust. He is obsessed with her orgasms, he demands her discharge. An example picked at random, from Joseph Heller's *Something Happened*:

> Women my wife's age . . . take up robustly with fellows much younger than themselves . . . The husbands . . . can't abide their wives humping a younger dick . . . Our dicks are so pathetic. (I felt that way early and was close to a truth. I felt need, not power . . . [scenario no. 2]) . . . (A girl can always find a man to lay her at least once.) I think they feel safer with teen-agers . . . grabbing the initiative with their tense, sharpened fingernails . . . I have a girl who goes way out of control every time she has an orgasm.[5]

Here the woman/victim is apparently no longer passive, but taking ('grabbing') the initiative, wanting it – as men do. Power alone brings only the cry of the victim; the modern hero experiences a need – and will use all his power as hero, as master, as subject, to fulfil that need, to coerce her pleasure out of her. Power is not abandoned, need is rather a surplus, since there is obviously still power invested in being a husband, a man older than teenagers and less safe for women. The ultimate goal, the holy grail, is as ever the subject's feeling of pleasure, his need is his feeling of life, but the woman's pleasure has become an intermediate goal in the attainment of the final one. Her pleasure, a bodily response to the vexation, a discharge in lieu of a cry, fascinates the hero: she 'goes way out of control every time she has an orgasm'. The woman's pleasure, translating itself into desire, imping- ing on her consciousness as an 'aesthetic' factor besides and beyond the pain of her body, constitutes a challenge, and thus an additional excitement to the male subject's power, yet her discharge at the same time confirms it: he has coerced her control away from her, she does not act as a subject with a will of her own, but *re*acts to his bodily imposition. She may have an orgasm, but 'I have a girl': I have her and I have her orgasm.

This new complication of plot, this new obstacle to be overcome by the hero, this new task to be accomplished in his pursuit of his prize, this new refinement of pleasure, provides so much dazzlement that all other factors are overshadowed. Heroes and critics are so overwhelmed by these new signs of life issuing from the victim presumed nearly dead that they mistake them for the discharge of a reviving subject. Alike they cry: equal opportunities! She has her pleasure now, so let us continue to pursue ours. She discharges – as men do. Barthes, the critic, notes and lays bare the fact that the whole hoax is a trick of rhetoric, but he continues to put the spotlight on the trick and to cast a shadow of oblivion over what is hidden behind the hoax. After the passage already cited concerning 'Sadeian meaning', he continues:

> The best proof is that when a sentence begins with the tale of a vexation, it is impossible to know who pronounces it, because it is impossible to foresee whether it will end in a cry or in ejaculation: the sentence is free, until the last moment: 'Verneuil pinched her buttocks with such cruel force . . .' (one expects something like: 'that the victim could no longer restrain her cries'; but what one actually gets from the syntactic machine, from the sentence-posture, is quite the reverse:) . . . 'that the whore discharged on the spot'.[6]

Barthes' syntactic analysis is faultless, of course, but what is curious is his claim that the speaker is put into question. The speaker is undoubtedly the same: the pornographer, reciter of the vexation. Who else could it possibly be? What Barthes seems to be getting at is that we cannot, until the last moment, tell whether we have unwilling or willing victim or, in sadean parlance, victim or libertine. But we need not even await the response of the victim to make our subtle distinction between cry and discharge: the speaker has already named her, has named her whore rather than victim. As speaker, as namer, as reciter of vexations, he still is the producer of sadean meaning and has not abrogated this privilege to the object-libertine. It is not she who is free: it is the sentence.

Barthes further notes that Sade

> does not define the victim by the practice in which she is caught ('suffering', 'enduring', 'receiving'); an exorbi- tant fact if one thinks of the current definition of sadism or the structural definition of character, that the 'role' is here held [to be] negligible. The victim is not 'he or she who submits', but 'he or she who uses a certain language'.[7]

Barthes notes how the sadean rhetoric leaves the orbit of logical analysis and gets into the customary sadean word magic, where He defines that the role should be neglected and the simulated victim-response become determinant, even though it lacks the structural capacity to determine anything. But Barthes no more than notes it. He neither corrects it, nor balances it up with his own discourse; instead, he follows his mentor out of the orbit, replicating his trajectory. He contines: 'In the sadean novel – like in the proustian novel – the population divides itself into classes, not according to a practice but according to language, or more precisely, according to their practice of language.'[8] The new and exorbitant analysis has become analysis, naturalized, and what is originally of Sade's, of Proust's making becomes an academic fact, a state of affairs. Note, not they, Sade or Proust, divide the population, but 'the population divides itself' – as if by natural law, objectively described, and like the victim, 'choosing' to do so by adopting a particular practice of language. Gone is the notion of 'role', of the fact that the victim, or the population, finds itself 'caught' in a particular practice which defines it. Gone is the notion that the discourse, even the simulated discourse (discharge) of the victim-object, is produced, is authored by the subject, and is structurally subordinate to an overall practice in which the victim is caught, the scenario in which the victim has become object. The sadean text, through association with the proustian text through likeness, has become literary – and so has the critic.

In an earlier literary tradition, the literary process was conceived as clearly defined: the master writes – masterpieces, literature, great works – the critic/reader reads, receives. The process is clearly transitive: subject – verb – object/recipient. Critical writing is called 'secondary literature' and serves the master literature. The author is the hero of the scenario of the literary.

*La nouvelle critique* sees itself as constituting a radical break from this tradition. It hails the 'death of the author' and the birth of the reader.[9] Its object is the pursuit, the exploration of pleasure, of desire. Not only the author-subject finds fulfilment in the medium, satisfaction of self-expression, but the reader too 'enjoys', *jouit*, engages in the process 'actively', wants it too, the pleasure, the orgasm, the *jouissance*. He leaves behind the 'readerly' text and progresses to the 'writerly' text, to writing, to *écriture*. With the concept of the orgasmic 'writerly' literary, the distinction between author and reader vanishes, as the reader 'writes' the text, constructs the meaning, as men do, as authors do. Sex/sexuality and writing merge: both are the project of the subject, the pursuit of his desire, ending in orgasm, *jouissance*. The writing of Lacan is at the basis of this new literary understanding; his most persistent question is, 'What does woman want?'. What does Lacan want that woman want? Like all other modern heroes, he wants, he wills, her pleasure. Like the others, he has arrived at this scenario no. 2 from a previous scenario no. 1: 'Lacan, who rarely delineates his divergence from Freud, is proud to make one distinction clear . . . "What I approach this year is what Freud expressly left aside . . . the *What does woman want?*"'[10] Where Freud was content to pursue his study of sexuality without ever inquiring after the 'attitude' of the victim, Lacan is after 'the other satisfaction, that which responds to phallic pleasure'.[11] Not, notice, after what woman might want, but after that discharge from the woman-object in response to the phallic vexation: her pleasure a response, and hence *his* satisfaction. The scenario in which she is taunted to want something is already defined, a strict imperative demanding a response, as Lacan's question – his 'sentence posture' or syntactic machine – demands an answer, syntactically preordained. There is no choice not to respond, not to submit to the vexation; there is only an 'attitude' to be chosen.

The modern American novel's anti-hero, in quest of sex and his sexuality (her pleasure his need), is also in perpetual quest for writing. He wants to be a writer, an author; he becomes a writer, writes a novel, modern, American. At the same time as critique proclaims the author dead in its quest for the reader's discharge, the author reappears in his own scenario of representation in the role of the novel's hero. The quest of the subject is dramatized through the hero's dual quest as sexual subject and as writing subject, a man in search of the woman's pleasure as a step towards his own, an author in search of his 'writing', in search of his reader's pleasure to guarantee his own pleasure as supreme subject. The two form a single quest: her pleasure, so consistently sought, so persistently wrought, informs the nature of his writing, which is *écriture*, that writing mixed with 'her' pleasure, with desire, *jouissance* – scenario no. 2.

Like the white man, author of the murder of Thomas Kasire, author of the representations produced for the pleasure of his guests, the writer-author puts himself inside the picture, dramatizes himself as hero in the represented scenario. Through his position within that picture, he offers the viewer a locus for identification, where the reader can join him as subject, to 'write' and compose the picture with him, to construct his pleasure and not to take notice of another possible locus for identification, that of the victim-object. For, the reader, formerly recipient in the literary scenario, servant to the author, now writes the text with him, helps produce the orgasm, produces the text, produces the *jouissance*, the meaning. Barthes has shown us how, in the transformation from scenario no. 1 to scenario no. 2, meaning is produced. Together, writer and reader-writer produce and write the scenario of 'woman's' sexual liberation (under orders from Sade), her pleasure that they will. The reader, once at the receiving end of a transitive process, 'feminized' in his literary role, turns round and produces his pleasure: chooses to ejaculate. This discharge, this orchestrated *jouissance* of the reader is the production of literary meaning. The literary is homologous with the sadean scenario, the offer of sadean 'choice', the pornographic vexation.

Within the traditional literary scenario, the vexation is the critic's particular plight: he suffers, passively, from the assignation to an inferior role, servant to his master. He is the one who has no choice in the action. He is served with works of art as if with rocks of nature. But according to the modern scenario, he has a choice of attitude, an improved opportunity within his role: to like his position of impotence, to help perpetuate it. The sadean/barthean name-giving is significant: the willing victim is called 'libertine'. Libertines are the white man's guests, Sade's guests. While he remains the supreme author, the *metteur-en-scène*, they are invited to the 'active' roles within the pornographic scenarios that Sade stages for them: to do as he does; and he puts them behind the Instamatic. Thus Sade, like van Rooyen, consolidates the axis of identification that runs from author via the hero to the reader or audience. In this way Sade masks the discrepancy in authority which leaves him the supreme author and ultimate subject, his libertine guests his recipient audience. And he thereby marks one kind of victim as collaborator-to-be. And Barthes, Sade's libertine guest, obediently follows behind him and informs us of the disappearance of his host once the play has begun: 'In the sadean film, no one – no "me" – is properly the subject of the sequence: nobody films it, nobody edits it, nobody projects it, nobody sees it: a continuous image gets into motion through no other mechanism than that of time, of the clock.'[12] The image, the sequence, the sadean film, has Come Into Being.

This production of the libertine, of the willing victim, also masks the fact that there still needs to be a victim for this libertine, powerless with regard to the action, caught in a practice already defined, just as the libertine guests are caught in the practice of hospitality as the receivers of services and benefits courtesy of the host. The collaborating, ejaculating victim is named 'libertine', derived from the Latin for 'freedman', a man made free, by one with the authority to do so. The language of hospitality applies to the remaining, unwilling victim as well, with Sade in the position of naming: 'There's not a woman on earth who would ever have had cause to complain of my services . . .'

The reader or critic, dazzled by the scenario – the represented action – overlooks the scenario of representation where he is the literary victim-turned-libertine. Delighted by the opportunity, the invitation to his illustrious host's party, he joins as a guest, with never a thought of criticizing the party. He returns the hospitality by choosing not to opt out of the binary, the inexorable categories of the literary which necessitate that there be hosts and guests, so that there may be a realm of fantasy and pleasure, a sanctuary from the real. Like Carter he agrees to suffer or to cause suffering, to belong to one half of the literary or the other. He develops a 'criticism' which is impotent within this scenario of political, of communicative coercion, accepting the plot and the binary choice as givens of nature. But the literary is no more absolute nature than the nature authored by Sade, the literary, like the cultural having been authored by patriarchy. But this literary critic wants 'liberation', wants equal opportunities within the given options, wants libertinism: he will orgasm, enjoy, accept with ecstasy the duty ordained by the literary, a devoted servant of art and the aesthetic, keeping strictly within the boundaries of the pleasure sanctuary. And he will participate in that endless repetition of the same, unchanging pleasure, the rearticulation of the sadean/patriarchal archeplot, the folktale of culture. For Sade, the patriarch, wants no change, change is prohibited, made impossible through the offer of only one option, the binary option, always the same narrative. Sade wants a timeless, eternal orgasm, tolerating only minor variations that do not alter the structure of the plot. Thus is the literary critic emancipated, liberated into the libertine 'writer', after the image of his author. Sade, responsible for the gender confusion of the ejaculating female, the victim/libertine, is responsible for yet another androgyne: the literary critic who thinks he has no gender, who thinks *jouissance* has no gender and aesthetics no interest; who wills himself to believe that the subject of reading is gender-free and neutral, 'human', after the image of his master – precisely.

The woman, object/victim *par excellence* in the structure of representation, is now being invited to join the readership and the spectators as a 'voluntary audience' of the great cultural fiction – the patriarchy represented – now that the structure of representation, the scenario in representation, have been defined and confined to the transitive plot, the coercive imperative, now that the (male) gendered act of viewing and of reading has been naturalized. The disen-franchised literary critic, recipient of the one-way aesthetic, has chosen to ejaculate under the vexation and transform himself into androgynous libertine, marking the text, partici-pating in the sadean scenario. The opportunity looks equal for the androgynized female: s/he can have her pleasure, a measure of subjectivity, and s/he can participate in the reading and even the writing, so long as that pleasure, that subjectivity, that reading and that writing, are those inscribed in the plot, are those plotted by the author, so long as they are 'equal'.

Example: We read that Danièle Dubroux, formerly a film critic, is now making films, her most recent one *Les Amants terribles*. Her interviewer, critic of *Le Monde*, makes sure the film as well as its maker are 'equal' and asks: 'Do you prefer suffering to inflicting suffering?' She replies: 'Do you mean as erotic jubilation or in general human relations? Generally speaking, I don't like to cause suffering, except if it is for a good reason,' and she proceeds to give three 'good reasons'.[13]

The feminist critic cannot recognize herself in nor accept the representation made of her and her pleasure, fashioned by Him and by him, by Sade the patriarch and his lackey libertine. She makes a choice not chartered by his master-mind: she chooses not to play. Choosing not to play in this scenario, electing not to choose between suffering and causing to suffer: this choice is the beginning of critique. The first question questions the options, the production of sadean meaning; it is critique with gender.

Feminist critique is directed at the structures which generate pornography, at the ideological, political organization of the society which produces it, at the literary organization which protects it. It reveals the connection between pornography and these structures, the homology of their organization. It shows up and criticizes the folklore nature of the pornographic plot, the rearticulation of an unchanging archetype, reiterated in the patriarchal culture at large, which recites the same tale over and over again, convincing itself through these rearticulations of the impossibility of change and of alternatives and confirming the eternal recurring. And since feminist critique disagrees with the literary critical self-censorship which stops short of critique, it will say that it does not like what it shows up and lays bare. It rejects the options offered, the equal opportunities proffered and questions them instead, disproving their inevitability so as to open up possibilities not preordained by the master-mind.

Feminist critique challenges the spurious division of labour which leads to the author's abrogation of responsibility, of critical, political responsibility for his writing, since his mirror-image, the critic, abrogates the same responsibility in return for being allowed to collaborate. Writing, for the feminist critic, necessitates political consciousness, not aspiration to the status of artist. Writing also requires that the writer have something to say rather than perform once more a variant of the cultural folktale. Critique thus ceases to be a beauty contest trying to establish who writes 'best'. Feminist critique reclaims writing as a form of communication: for change, not for the maintenance of the eternal same.

Political consciousness means recognizing no sanctuaries from political reality, no aesthetic or fantastic enclaves, no islands for the play of desire. Political consciousness includes owning up to personal politics, to one's political and historical determinations as writing subject, as literary politician, and it means owning up to one's gender and the history of that gender. It means giving up the fantasy of the literary androgyne.

# Collaboration

The modern capitalist consumer society has a simple basic scenario: there are producers, with economic power, the means of production, on their side, and there are consumers, recipients, powerless with regard to production. The process between them is one way, transitive: from producers to recipients. It is to that extent a coercive structure, with an obscene power disequilibrium between the two.

The pornographer is a producer, the published author is a producer; the reader is a recipient. The process is one-way. The literary critic looks like a hybrid in this institution, as are the marketing lackeys of the manufacturers who establish 'consumer needs' but are paid by the producers. A reader in the literary scenario, he fashions himself into the author's 'ideal reader', the expert among readers. The reader proper is a powerless consumer in a one-way process. Readers may choose among the products offered, but they have no say in the production, have no access to the means of production. The androgyne critic interposes himself between author and reader (like the libertine between master and victim), making himself half a writer but posing as the spokesman of readers. He wants to participate actively; like the victim-turned-libertine who betrays the remaining victim, so the critic betrays the reader: he is a collaborator. He would rather share in the power of the author than defend the interests of readers. While the willing victim is a product of the pornographer's imagination, the critic is for real, a political agent in the world. But he is also an invention of the literary imagination, an outgrowth of the great artist-ego, the aesthetic subject.

Sade is indeed a great forerunner. Having set out the sadistic master-scheme, the inexorable structure of oppression (scenario no. 1), he has also delivered the blueprint for containing the anticipated rebellion of the victim: the invitation to collaborate. It is a political schema *par excellence*, played out in history many times to the letter. Kate Millet, in *Sexual Politics*, traces the same structure in Jean Genet's later work which makes the collaboration of the slave its theme:

> Oppression creates a psychology in the oppressed. Marxism, though adroit at analyzing the economic and political situation of such persons, has often neglected, perhaps out of nervous dismay, to notice how thoroughly the oppressed are corrupted by their own situation, how deeply they envy and admire their masters, how utterly they are polluted by their ideas and values, how even their attitude toward themselves is dictated by those who own them.[1]

Remember the literary critic. Millet continues that Genet's play, *The Screens*,

> accuses the revolution of becoming the very pattern of its colonial predecessors, leaving the masses, Said and the women, as wretched as before. The last scenes are a duel between a group of prophetic matriarchs, grand in their poetic rage and their vision of an ongoing revolution, and the pale and automated males of the new order, carbon copies of their French enemy, bursting with narcissism and military discipline, *la gloire*, and the organized slaughter called valour.[2]

The revolution, anticipated by Sade as by Marx, becomes the transformation of scenario no. 1 to scenario no. 2 and witnesses the birth of the libertine. The slaves conditioned to see only one choice, to be master or slave, to cause suffering or to suffer, ensure the very continuation of the Master even in his *coup d'état*. Locked into the mutual mirror-gaze of master and slave, the two will see-saw endlessly, changing places now and then, leaving the structure intact. The slave has accepted the master's law that there shall be masters and slaves, he has agreed to play. And Sade, the author, is content, the game remains the same, guests and victims sometimes changing places, but playing the game, agreeing to the equal opportunities offered, to being exploited, as Williams notes, on equal terms.

For Sade as for Marx, the focus in the second scenario is on the libertine, the collaborator, the 'males of the new order' who prepare themselves to take over after the revolution, as men do, as masters do. The focus is off the remaining victim, the 'masses', highlighted by Genet through the character of Said 'and the women'. As if by chance, the remaining victim, apart from the hero Said necessary for the play, consists of 'the women', a gender class left behind by most revolutions in history, even where it fought in the liberation struggle. Scenario no. 2, the scenario of transformation, the scenario with plot, with historical process, masks a double oppression, masks the fact that oppression remains despite a superficial change, a change-over of the masters.

In the USA at the turn of the century, the competition between black men and white women for the privilege of an equal powersharing with the white male is a demonstration of the quest for libertinism under the white male vexation: black men were content to perpetuate the oppression of women if they could become 'equals' of white men, just as white women were content to perpetuate racial oppression if they were granted equal status with white men.[3] Their respective liberation was predicated upon the maintenance of inequality elsewhere in the system; neither fought their campaign on the premise of equality for all, liberation of everyone. Though they might have upheld universal equality as the ultimate ideal, when it came to political realities – the options available in the white man's scenario – joining the powerstructure rather than abolishing it became the practical choice. Suffragist Elizabeth Cady Stanton is explicit in her disappointment at the black male franchise: 'If Saxon men have legislated thus for their own mothers, wives and daughters, what can we hope for at the hands of Chinese, Indians, and Africans? . . . I protest against the enfranchisement of another man of any race or clime until the daughters of Jefferson, Hancock, and Adams are crowned with their rights.'[4]

In the very fight for women's rights, those rights are reduced to benefits courtesy of the host, the rights of mothers, wives and daughters of the white men who hold them in bondage. The category of black women has disappeared from Stanton's scenario, which figures white men, black men, and relatives of the former. In the early twentieth century, some white American suffragists were opportunist enough to play the card of racism openly in order to advance their own cause, which 'would ensure immediate and durable white supremacy'.[5] Similarly, black men did not object to the enfranchisement of black men only, ensuring immediate and durable male supremacy. The only ones who could not but envisage total equality and an 'on-going' revolution of the power structure itself were the victims of a double oppression, namely black women, since neither the liberation of black men nor the liberation of white women would free them of oppression, and since in the libertinism of either they were destined to be the victims. Both the (white) women's franchise and the black (men's) franchise were fought for through appeal to the bond-master to grant them liberties, like the pornographic victim appealing to Sade to grant her improved status: permission to cause suffering rather than suffer. It is no surprise what history has shown, namely that neither the franchise of black people nor that of women has led to their total freedom or to equality. The masters are still in place, the scenario is scenario no. 2.

While Sade and Barthes are busy offering the victim improved status by calling her libertine – ascension to the rank of guest – it has to be remembered that the association works both ways and that the libertine, too, shares in the colour of the victim. Thus in the passage cited above, where Barthes educates us in the nuances of victim-attitudes, he gives us an alternative to the pair of victim/libertine: before the quoted victim has time to reveal herself libertine, she is named whore (*putain*). The difference between the unwilling victim of rape and vexation and the willing victim is that the latter 'prostitutes' herself, agrees, like the libertine, to be victim in exchange for some additional currency: the glory of guest status, the payment by the master.

What we are witnessing, moreover, is a process of nomenclature, a choice of name, i.e. of masculine meaning. On certain occasions the willing collaborator is named libertine, a term of indeterminate gender, capable of becoming, in the historical process, that of 'liberationist'. On other occasions, the willing victim is termed whore, a name of unambiguous femininity. We use the term prostitution metaphorically to describe collaboration, libertinism, selling out. The different terms in this system of masculine semantics carry different connotations, in particular, connotations of differing degrees of blame. This naming is based on the look at the represented scenario, with the customary focus on the hero and his objectified victims, at the expense of the structure of representation in which it is embedded, and so leads to the absurdity of blaming the victim for taking a certain attitude: she 'makes herself' a victim because she 'chooses' to cry; she bears the burden of prostitution because she chooses to collaborate. Authorship, the choice of vexation, has disappeared from view. Responsibility has been hidden in favour of blame. Just so the formulation of the principle of the master–slave dialectic is a slur on the memory of real slaves. It attributes blame for a 'slavish' attitude to the victim. It is not a feature of slaves to assume the negative imprint of the master's image, just as it is not a feature of women to be the masochistic counterpart to the male sadist or the prostitute to his patronage. The categories of slave-complement to the master, of the woman-masochist-complement to the male sadist, are the result of conditioning under the vexation inflicted, are an invention and creation of the master-mind. They may be presumed strategies for survival, but they are engendered by the master plot, with which the responsibility remains. They are not in any proper sense of the word choices.

Genet's play has two kinds of victims: those who head the 'revolution' and who are the future oppressors, and those like Said and the women, part of the masses, who have and retain a vision of an on-going revolution which will abolish both masters and slaves. The latter are proof that the conditioning of the 'master–slave dialectic' is not absolute, a feature of slavery and oppression. The element of 'choice' that Said and the women introduce is not the choice offered by the master plot, for the latter offers only the place of either master or slave. The choice is one that bursts the frame, that breaks out of the boundaries of the master structure. Within the given frame of vexation, responsibility can only be attributed to the rising libertine in the measure to which the latter acquires power, the power embodied in the leadership assumed by the men heading the 'revolution' over the 'masses' they purport to lead. They have assumed responsibility for the oppressed, and they have to that extent to bear the responsibility of selling out their own class. They could be said to 'prostitute' themselves to the master-structure.

Yet such aborted revolutions, bids for a share in the power structure by male bourgeois elites of colonized people, or those by black men and white women in the USA, seem to escape the full brunt of the accusation of prostitution. These historical agents of 'liberation' (like the term 'libertine', ambiguous as to gender, and the term 'collaborator', masculine of connotation) manage to shed the ultimate shame and baseness which the term prostitution implies. What is it, then, that makes prostitution, the 'oldest' livelihood of women, the very lowest form of collaboration with power, the very worst instance of selling out? What is it that white-washes the libertine but stains the prostitute?

The feminist argument against pornography and the oppression of women is not only about sexual politics. It is also about the sexualization of the political. Sexual politics lends the most powerful metaphor to politics: a sexual difference (in the superficial anatomy) grounded in nature – male/female. Genderize political difference, the disequilibrium of power, according to Sade: power and powerlessness, master and victim/slave, subject and object, and naturalize it as masculine/feminine. The places are given, their gender established: henceforth the roles can be taken by anyone: man, woman, libertine, prostitute, black, white, Aryan, Jew or Palestinian. The revolution is contained in the exchange-ability of the roles, the either/or of the binary option.

The cultural metaphor which genderizes oppression has become such a dominant outlook that it makes us view any other form of oppression in its analogy, allowing us thereby to obscure the whole set of relations in which it is embedded and which it in turn subsumes. It is a commonplace to view the oppression of black people under slavery as an emasculation, the white master beating the black slave into submission like a woman (scenario no. 1). It is a commonplace to describe colonialism in the same terms. It means that the categories of white women and black women disappear from view, and with them the power relations that hold between all four categories. Bell Hooks writes: 'Sexist historians and sociologists have provided . . . a perspective on slavery in which the most cruel and de-humanizing impact of slavery on the lives of black people was that black men were stripped of their masculinity.'[6]

The perspective is familiar, it is based on the view that human status equals male status and that it is natural to see the status of women as a form of dehumanization. The status of slave, it appears under this perspective, is not in itself objectionable or dehumanizing, it is so only in the context of a male being held slave, that is to say, held like a woman. For a woman to be a slave constitutes no such stark contradiction, which is why there is very little mention and less analysis of the history of women as slaves.[7] The image of humanity, of full human subject status, has been worked out and shaped, has been constituted, through the scenario of oppression, the assignation of object status to the Other. Subjectivity as envisaged in patriarchal culture is attainable but through oppression and objectification: subject status equals supremacy over an other, not intersubjectivity. Only then does it produce the feeling of pleasure, the feeling of life. How can the subject be sure that he is high if no one is low, how can he know he is free if no one is bound? For the male subject, the blueprint for the scenario of oppression, for the constitution of his being, is provided by the 'natural' scenario of the oppression of women as a gender. His understanding of gender relations is at the very bottom of his understanding of himself, it informs his understanding and organization of society, and it informs his semantics, his symbolization of it.[8]

In our modern artistic culture, the writer, the great symbolizer and name-giver, has become the epitome of the supreme subject: having sorted out his sex life as a young man, he finds ultimate fulfilment through self-expression, the supreme self-expression made possible exclusively in the aesthetic sanctuary which frees him of any human, any political responsibility. The subjectivity we aspire to, the role model of the human subject, is thus not the acting subject in any scenario, the libertine who derives temporary (sexual/ dominating) pleasure: it is Sade the Author, the orchestrator of human destiny, the one and only master of the game. The hierarchy of subject and object, in the context of humanity, of a society, must needs lead to an extended, proliferating hierarchy that leads to the supreme ruler. The result is the proliferation of victims we have observed, a ladder of hierarchically ordered positions in relation to the ultimate power, and it should not surprise us that this hierarchy is polarized in terms of gender. When the male is subjected to oppression, he is emasculated, feminized. When the generic victim collaborates with power, she ascends to the gender-neutrality, the androgyny of the libertine. Yet this leaves us still with the problem of why the collaborating victim, in some cases, is not masculinized upward to androgyne, but feminized down to the very bottom, the place of the prostitute.

The original definition of the term pornography is based on its components porno (from Greek porne), prostitution, and -graphy, writing, adapted from representation (drawing or writing). The *Shorter Oxford English Dictionary* (*OED*) gives the following definition: 'Description of the life, manners, etc. of prostitutes and their patrons; hence, the expression or suggestion of obscene or unchaste subjects in literature and art.' Collaboration/prostitution is at the very basis of what is deemed 'obscene' or indecent in polite society. (Note also that art and literature are closely connected with pornography.) We are focusing on a scenario which is distasteful, we therefore try to ban the circulation of the representation of that scenario ('description'). We discriminate between this and similar representations on the basis of the victim-object in the scenario, the prostitute; she, in real life as in representation, bears the burden of unchastity. We never inquire into the authoring of scenarios which feature prostitutes. The attribution of blame deflects from the question of responsibility. Only in the second half of the definition is there some discrimination between different kinds of authorship. For, according to the first part, a sociological study of prostitutes would be pornography, while a representation of a father sexually abusing his daughter would not qualify. The second part of the dictionary definition takes care of this problem, introducing the term 'obscene', very much less precise than that of 'prostitution' and evaluative rather than descriptive. With 'obscene', however, the offending quality has been located in the subject matter of art and literature, i.e. in their content.

The derivation of the term pornography from prostitution is highly significant. The presence of the root 'prostitution' indicates the centrality, in pornography, of a relationship of power and exchange, an emphasis clearly over and above 'sex' (which may feature in art and literature under the name of erotica). The *OED* is further candid in calling the male role in prostitution that of 'patron' rather than the customary one of 'client'. The roles of prostitution are gender-specific: the prostitute is a woman; the patron, pimp or client, is a man. As man, as patron, he has the power of a male in patriarchal society. A patron, according to the *OED*, is

> one who stands to another or others in relations analogous to a father; a lord or master; a protector . . . The former master of a manumitted slave, who retained certain legal rights upon him . . . A person of distinction who protected a client [sense 1 of the word 'client': a plebeian under the protection of a patrician, a dependant] in return for certain services . . . One who supports a practice, a form of sport, an institution etc. Also (in tradesmen's language), a regular customer.

The patron is in a fatherly relationship to the prostitute, lord and master, also her protector. Her status improved from slave to manumitted slave (from scenario no. 1 to scenario no. 2), over whom the patron retains certain rights. His status is that of a person of distinction, the patrician to her plebeian; his protection is granted in return for certain services, for he supports a practice, a form of sport, an institution, to which he is a regular customer. He has the money to pay the prostitute and buy her cooperation and compliance. The prostitute has no power: not only is she a woman (manumitted slave), but a woman 'outside society' as that society defines itself. She needs his cash, however, for despite everything she lives *in* the society – not the social, but the economic society – of her distinguished patron.

The relationship of prostitution is the paradigm relationship of pornography, to which all variants can be led back. The father abusing his daughter, the adult man abusing a child male or female, man using woman, are all patrons in a relationship of prostitution: they buy the compliance of the other (where they do not force it) with the power at their disposal. They can patronize.

The libertine, the willing collaborator, is bought with the prestige of the author/patron: a little reflection of glory and of power buys the cooperation of the already dependent victim. The prostitute alone is bought with money, the culture's most ambiguous symbol of power. Here lies her fundamental 'obscenity', for the dirty secret at the heart of our culture is not sex, but money.

The willingness of the victim is a tricky business: it is difficult to establish in an object that is supposed to be deprived of all will and subjectivity. To understand the will and willingness of the woman-object, we need to look at the economy of that object as understood by its male owner. The woman-object consists of body alone, without the dimension of a human will. When it is new, unused, intact, it bears the seal of its 'unwillingness' in its virginity. Scenario no. 1 is a reflection of the male culture's historical obsession with female virginity and the act of deflowering: breaking what is intact, the object's state of being, an act of destruction, an imposition. Once the seal is broken, however, the woman-machine gets going, responding to its use. The presumed unwillingness was only a state of inexperience. The under-lying presupposition concerning women's biology is that the body is insatiable, unrestrained by the constraints of phy-siological limitation of the male body.[9] Where a modicum of 'will' is attributed to the virgin and the nun, this is soon revealed to be only the most superficial effect of a social conditioning to chastity, overridden at once by the body's much more powerful biological urge. The unwillingness of the woman-victim is thus the cultural state of woman, coded by the patriarchal economy of the exchange of women, its laws and its religions. The willingness of the woman-object is the natural state to which she has been returned through the offices of men. Willingness and unwillingness are thus expressions of her body, not determinations of her mind. The 'willingness' of the woman-object is often portrayed as the triumph of the body over the rudiments of the female mind, her social conditioning, in the plots of tales from pornography through literature to romance.[10]

The willingness of the prostitute is obscured by the factor of money. Popular mythology presents the prostitute as the omnivorous sexual desirer, especially in the nineteenth century, where she is the counterpart to her respectable frigid sister, the angel in the house.[11] Yet despite this colourful picture, it springs to the eye that the prostitute collaborates not out of desire, but for economic reasons. Money is the most abstract, the most symbolic, of man's possessions. It consists exclusively of exchange value. Where the libertine collaborates in exchange for something of use-value – guest status, prestige, a share in possessions – her willingness can be believed in, her willingness has foundation, in particular, it is linked to capital, the surplus power of the male. What the prostitute gains is only cash, determined by the demand: what her service is worth to the patron. It is a wage.

Exchange is the preferred term characterizing commercial relationships and the economic market. It is a word like 'criticism', most inappropriate. Exchange implies two agents, exchanging objects between them, *inter pares*. The original idea is also that you exchange like for like. The dominant form of exchange in our economy is one of goods or commodities and services for money. 'Third World' countries exchange raw materials and cash crops for foreign currency – sometimes more, sometimes less for the same goods. The 'First World' is in possession of the hard currency, it is the patron. The developing country, like the woman, is in need of the hard cash, for like the woman, it is 'outside' the 'First World' but participates, economically, in the world of the patron. It receives the variable cash in exchange for something real, something of use-value, indirectly its own subsistence production. In both cases, one gives what he has a surplus of and no use for except in exchange, and which is not of himself. The other gives of itself, of herself. The exchange is unequal, it looks remarkably like prostitution. Prostitution, which is not so much a special case of economic exchange, but rather the paradigm of the cash nexus.

In the cash nexus, it is the one with the surplus (capital) who decides what is 'like for like', who fixes the price according to his demand. He decides what to buy, and what is a commodity. He writes the possible scenarios, and determines how they are viewed.

One might have taken sexual relationships to be relationships of exchange. But it is not apparently so, the master author wills it otherwise. Let us look at prostitution: he gives money, and receives in return a service; she sells her part of the sexual relationship – while his seems to be for free. Instead, it is not counted in the scenario of exchange. He likes to think that he gives nothing of himself, just money which is of no use-value to him. His view of heterosexual relationships in general is that he takes, while she gives. She loses in the exchange. Because he chooses to inflict the vexation. taking what he wants, he apparently never gives anything away, never 'goes way out of control', because he keeps the authorial control over the scenario and over the woman. He remains the subject, and he buys her subjectivity away from her. Which goes some way towards explaining his need to cling to his preferred representations of sexual relationships as essentially aggressive, transitive, coercive, predatory, a certain conquest, an assured victory. If she resists, he will 'take' her (scenario no. 1); if she 'yields' (her form of willingness always a response), he has 'had' her (scenario no. 2); taken and had she remains. Her perspective of the matter does not exist, for she must not be acknowledged to have any subjectivity. Her tale, and the prostitute's tale, might be quite different. Hence the representation must be made from his perspective, the verbs defined through his agency. To be taken, to be had, mean humiliation; but this passive verbal construction allows only for a feminine grammatical subject: a man can neither be taken, nor had.

Throughout the 'sexual liberation' this pattern persists, for it is not the liberation of women, but the liberation of the female sex-object, which is now expected to orgasm (in response). She can be had, together with her orgasm. The sexual story may be written from the female-object's point of view, an enticing variant of the male writing of her pleasure. She may write it because, as libertine, she will have acquired the point of view of the scenario, the perspective of the master: she will write it as a male cultural subject, as author, as artist. Erica Jong has given us an example, and men do not tire of pointing it out to us: the female point of view, as we like to see it, the libertine discharging.[12]

Historically, that is under the dominance of scenario no. 1 when women were by definition (and by social organization) objects, produced by fathers for exchange, there were straightforward reasons why this economy of sexuality was to apply. A certain use-value was put on women's bodies (on women-objects) that would determine their exchange-value as 'first-hand' or 'second-hand' objects, while no such value was assigned to men's bodies and their sexuality since these were never exchanged. Rather, they were the actual means of consumption that would use up the women's use-value. For Marx, women were as naturally an example of commodities as they were for Kant examples of products of fine art. Julia Swindells has traced the constitutive role women play in Marx's notion of commodities and exchange, in a close reading of the following passages from *Capital*:

> Commodities cannot themselves go to market and perform exchanges in their own right. We must, therefore, have recourse to their guardians, who are the possessors of commodities. Commodities are things, and therefore lack the power to resist man. If they are unwilling, he can use force; in other words, he can take possession of them.[13]

And Swindells quotes the following footnote of Marx's:

> In the twelfth century, so renowned for its piety, very delicate things often appear among these commodities. Thus a French poet of the period enumerates among the commodities to be found in the fair of Lendit, alongside clothing, shoes, leather, implements of cultivation, skins, etc., also *'femmes folles de leur corps'*. (His emphasis)[14]

And Swindells comments:

> Coaxed into a grin, we learn (if we had not already known or guessed) from the modern editor's note that 'femmes folles de leur corps' are 'wanton women' (Marx 178). Male-subjected humour, in a leap which is also a continuity from the 12th Century to the 19th Century, thus reveals its ideological colouring. The shade of the joke, that is, albeit against the hypocrisies of 'piety' and pious historiography, affords us a glimpse not only of that sexual ideology which circumscribes Marx's writing, but additionally that which is both specifically characteristic of the mid 19th Century (woman annexed to particular notions of commodity, but uncertainly – nudge, wink), and more generally characteristic of a historical continuity called masculinity.[15]

The subjects involved, in exchange, in poetry, in historiography, and in the jokes, are all the subjects of culture, also
called masculinity. It is further interesting to examine the
economy of Marx's discourse in the light of our present
discussion. Note that the relationship towards commodities
is one of guardianship and possession, a fatherly, patronly,
patriarchal relation. Commodities cannot themselves go to
market or perform exchanges in their own right. They do
not have subjectivity which would enable them to be
subjects. Not really surprising, for they are *things*, that is,
objects rather than animate beings. Their guardians are their
possessors, their owners. One would have thought the case
was amply and unambiguously circumscribed.

Yet Marx adds: 'If they are unwilling, he can use force; in
other words, he can take possession of them.' Before we have
learnt of the curiosity of *femmes folles de leur corps* among the
commodities, Marx provides for the case of objects which
nevertheless manifest curious symptoms of subjectivity: they
are unwilling. Scenario no. 1: the object resists, is unwilling,
the subject can use force, take possession, can take the object,
can have it. We thought that the guardian *had* possession, that
he was already the owner of commodities; yet he needs to
assert his ownership by simply taking possession by means of
superior force. 'Commodities are things, and therefore lack
the power to resist man' – so why do they resist and are
unwilling?

Rather, the patriarchal definition is as follows: 'Whosoever
and whatsoever lacks the power to resist man, shall be his
possession, his thing, his commodity.' His power may be
muscular power, it may be intellectual power (see Berger's
article on the relationship of man to animal, as representative
of his relationship to nature in general), it may be political
power, but more importantly, this power is not an inherent
quality of the species of the male, it is a socially, politically
and culturally constructed position of power, reinforced by
military and technological means of exercising it. Not every
white man is muscularly stronger than every white woman;
he is likely to be weaker than his black woman slave, and

bound to be weaker than his black male slave. Yet Marx writes as if the lack of power in the commodity to resist 'man' were inherent in the commodity, and inversely, the power to dominate inherent in 'man', the operator of exchange. He talks as if this power of 'man' were gender-specific, as if it were his by natural law, by natural selection of those fittest to dominate and patronize, rather than the result of a particular social and economic organization which endows some men with the requisite power.

The focus once more is on the object-victim in the commodity scenario: 'it/she/he make themselves into commodities, because they choose to resist and hence force has to be used against them; if, under the same vexation, they were to co-operate, they could be willing objects of exchange, libertines in the market place.' Just such a one is the woman *folle de son corps*: she takes pleasure in her object status – her body – and makes herself willingly into an object-of-exchange. The 'wanton woman', so the expression suggests, is wanton of her own free will: she has chosen an attitude under the vexation of being a woman in a social organization where women are objects of exchange.

'Wanton', the *OED* tells us, has several suggestive meanings: '1. Undisciplined, ungoverned; unmanageable, rebellious . . . 2. Lascivious, unchaste, lewd . . . 3. (Chiefly *poet.*) of young animals: Frisky, frolicsome. Of moving objects, viewed as if endowed with life: Sportive, impelled by caprice or fancy, unrestrained.' First sense from scenario no. 1: unwilling, resisting, ungoverned, rebellious; the following senses appropriate to the 'wanton' victim of scenario no. 2. The last of these seems particularly appropriate: the woman object is viewed, appears under the patriarchal perspective, as if endowed with life; the surprise is the same as when the victim believed to be dead manifests symptoms of life by crying or discharging: the wanton commodity going to market and performing exchanges in her own right! This attitude of the commodity yields a certain sport, through the sportiveness, the caprice and fancy, the willingness to play manifested by the moving object, a sport of which the man of the market place is to become a distinguished patron.

Bell Hooks writes of the sexual exploitation of black women by their white masters during slavery: 'White male slaveowners usually tried to bribe black women as preparation for sexual overtures so as to place them in the role of prostitute. As long as the white slaveowner "paid" for the sexual services of his black female slave, he felt absolved of responsibility for such acts.'[16] The white slaveowner does not have to pay for the services of his black woman slave. She is already his double commodity, he is already her owner and her possessor. If she resists, he can use force: he has got the superior force, in plenty. If he pays the black woman slave, it is to place her unambiguously in the role of prostitute, to make sure that through his invitation to her to collaborate, she does not consider herself the white man's guest, the libertine who, through cooperation, ascends to the guest status of her host. If he pays, he is giving nothing of himself, except cash, of no use-value to him. He is not, above all, entering a relation of sexual exchange: the exchange, on his part, is strictly contractual, commercial. She, on the other hand, is seen to give her share in the sexual relationship willingly, wantonly, not because she is a slave and cannot do otherwise, but because she is a 'whore'. She 'humiliates herself' by 'choosing' to take money. She feminizes herself to the bottom rank, worse than woman, worse than slave, worse than woman slave.

Whether caught in the practice of slavery or caught in the practice of patriarchy, which exclude women and slaves from subject status and from ownership and exchange, accepting the bribe of payment apparently shifts the responsibility for the overall scenario, the practice in which the victim is caught, on to her shoulders. Willingness is deduced from signs of apparent collaboration, that is, absence of resistance, without regard for the available options, where the only available option for the victim is rape – the same vexation, with violence, without payment.

Man identifies with his possessions of use-value, they are

part of him, part of his identity, and when he throws a party, he is a generous host. When he loves, he gives 'himself'. When he acquires a wife, he gives of his status and his estate, for the willing collaborator to share in. But when he pays in cash, he ceases to identify with his gift: he is no longer a host, he gives nothing of himself but 'takes' from the collaborator who prostitutes herself for exchange-value rather than use-value. He considers her venal.

Culturally, ideologically, the supreme subject does not want to acknowledge his responsibility for his relations with the Other. In the modern age, where the Other is theoretically considered to have become a subject as well, he wants to convince himself that his position of power and supremacy, and his acts of domination and oppression, are the will of the newly enfranchised subject. Her willingness is his need, a justification for his unchanged supremacy, his continued domination. If he can bribe her into willingness, according to scenario no. 2, he can read from it her agreement.

Representations, compositions that determine our perspective and how we look at things, are a crucial strategy in the supreme subject's endeavour to maintain his position of power and privilege and the social, political and economic organization that supports it. Among the whole gamut of coercive structures in patriarchal capitalism, the scenario of vision, the representational structure imposed on them, isolates a partial 'content', framing part of a phenomenon, so as to exclude possibilities of analysing the larger network of structures in which it is embedded. Thus we have, for instance, the focus on the willing victim, the spotlight on the prostitute's venality for cash, so that these may be the readiest loci for the attribution of blame and responsibility. The larger context and its source of responsibility conveniently fall outside the frame.

The arts, as expert domains of vision, perception, representation, lead the way. We take the artist to be a pure creator of visions or images, disconnected from the social and economic fabric in which he produces them and into which they enter not only as cultural, but also as economic entities.

We think of a writer as simply a writer, but the writings which form the object domain of the arts are published writings, where publishing is an entire mode of production not contained or considered in the concept of 'writer'. Artist, critic and writer can therefore not simply be seen as roles in a literary scenario, the innocent, idealistic devotees of the aesthetic sanctuary, since they simultaneously have a double role within a production and consumption scenario. When we blame the literary critic for his libertinism, for his betrayal of the common reader, it is not through the reflex of blaming the willing victim. We do not just blame him for the somewhat understandable lapse into the admiring and narcissistic mirror-gaze of the master-slave dialectic which derives from his role in the literary scenario. We blame him because as critic he has access to the means of production to which the common reader has no access. Like the colonized revolutionaries in Genet's play who sell the masses (Said and the women) by turning themselves into carbon copies of their oppressors, revelling in *la gloire*, so the literary critic, who of course is a published critic, sells the reader when he chooses to waste his chance that the access to production would have offered. Libertine like the white man's guest, he prostitutes himself for glory, for use-value, for self-interest.

The domain of art and literature as we know it is a commercial enterprise where communication is for sale. Communication is industrially produced, under the order of the transitive consumerist scenario. The speaking function is turned into a means of production, the listening function into consumption. The only means of expression the reader has is consumption – the right of reply in the consumerist scenario, silence in the literary scenario – that is, buying books, in 'response' to the communication received. The critic, masquerading as the 'ideal reader' and mouthpiece of the audience, is a producer like any other author, a writer whose voice is published. Yet the literary sanctuary prefers to highlight his literary role of reader, so as not to alert to the production machinery of publishing, of industrialized voice.

# Communication

It is not without reason that the key term of contemporary analyses of communicative products, be they verbal or visual, is 'representation'. Neither in the study of art and literature, nor in the better part of the study of signs, is the emphasis on communication, although cultural products and signs are embedded in communicative processes and produced by and disseminated through media and means of communication. The emphasis on representation as a focus of anlaysis is appropriate and reflects a reality: the reality of the status of communication in our society. For an increasing domain of communication is given over to the modus of representation, namely the domain of public communication, the Arts and the growing commercial sector. What the state gets free in terms of the channels of communication, the commercial sector can buy. With this expanding influence of public forms of communication, communication in its common or ordinary meaning is going on almost exclusively in the 'private' domains of society. More importantly, the two different modes of communication do not develop in isolation, but influence each other. The influence, however, is unequal: it is above all the public mode of communication which is exerting pressure and leaves its traces on private communication, while a replica of private communication turns up in official communication only as a travestied semblance: a fragment, employed as rhetorical device, designed to allude to, remind of, feign familiar contexts of private communication and to veil the blatant otherness of its structure of communication. Thus the homely advertisement shows us two housewives exchanging notes on their washing, the happy family commenting on mum's dinner, the family doctor extolling the virtues of a drug, so that we may overlook the peculiarity of the ad's own communication to us as the voice of truth, monolithic, the word incarnate.

Representation means the reification of the message. The medium-and-message is foregrounded, at the expense of the communicators, the two speakers who take it in turns to listen and to speak. Representation foregrounds content – the representation 'of' – and obscures the agent of representation. The expert domains, art and literature, have a concrete body of 'works', with the workers bracketed out as abstracted, incarnated Artists. Yet the history of these domains shows an obsessive concern with the person of the artist, a concern which mostly overshadowed the concern with the work itself. It is only with the beginning of the twentieth century that the reification of the work of art has come into fashion, where poems are said not to mean but to be. To be like rocks of nature. With the advent of *la nouvelle critique* and reception theory in the latter half of this century, we are beginning to turn our attention to the reader, the libertine critic. We are taking it in turns. What is striking is that in the context of art the communicative situation is being chopped into segments, that we seem to be able to deal only with one part of it at a time, never with the whole communicative act. Were we to view works of art as whole communicative processes, we could no longer isolate them in an aesthetic sanctuary; they would be seen to belong to a communicative context which is reality rather than fantasy. Fiction is only fictive with regard to representation; as communication it is real, a fact in reality.

Language is a means of communication, that is to say, primarily an instrument of collectivity, of social interaction, of establishing intersubjectivity – as Berger notes, the means by which 'man recognizes man'. There are two points of access to communication, through the roles of speaker and listener. One of the more endearing features of language is that these places are not assigned, not fixed in language, are not owned, but are infinitely exchangeable. I or you may mean you or me or either or both. We really misrepresent the structure of language when we teach our children that there are six personal pronouns or 'persons': first person, second person, third person singular, and the same set again in the plural. There is a fundamental difference between 'I' and 'you' on the one hand, and it/he/she/they on the other. The latter function like other shifters such as 'this' or 'that': they refer to 'objects' of representation, and are optional depending on whether such objects feature in what is to be represented. 'I' and 'you' and their derivations may be such shifters also, but they are always more: they are the indispensable poles without which no communication can take place. Whether or not these pronouns feature in the message, whether or not they are articulated, they are inherent in the existence of the message itself, they are implicit in the very fact of communication. The presence of the message bespeaks the presence of its source and its destination.

As Raymond Williams notes in his book *Communications*, we use the terms 'means of communication' and 'communication' in many different senses. The 'oldest meaning' of communication is speech, 'the passing of ideas, information, and attitudes from person to person'.[1] One might therefore call language the medium of communication so as to distinguish it as the primary mode of communication which is of a different logical order from the various 'means' of communication we call 'media' today. Writing as a notation of language permits an extension of the communicative situation beyond the here and now of speech and of face-to-face interaction. The 'listener' may be far away beyond the reach of a human voice, and may 'listen' at any time after the 'speaking' time of the production of the message, since the message has been recorded. But while writing thus extends the possibilities of listening, it in turn deprives the listener of the potential twin-role of speaking and interacting, of responding to the message within the framework of dialogue. As a reader of writing, the 'listener' can only in turn, and in sequence, assume the role of writing too, can only let another monologue follow the monologue received. Writing is thus a first step towards the reification of the message: through it, the message is recorded and made permanent, and at the same time made interaction-proof.

Technological inventions have provided further means or channels of communication which amplify particular aspects of the communicative act. Printing allows for an effective distribution of the recorded message to a large number of potential listeners, extending not only the 'now' of the speech situation, but also the 'here' of the physical presence of the message. Other means of communication are aimed at amplifying the human voice – the articulated rather than the written message – beyond the natural reach of the voice and for a multiplied audience. The development of technical means of communication and their uses shows that amplification is directed both at the message itself and at the listening function, but not at the function of speaking. As Williams notes, however:

> In modern Britain, we have a whole range of uses of printing, of photography, of television, which do not necessarily follow from the technical means themselves. Many have been shaped by changing political and economic forces. Many also have been shaped by what are really particular communication models: the idea that speaking or writing to many people at once is speaking and writing to 'the masses' . . . These arguable assumptions [of clear types of people and interests] are often embodied in solid practical institutions, which then teach the models from which they start.[2]

Because particular forms of communication by means of technical amplification have become rapidly institutionalized, they appear 'natural', the logical consequences of these technical innovations. But they are not. Williams also points out that 'the development of powerful new means of communication has coincided, historically, with the extension of democracy and with the attempts, by many kinds of ruling group, to control and manage democracy.'[3] In other words, behind the extension of 'democracy', of the equal opportunities for all, there are subjects apart from that democracy who endeavour to manage and control these equal opportunities for the rest of society, constituting that Subject we found behind Bernard Williams's equal exploitation of women and men. Such control and management, not itself among the equal opportunities of the citizens of democracy, aims at restricting the function of speaking to a few, aims at controlling and patronizing the voice and extending the role of listening to the 'masses'.

More particularly, these functions of speaking and listening are becoming fixed roles, institutionalized social identities belonging to certain individuals and losing that potential of interchangeability which characterizes language and communication. The community of communication is chopped up, segmented into distinct individual roles. In terms of the communications produced we can observe a general cultural tendency towards monologue in lieu of speech and counterspeech, in lieu of dialogue and interaction.

Literature as a privileged form of verbalization and a locus of the production of values can be seen to have contributed to the control and management of democracy in the domain of communication. Its aesthetic framework is constitutive of the reification of the message and the monologuization of communication. As we have already seen, works of literature are regarded as the word incarnate, produced by a 'pure gesture of inscription',[4] rather than as speaking acts by individual subjects. The message is viewed as complete, perfect, unalterable, not susceptible to the communicative interaction by a listener who might want to clarify, question or comment upon particular parts of the message. Within the aesthetic sanctuary there is a taboo concerning communicative interaction, comparable to the taboo of incest in kinship relations.[5] The only interaction permissible is the exchange of texts (monologues), but a direct dialogue between author and critic/reader is prohibited. The listening attitude to be adopted towards the literary text is that of scriptural criticism, of examining the message's internal cohesion and structure of meaning without recourse to any extrinsic mode of feedback or illumination. The word of the text, in other words, is taken as the ultimate word, a final monologue; the communicative process is frozen in the message.

The aesthetic conception of art is by no means as old as 'art' (a practice of art) itself, but has evolved alongside a growing secularization of culture and an increased emphasis on individualism. The fact that products of art from an earlier era have been incorporated into the modern aesthetic canon of art as objects of a kind creates the misleading impression of a historical continuity. However, where art was once a matter of skill, it has become a matter of expertise, congruent with other forms of professionalization. Where art once ranged among the products of culture in general and had a useful (often religious) besides an artistic function, art today pertains to a special sub-category of culture, namely 'high culture' and is limited to a purely aesthetic function (leaving aside its economic dimension). For the visual arts we have museums, institutions specifically dedicated to the aesthetic function, built, like zoos, for the exhibition of objects without any other function or role in society. Literature has been banished to the pleasure island of non-fact and non-reality, a zoo of words to go and look at during leisure hours.

There has been a parallel transformation of the producers of art from artisan to artist, which in the domain of verbal art is an even more complicated phenomenon if we take earlier oral forms of literature into consideration. There, the 'author' is not only potentially anonymous, but essentially collective: verbal folklore could be said to be authored by the audience, that is, by the community, which only falls temporarily into the categories of listening audience and a speaker in a situation of performance, which itself retains the potential of dialogue and interaction.[6] (The demure, passive, non-interactive audience of the theatre and the concert hall is an invention of polite society, in scandalized contrast to the active, vocal and participating audience of pop concerts and other 'mass' events.) However, the tradition of written literature has brought with it a singularization and identifica-tion of the author that is synchronous with the growing individualism of the culture at large. The stature of the author has grown together with the demand for originality and innovation in the work itself. Romanticism may be seen as a culmination of this development with its explicit emphasis on the individual artist's sensibility, which finds expression in a work of art of which the artist himself is the hero. Its aesthetic conception negotiates the relation between work and artist in such a way as to permit the twentieth century to shift its orientation to the work of art without having, in effect, to dispense with the artist-hero. By the time of Romanticism, artists have become a different species of men, marked by a 'sensibility' not shared by common people. Frank Kermode writes: 'Occasionally one encounters the paradox that the artist is magnificently sane, only the quality of his sanity distinguishes him from other men. His *sensibility* (in Henry James's sense, the "very atmosphere of his mind") is more profound, subtle and receptive, and his powers of organizing experience very much greater.'[7]

No longer is the artist distinguished by his exceptional skill in handling a particular medium, it is his capacities as a human being (or man) that mark him out from common men. His power of organizing his own experience is greater, organizing it as experience rather than as representation specifically. The common man's experience of life is dull in comparison, his suffering of pain and poverty nowhere as acute, profound and subtle as the poet's suffering as the most individual of individuals. And let me emphasize, with Kermode, that we are not discussing the caricature of a 'vulgarized bohemian tradition', but a concept which is 'a serious belief held by and about artists'.[8]

Life, or experience itself, has become an aesthetic matter, which the sensitive artist-subject represents to himself as a painfully wrought 'vision': 'He is thrown back into himself and his own thoughts. He lives in the solitude of his own breast,' as Hazlitt observes.[9] Communication is the least of the poet's worries, for his 'motive and subject is his struggle with himself'.[10] His vision, his perception, is a representation to himself, author and receiver of the representation conflated in his magnificent soul. He is the creator of *images*. As Kermode notes, 'the artist's devotion to the Image developed at the same time as the modern industrial state and the modern middle class.'[11] The emphasis, however, is commonly on the artist's alienation from that bourgeois middle class and the restricting state which drive him into isolation and solipsism, rather than on the poet's participation in that industrial state in which, as a producer of images, he contributes to the reification of communication. There is a joint indulgence on the part of critic and artist in that isolation of the new species, which is held together through commiseration. D. H. Lawrence, commenting on Beethoven, speaks of 'crucifixion into isolate individuality' and adds '*poveri noi*' (poor us).[12] Kermode explicates the requirements of the artist's condition: 'He must be lonely, haunted, victimised, devoted to suffering rather than action – or, to state this in a manner more acceptable to the twentieth century, he is exempt from the normal human orientation towards action and so enabled to intuit those images which are truth.'[13]

Yet the artist is not, of course, a sheer masochist who suffers for the sake of suffering. His other distinguishing characteristic is that 'Some difference in the artist gives him access to this [to "vision"] – an enormous privilege, involving *joy* . . . But the power of joy being possible only to a profound "organic sensibility", a man who experiences it will also suffer exceptionally'[14] (Kermode's emphasis). For all his difference, for all his professed separateness from the industrial state and its middle class, the artist is acutely conscious of its dominant form of exchange and the fact that everything has a price. The language of commerce is the one that naturally suggests (transmits) itself to the critic, who tells us that Arnold 'knew about the Image, and what it costs', that 'Pater also knew the cost of this intensity . . . "a very costly matter"', that 'Keats . . . seems . . . to have been the first to achieve in English a characteristic poetic statement of the joy and cost of the Image', and that 'the free, self-delighting intellect . . . knows what pain is the cost of its joy.'[15] Once the price is fixed, you can go and buy the goods, like Keats, who resolves 'to live like a hermit' and to 'bear anything – any misery, even imprisonment' in order to earn his joy.[16]

To achieve the joy of vision 'demands', in the words of the critic, 'intense individuality, a cultivation of difference and indeed conflict with the world at large'.[17] Where we might have thought the intense individuality to be a distinguishing feature of the species artist, it turns out that the artist must cultivate it, must forge a difference and a conflict with the world at large, as a payment that will entitle him to the particular privilege. Yeats continues to emphasize the price – self-sacrifice, renunciation – the down payment, to convince himself of his artistic entitlement.[18] And as with the white slaveowner, who 'paid' for the sexual services of his black female slave and hence felt absolved of any responsibility for his acts, so the artist, on account of his payment, feels absolved from any responsibilities as a human being and a member of society. For, as Kermode put it in a twentieth-century idiom, what the artist also buys is exemption, exemption 'from the normal human orientation towards action'. We are therefore hardly surprised to find the thought of prostitution not far from this selfconscious payment:

> The poet, though devoted to the Image, belongs to the city, his place in which Baudelaire notoriously compares with that of the prostitute. All men, he says, have an 'invincible taste for prostitution' . . . the poet is different in that he wants to be alone, but this is only 'prostituting yourself in a special way' . . . and the poet can claim . . . only difference in the manner of his prostitution.[19]

If ever there had been any doubt about it, there certainly cannot be doubt any longer that we are witnessing a particular project of the male-gendered subject, who shares with 'all men' an invincible taste for prostitution. As poet, as author, he exceeds the ordinary man's taste for prostitution in that he has also a taste for imagining himself into the place of the prostitute, the willing victim, the joyful sufferer produced by his own scenario. The difference in the manner of his imaginative prostitution is that 'he wants to be alone', wants, in 'this attempt at unity in solitude'[20] to be patron and prostitute at once (remember the men in the peep-shows).

In this adventure of prostitution, the 'wife and child' are the most conspicuous obstacles, besides representing the common bond of a bourgeois society. In Hazlitt's words, the artist is

> a limb torn off from society. In possession of eternal youth and beauty he can feel no love; surrounded, tantalized and tormented by riches, he can do no good. The faces of men pass before him as in a speculum; but he is attached to them by no common tie of sympathy or suffering. He is thrown back into himself and his own thoughts. He lives in the solitude of his own breast, without wife or child or friend or enemy in the whole world . . . He is himself alone.[21]

It looks nicer, of course, to represent himself as a limb torn off, so that he *can* feel no love, *can* do no good, rather than to admit that he is a limb of society that tears itself off, by way of payment, so that it *need* feel no love, *need* do no good, and so that he *can* wrench that common tie of sympathy and suffering. Like Sade, he removes himself above and beyond his fellow humans, who become the objects of his representations, passing before him 'as in a speculum'.

The favourite prostitute of the artist is the Muse, significantly endowed with a gender and exacerbating the man's guilty relations with his 'wife and child'. Kermode reports that 'Yeats said that he had seen more artists ruined by wives and children than by harlots.'[22] Marion Glastonbury, in 'Holding the Pens', records a few more of the specific invectives by poets against 'wife and child', and of critics and artists combining in the chastising of wives who are said to stand in the way of their poet husbands. T. S. Eliot's biographer asserts that Eliot's wife became 'the emblem of the material world against which [Eliot's] religious impulse struggled to free itself'.[23] Cyril Connolly 'deplores the inability to live alone which leads the unwary into the marital trap',[24] seduced, it turns out, by one of those products expected to stand on the footing of fine art:

> Writers choose wives not for their money nor for their appreciation of art, but for their beauty . . . After seven years or so they divorce and their talent is given another chance . . . there is no more sombre enemy of good art than the pram in the hall.[25]

For, it turns out that

> the baby is even less capable than a wife of seeing the artist's point of view.[26]

If they did not divorce and/or give their children away as Rousseau did,[27] writers

> felt that their heroism merited congratulations and condolence. During his wife's pregnancy, Tolstoy bewailed 'the troubles of an eating house, baby powders, and jam-making along with grumblings . . . All this is not merely wrong but dreadful compared with what I desire.'[28]

However, as Glastonbury's analysis shows, artists not so much dispense with wife and child, as with the latter's claim upon them as husbands and fathers: they have, we remember, bought exemption from such ties. Only, as Glastonbury also shows, 'the life of the mind must be physically sustained', so wives have their usefulness as sustainers of those bodies whose minds soar high above.[29] According to Connolly,

> Marriage can succeed for an artist only when there is . . . a wife who is intelligent and unselfish enough to understand and respect the working of the unfriendly cycle of the creative imagination. She will know at what point domestic happiness begins to cloy, where love, tidiness, rent, rates, clothes, entertaining and rings at

the doorbell should stop, and will recognise that there is
no more sombre enemy of good art than the pram in the
hall.[30]

The angel in the house, spiriting away the pram and all other
signs of earthly existence so as to prepare a sanctuary for the
creative imagination, her holy ghost of a husband.

Henry James has dramatized these complex dealings of the
writer-man and Muse in a series of stories, where he puts the
two 'females' in direct rivalling competition. In his scheme,
in the aesthetic scheme, the artist-man has to choose between
intercourse with the Muse and intercourse with the wife,
between being an artist and being a 'man', the two apparently
incompatible.[31] Quite apart from the domestic debris which
is the charge of the angel in the house, the angel in the bed is
also a disturbance; as Connolly notes, she has to be divorced
to give the talent a chance. This binary opposition is usually
called Life versus Art or, in Kermode's words, 'the normal
human orientation towards action' versus the Image, vision,
joy. James's close association of art with sexuality, its rivalry
with the sexual female, already throws a somewhat new light
on that joy gained through renunciation of 'the world',
foreshadowing the Freudian concept of sublimation and the
subsequent sexualization of writing and artistic *jouissance*.
The real woman stands in the way of the highbrow artist's
consummation of his joy, just as she stands in the way of the
pornographic subject's sexual gratification. Yet, just as the
latter masturbates into his bucket in the real world rather
than in fantasy land, so the romantic artist remains a
producer of Images in the world he apparently has
renounced. It would be as wrong to see him as outside the
sphere of human action, as it is wrong to regard pornographic fantasy is not of this world. Contemplation and
imaging are as clearly human actions, as the Romantic poet's
choice to abstain 'from any attempt to alter the social order'[32]
is a decisive political stance. But artists as well as critics are
together forging an aesthetic sanctuary from the world and
from women, a pleasure island for the male subject to frolic

in with his imaginary Muse-prostitute and let his desire play free from any interference by any other subject, free, most importantly, from the claims of that subject he terms the Other.

'The Image is the reward of that agonising difference,' in the words of Kermode,[33] the reward for being that subject with a difference – the sole, the solitary and the supreme subject, in need of no interlocutor other than his own breast. The image is not forged for purposes of communication, but for the joy which is the subject's. The subject and the medium are self-sufficient: 'The artist or the "aesthete", so elevated above all others, "refines" the instruments of "intuition" till "his whole nature" becomes one complex medium of reception; what he receives is the vision – the "beatific vision."'[34] The artist, the subject, is himself part of the medium, the medium of vision, of imaging. Language, the means of communication of ordinary humans, is but an auxiliary to that medium of vision but with its communicative aspect atrophied. It serves the interest of self-expression, of auto-communication, of the subject's vision. The verbal representation of the poet incarnates the vision, hence incarnates the subject; through them, the supreme subject constitutes himself. The Image is an icon of the subject.

Roland Barthes, for whom 1850 marks a dividing line between a classical-realist understanding of art and our modernist conception of the artistic, distinguishes between ordinary writers (*scripteurs, écrivants*) who write *about* something, and the writer (*écrivain*) who simply writes. This mirrors the romantic shift away from writing about reality and to writing as self-expression and verbal incarnation. Barthes describes the two modes of writing respectively as transitive (writing about something) and intransitive (writing *tout court*). The notion of transitivity, however, applies even more directly to the communicative process itself, where we can distinguish between writing to a reader, a transitive process, and writing as an intransitive process, self-sufficient in itself, in no need of an interlocutor. Terence Hawkes, quoting from Barthes, describes the distinction as follows:

Unlike the writer (*scripteur, écrivant*), who writes for an ulterior purpose in a transitive mode, and who intends us to move from his writing to the world beyond it, the *écrivain* has as his field 'nothing but writing itself, not as the pure "form" conceived by an aesthetic of art for art's sake but, much more radically, as the only area for the one who writes'.[35]

The sense in which this conception of *écriture* is much more radical than an aesthetic of art for art's sake, is that not just the art, but the artist himself, has been moved out of this world and into the pleasure sanctuary of writing. And with the removal of 'reality' from its role as a purpose in the mimetic or realist conception we, the readers, have also been sacked: we are not told that we are intended to stay in this area of writing from which we formerly moved beyond, since this area is 'for the one who writes' only. What looks principally like a shift in concern with content – what writing is about – a shift from reality to expression of sensibility, effects a much more radical reconceptualization of the communicative process itself. Author and writing become one – intransitive – the reader is a superfluous element. Hence if a role is to be found for the unemployed reader who still wants to play, it can only be the one and only role that exists: that of the author of the text, the *écrivain*, the *jouisseur* – the libertine reader who 'produces the text'.[36]

The literary scenario has apparently become intransitive, the writer no longer needing his subservient reader as he produces his writing, his monologue. It is the author who needs his reader, also called buyer of books; in the economic scenario, the process remains transitive. The silencing of the reader is doubly ensured: through the writing process, and through the consumer process. The message is doubly reified: as the final monologue of artistic writing, and as book object for sale. The communication and exchange is doubly interaction-proof. The equal opportunities provided by the exchangeability of the speaking and listening role of language have effectively been managed and controlled.

The self-sufficiency of the writing subject, of the romantic visionary, has been achieved at the expense of women. Throughout, the romantic poet is a man rather than an individual, the world he renounces, the obstacles he contends with, the people from whom he severs the tie of sympathy and suffering, are 'wife and child'. Cutting that tie means representing these others as objects passing before him as in a speculum, erecting the sadean barrier against intersubjectivity. The achievement of subjectivity through writing, through self-expression, is a male-gendered project. It suggests itself that the role of the superfluous reader, the dispensable interlocutor, acquires the gender of feminization.

The reification of the message, the transformation of a communicative process into a thing – Image, Text, intransitive Writing – is not, however, just a romantic affair, nor exclusively a highbrow one. Reified messages abound all around us, and the truncation of communication to monologue has become so naturalized as to seem inevitable. We have moved into an age where monologue (discourse) seems the natural form of language. *Le Monde* reports the production of a play at a Paris theatre, 'Peter Handke at the Theatre de Chaillot' (the author his play).[37] In this modern instance of the genre of the dialogue 'there are no dialogues, in the strict sense of the word . . . no give and take. Each of the characters . . . speaks at length one after another, each searching his memory, retracing his life . . . revealing his anguishes and dreams.'[38] The literary movement of modernism foregrounded the breakdown of communication; postmodernism leaves the pieces behind and decidedly moves on to the quest for self-expression. The (post- ) modern hero wants to be a writer, and in this era of equal opportunities an increasing number of female heroes also do. Their modernist forebears already did, but the modernist novel mainly dealt with the becoming of a writer, the portrait of the artist as a young man, while the post-modernist novel emphatically includes the successful achievement. To the modern imagination, finding oneself equals expressing oneself, in print. In the project of self-expression, the interlocutor is dispensable, alluring only in the abstracted and objectified notion of a reading public that confirms success.

It would be more accurate, however, to say that the interlocutor is undesired rather than dispensable. Becoming a writer rather than an accomplished social speaker and user of language signals the privacy required by the writing subject: the listener, with the potential of assuming the speaking role in turn at any moment, must be held at arm's length. That other subject might disturb the subject in the very process of constituting himself, as Mrs Shandy interrupted Mr Shandy Sr claiming his marital right.

Holding the interlocutor at arm's length is, as we have seen, a specific feature of writing, yet the effective silencing that has become institutionalized is not as inevitable a consequence as it seems. Letter writing furnishes an example of fairly equitable turn-taking in the speaking and listening roles. Print, however, seems to add a measure of authority to the speaker which more powerfully silences the reader. The fact that print seems to carry such authority, often noted, has more to do with the particular institution of printing in our society than with the intrinsic fact of print.

Julia Swindells, in *Victorian Writing and Working Women*, reports a vivid exchange of views and poems between Ellen Johnson, working-class poet with a regular column in a newspaper, and her readers.[39] In this case, the readers found as easy access to the newspaper's print as their columnist, and they seemed unintimidated by the aura of authority and professionalism that attaches to print today. Today, we only know the much reduced format of reader participation in newspapers in the rubric 'Letters to the Editor', prefaced by a deferential 'Dear Sir'. A definitive, hierarchical distinction between professional writing and amateur commentary is made among the paper's print, through the designation of the reader's writing by the label 'letters'. Letters are writings from the private domain, and the reader's writing remains private even in the event of being published in a newspaper. Readers, at any rate, cannot dialogue with the particular author of an article with whom they take issue; they can write to daddy Editor to complain about one of his crew. (I assume here, for the sake of argument, that most letters are replies to and comments on articles previously published by the same newspaper; letters to the editor which initiate topics are comparatively rare.) The letter-writing reader is also unlikely to receive a further dialogic response to her or his writing, although some, especially literary review papers, send letters to the particular contributor so as to print the contributor's answer alongside the letter from the reader. But the effort at dialogue on the part of the reader is a lost cause, since the imbalance in the hierarchization of writing and of authority make it easy for the newspaper professionals to have the last word. Factors of time and place are also involved, the letter-writing reader at the particular disadvantage of the distance and delay typical of letter-writing. Similarly, audience discussions in broadcasting and television tend to be an uneven match between the members of the public and the professional convenors and contributors, since the public's contribution is restricted to the unique here and now of the exceptional opportunity, while the professionals' access to the media is continuous.[40]

With book printing matters are even worse. Raymond Williams pays tribute to this situation in his book *Communications* in the following paragraph ending chapter one:

> I said in *Culture and Society*: 'I shall be glad to be answered, in whatever terms . . . When we consider how matters now stand, our continuing interest and language (sic) could hardly be too lively.' I have greatly valued the very many answers I actually received, agreeing and disagreeing. The original invitations stands.[41]

This highlights the problems of creating a dialogic situation through a medium which proliferates the readership and gives a publicly recorded voice to the author. For all the author's willingness to exchange roles with his readers and become listener to their voice(s), the character of their voice is considerably different from his. Their voice does not have access to the same medium; they cannot assume a reciprocal speaking role. The readership's voice is necessarily fragmented into the individual voices of particular letter writers, and the individuals do not know of each other's responses. Their messages remain private, accessible only to the listening author. Their messages do not become reified in the public discourse in which the author spoke, unless he chooses to amplify such private messages in a future book of his. Responding to an author's work through private correspondence remains a matter of personal gratification for the reader and the person of the author, but the medium of book publishing does not itself provide for dialogic response. The only equitable response to a published book is another published book, which requires of the listener a great deal more than assuming the speaking role in turn: it requires becoming an author, that is to say, a published author. While every 'you' of speech can become an 'I' speaking in turn, not every reader can become a published author. We are spoken to in ways in which we cannot answer. The dialogic potential of language has been virtually excised from institutionalized forms and models of communication, it is being controlled and managed through the organization of those institutions. As members of society, you are either an author or a reader, with the two being unequal, hierarchically differentiated roles. While the author can be a reader too at any time, the reverse is not true.

This state of affairs is reflected in our use of language. We talk of authors, writers, artists as if they were a special class of people, their roles an identity. Published authors are of course a professional group, whether or not they earn their living exclusively as authors. Literature, however, does not like to make its professional structure visible, since the dominant myth of Art as Value presents artistic labour as disinterested. 'Anybody can become an author, provided they have talent,' talent apparently the only determiner in art. Yet in our commonsense attitudes, and in our use of language, we seem to have become entirely resigned to the fact that only some 'special' people are authors, indebted of course to the powerful image of the romantic hero-poet forged in high literature. Raymond Williams reflects this in his book *Communications*, in the very attempt to discuss a possible democratization of the media. In a sub-section entitled 'The Contributors', he writes:

> Surely the people who really matter, in any culture, are the contributors. Why do we talk always about publics and audiences and cultural systems? Surely the only way to get good culture is to have good artists and performers. And is there really anything we can do about getting them? Perhaps the most we can do is to try and create a society in which artists find it worth living.[42]

Williams might have talked of people who contribute to culture. Instead, he talks about 'the contributors' – a well-defined guild, clearly identifiable. They seem to exist somewhat platonically – or perhaps they live in the aesthetic sanctuary. If we construct a society congenial to them, they might come and live with us. And the implication is: if we don't, they won't. Clearly, what Williams must mean is that we should create a society which encourages artistic practice, so that members of the society find it worth their while engaging in it, making contributions to culture. But through his particular choice of language (us and them), Williams indicates that he takes it for granted that some people *are* contributors (born artists?), a special group (like 'the immigrants'), while we are the society, or rather, responsible for it. If we are good, we 'get' good art. Williams continues throughout to presuppose this guild, and distinguishes four categories: 'the creative artist, the performer, the reporter, the commentator or the reviewer',[43] in other words, professional groups. He seems to accept, in other words, that culture will be the product of professionals rather than the practice of a society.

> In their different ways, the reporter, the commentator and reviewer, the performer, and the artist need a guaranteed freedom to communicate what, in terms of

*their own* understanding of their work, needs to be communicated. This sounds like, and is, a definition of individual freedom. But it is not only for the sake of individuals that this freedom should be guaranteed. A good society depends on the free availability of facts and opinions, on the growth of vision and consciousness – the articulation of what men have actually seen and known and felt.[44] (Williams's emphasis)

Williams recognizes a need to communicate (to monologue) on the part of 'the contributors', and assigns a need for the reception of 'facts and opinions' (not to mention 'visions') to society. The need to communicate – express and receive information and opinions – is not apparently a human need (or right), but is split into different portions: some need to communicate, others need to be communicated to. Those who need to communicate are the contributors, and they are also the individuals of individual freedom. The others are the public, the audience, the society who should not interfere with the freedom of individual contributors, and they do not seem to be individuals themselves. The options are rather limited. While I agree with Williams that it is not a good idea to interfere with contributors' need to communicate, I hold that sitting back and listening is not the only alternative to obstruction and censorship. Williams's efforts are aimed at reducing the interference from commercial structures (and the law) with the designated contributors. My aim is to lessen the difficulties of 'the public' in gaining access to the role and means of contributors, so as to make communication a dialogic practice *in* society rather than a professional (monologic) lecture *at* 'the public'. It is not simply the merciless laws of the market which define the contributors and their freedom, but the professional structure in the hands of these contributors. 'The professional and the racist ethos converge,' writes one analyst of professionalism.[45] 'And the analogy with racism quickly extends to gender,' adds Julia Swindells in her critique of literary professionalism.[46] The professionals, always defined with reference to 'the public', are the professional Free Individuals, 'preaching', as Glastonbury writes, 'the doctrine of Individual Freedom which is the official religion of class society – the exception proving the rule'.[47]

Williams later admits that 'of course things are not so formal, in reality. There is not society on the one hand and these individuals on the other.'[48] Yet in his theoretical conception and through his use of language, he has established 'the contributors' as a guild, and whilst he concedes that they also share in the life of society,[49] he never conceives of the option that the society share in the practice of the guild and the freedom of its individuals. Williams hopes to democratize communication whilst leaving the undemocratic professional categories of 'the contributors' and 'the public' intact (for the public have become the institutionalized listeners). 'The contributors need the support of the wider public,' he advocates, and this means that 'the principle should be that the active contributors have control of their own means of expression.'[50] This supports the claim of the critics of professionalism that these contributors, 'far from existing to meet service demands made by the public, exist to *create* those demands',[51] and create the very category of their specific 'public' in order to meet their own demand, their need to communicate. No mention that the receiving public should have control over the 'means of being communicated to' so as to safeguard the 'free availability' of information the *public* needs and wants, their right to know at the mercy of the contributors' own understanding of their work, at the mercy of the cultivated capriciousness of their inspiration and their eccentric individuality.

The only positive terms in this analysis are the needs of contributors, what they may wish to communicate; the public can either listen or suppress (if they can). What is lost from this analysis is what the public may wish to know, but contributors happen not to want to communicate, as well as what the public might wish to communicate, by way of facts and information, growth of vision and consciousness – the articulation, even, of what women have actually seen and known and felt. The former is a problem the British public is increasingly becoming aware of with the suppression of television programmes and official information (e.g. on the sinking of the *General Belgrano*), though only because there is a split amongst 'the contributors', a disagreement between the government and the media in their understanding of the contributors' work. The second problem is very much harder to become aware of, since the public's need to communicate has disappeared from the analysis and disappeared from our language as we use 'to communicate' as a synonym for speaking with an amplified voice to a silent audience. As an invisible category, what the public may wish to communicate has given rise to an invisible form of communication. For, the contributors sometimes do wish to know what the public may want to express, and the contributor we call the government has arranged this by means of a professional ear, the MI5. This assures that the communication (yours) remains private, unheard by the rest of 'the public' (save your immediate private addressee). It is speaking with a partially amplified voice where you have no control over and indeed no knowledge of the amplification. Other contributors sometimes elicit your thoughts through opinion polls and market research, which similarly syphon your communication into the contributors' ear rather than that of the general public.

In the domain of public communication Williams is concerned with, 'to communicate' means speaking in an amplified voice to a silent mass audience. The contributors are monologuers, their contributions are monologues, their need to communicate is a need to monologue. Communication has become a one-way process, a transitive transfer of information, 'facts' and opinions (representations). The term 'communication' is most inappropriate and should be replaced by 'self-expression' if not 'monologue', although both these terms fail to make explicit the coercive aspect of the process with regard to the receiver group – the 'general public' or, as it is known among the professionals of the media, the 'target audience'.

In communicative terms, the listener has been dispensed

with but in economic and social terms is essential as the willing victim category who will 'support' the urgent need of the contributors with public funds. In this connection, I like D. M. Thomas' own term for its explicitness with regard to the effect of his contribution on the reader: 'It's . . . got to have . . . impact, so that the reader is left shaken by it.' And his editor's term, similarly cataclysmic: 'My editor says my novels are like explosions.' Where once the genteel *poètes maudits* were content to *épater le bourgeois*, to rob the good citizen of his feet and floor him, the contemporary contributor's need is summed up, rather, as 'dynamite the public'. In order to do this, your message needs to be pretty solid: reified, like a rock of nature.

The tendency towards an increasing monologuization of communication can also be observed elsewhere, not just with the designated contributors. The solidified messages of advertising bombard us from all quarters, even where we deem ourselves outside the presence of the contributors. Here the message is solid indeed, it no longer has a subject; it is Word, the truth revealed, vision manifest. 'We', needless to say, are an involuntary audience, unprotected by the law's Indecent Display (Control) Act. We are, decidedly, an unwilling victim, in contrast to the book-buying, theatre-going, museum-visiting audience. Nobody particularly asks after these contributors and their right to force their 'communications' upon us, or our need to have these visions communicated to us. Not in need of our public funds-support to guarantee their freedom of expression, they can buy the necessary communicative space to assume a thundering voice. The struggle for the place of the speaking 'I' leads not so much to the survival of the loudest, as of the richest. And they shout louder, the smaller the audience (the less voluntary?); as Williams notes: 'Much of the most relentless advertising is in fields where need and demand are marginal, or where there is an actual contradiction between the priorities of productive investment and this more immediately profitable investment.'[52]

The 'demand' which is marginal is 'us'. Williams fails to

mention the contradiction between the public's interest, which is different from demand (and which admittedly the public has no means to 'communicate' – work out and express) and the company's interest. Take, for instance, the case of the tobacco industry, one of the loudest, and one which manages to restrict even the government's speaking-space and volume, since it can not only buy speaking-space for itself, but buy off the government's through its large contribution to revenue (it successfully opposes more out-spoken government warnings on cigarette packets, for instance). What is particularly interesting is the industry's relationship to its own audience, for whilst in commercial terms it ought to be interested in enlarging that category, it is very effectively engaged in reducing it: 'This . . . industry produces a commodity that, by [Peter] Taylor's count, "has wiped out more people than all the wars of this century".'[53] At this point we need to remember that representations are not only produced with a view to selling them and selling commodities, but as a means of self-representation. With a demographic impact of this kind, an industry has some need to communicate a more acceptable, socially friendly image of itself, 'to reinforce its own myth that smoking is a socially desirable habit'.[54] Like patriarchy's self-representation through high culture, convincing itself ('communicating') that men are heroes.

Governments also have an ever more urgent need to 'communicate', to transfer facts and opinions to the masses. In the case of the US government, 'the masses' are not simply the American public whom it governs, but the world public. For its needs it has developed 'Worldnet', 'the expensive new media toy developed by Mr Charles Wick, head of the United States Information Agency, a former tycoon and long-time crony of the President.'[55] It allows US government officials, such as the Assistant Secretary of State for Inter-American Affairs, to be 'hooked up by satellite to American embassies' elsewhere in the world for a special kind of 'news conference' to broadcast his government's view of US intervention in Central America. Journalists at the respective embassies can see him on a screen, and speak on a telephone line, 'heard, but not seen, by [him]': 'One of Mr Wick's uses for the device was what are known in US government jargon as 'non-interactive' closed-circuit sessions. Journalists could watch things happening in the US – but not speak.'[56]

This proved to be unpopular with journalists, themselves used to being among 'the contributors'. 'The press conferences have been more successful. But to call them "interactive" was a joke that did not amuse many of the British journalists.'[57] The promise that 'the new Big Brother technology' would provide 'a unique frisson of direct contact' was discovered to be an illusion:

> Each Worldnet hook-up covers at least four countries. Control of the microphone is in the hands of the host [i.e. US] embassy, and journalists have no eye contact with their interviewee to press for follow-up questions or ask for their first question not to be evaded. As a result of the rationed questions among too diffuse and separate an audience, the US government official comes out almost unchallenged.[58]

The access to speaking is controlled and patronized by the supreme speaker, in this instance the US government. There seems also a dawning awareness that there is more to face-to-face communication than messages, other means of subject-to-subject interaction which are absent from this artificially mediated 'contact'. As with the readership of a book, the fact that the audience is vast and diffuse, puts the audience at an insurmountable disadvantage when 'it' wants to assume the voice in turn: the voice is fragmented and diffuse, divided and ruled. And as with audience participation in media events, the audience is at the particular disadvantage of one unique access when those in command of the media have continued access:

> An astonishing statement in Mr Motley's [the Assistant Secretary of State for Inter-American Affairs's] Latin-American hook-up that 'nobody participated but the Sandinistas' in last month's elections [in Nicaragua]

(there were actually six other parties in the ballot) was able to go unchallenged for two weeks until under pressure in the London hook-up he conceded he was wrong.[59]

With enormous delay, this particular feedback pointing out a falsehood could eventually succeed – but the audience who witnesses the correction is of course no longer the same as those who were fed the untruth for the preceding two weeks.

The advantage is also captured economically: 'the 75-minute hook-up . . . cost close to £30,000 in rented satellite and telephone time.'[60] Difficult to compete with for the individual citizen with a need of 'facts' and 'opinions' and especially 'truths', on that economic count alone.

Not only the medium of writing, but also the media simulating 'contact' hold the watching and listening interlocutor at arm's length, aim at making the message, the subject speaking, interaction-proof. Those who speak usurp the entire potential for speaking, expand into the available public space of expression. And expression is certainly not for free.

Institutionalized forms of 'communication', or better, of monologuing, have contributed to a systematic development of the speaking function, which is strictly controlled, and the reified message, at the cost of the listeners and their right to the interchangeability of roles. The speaking function is patronized – it has a patron – and the turn to speak is refused. The arts, with their glorification of the artists and of the artisitic object, have led the way, naturalizing the notion of a frozen communication which today is the norm. But while there is commonly, among 'the public', some suspicion of the power and the interests behind advertising and the news media, no such suspicion extends to the sanctified artist and his institution. Yet it is arguable that the model of the arts has as strong an influence on everyday and private forms of communication as do the media and advertising.

Private and everyday forms of communication show similar tendencies towards monologue, spieling, talking at rather than with interlocutors. We educate verbally gifted youngsters towards holding their own, expressing themselves. The successful student is the articulate one, the one most able to talk and to persist in the face of others' competition for the voice. Every public meeting evidences a struggle for the 'word', and holding the floor is an effective means of manipulating public consensus. I know of no systematic effort in formal education to train the listening or interacting functions of verbal communication. But the training exists – in gender training. The speaking function is masculine, the listening function and silence are feminine, as is also the function of convening the turn-giving executed by the fine hostess. Conversation itself is almost a feminine art, on account of women's presence in it – compare it with talk, when it is serious and becomes discussion. Anne Karpf describes women's traditional function in conversation as follows:

> Her eyes are fixed intently on the male speaker, her face is glazed with an interested smile, she nods at choice intervals to signal her rapt attention, and she interjects the odd key question to lubricate his parlance. Women are the midwives of male speech: we facilitate the birth of orations [monologues] to which we have to listen.[61]

'If this seems waspish', she adds, 'it is meant to be' and derives 'not from any contempt for the noble art of listening, but simply from the annoyance that they don't do it back'.[62] Women notice the absence of turn-taking, as well as the resulting quality of reified speech, of monologue, of oration. Women are 'the dumping ground of men's discourse', says Karpf.[63] Notice the impact, and the direction from above to below. Dale Spender has analysed the gender effect on the distribution of the speaking role in apparently egalitarian situations, such as mixed conferences of 'assertive' feminists and self-conscious 'non-sexist' men, in *Man Made Language*:

> Present at the discussion, which was a workshop on sexism and education in London, were thirty-two women and five men. Apart from the fact that the tape revealed that the men [13,4 per cent of participants] had talked for 50 per cent of the time, it also revealed that

what the men wanted to talk about – and the way in which they wanted to talk – was given precedence.[64]

Other studies of mixed sex conversations show that '98 per cent of interruptions . . . were made by men';[65] an analysis of husband/wife conversations 'that it was often impossible for women to talk when men were present – particularly if the males were their husbands'.[66] And Spender quotes Phyllis Chesler who notes that 'very rarely . . . do men listen silently to a group of women talking,' while women listening silently to a group of men talking 'is a common occurrence in our culture'.[67]

Speaking, self-expression, is the project of the male cultural subject, and men have effectively usurped it as their exclusive prerogative through the very gendering of the roles of speaking and listening. The whole drive of the cultural education of women is towards presenting silence as the highest *female* virtue and the necessary component of female beauty. The gender repression of patriarchal culture follows scenario no. 1: silence is imposed on women by force, through the coercive structures of a discriminatory social organization which prohibit women the vote, access to the training of their expressive faculties in education and later to public and professional positions. But scenario no. 1 is refined into scenario no. 2: the suffering, silent victim has to become an 'active' and willing victim: she has to listen. In order to fulfil their destiny as human subjects, men need women to be 'linguistically available' to them as listeners, in the words of Pamela Fishman.[68] Women must furnish their 'share' of the communicational 'exchange', the passive masochistic counterpart to men's aggressive and sadistic linguistic assault; women are turned into men's 'speech objects'. Men will their women victims' communicational pleasure under the vexation; women must choose an attitude and discharge – 'with an interested smile', with 'rapt attention', with lubricating 'questions' of 'oh really?' and 'how interesting'.[69] If you are an unwilling victim, 'if you reject the role, the penalties are high', as Karpf observes: turning away from a conversation between two men, to which she was 'clearly expected to be an audience', Karpf was reproached for being 'rude'. 'Simply my withdrawal from the conversation was taken as an act of aggression! Why risk such appellations when listening seems to come "naturally" to us, we do it so easily?'[70]

Charming sex – do not withhold yourselves!

The male demand that women be 'linguistically' or communicationally available to them as they are sexually available to them or, in other words, the homology of the communication vexation and the sadean vexation, suggests a parallelism and a connection with sexuality, which shall be the next problem for our scrutiny.

# Sex/Sexuality

The most 'Freudian' of Freud's achievements, what makes him a radical innovator who divides the 'pre-Freudian' from the 'post-Freudian' era, is 'his concept of a sexuality that is not inscribed within the bounds of actual interpersonal relations'.[1] As Jane Gallop, whose formulation this is, further emphasizes, following Juliet Mitchell: 'The "Freudian" Freud placed a premium on "psychical reality" over actual "reality". Freud's contribution to man's understanding of himself is a description of the human being in culture, not of the natural animal, man.'[2]

As thorough post-freudians, we have already become quite accustomed to the reality of 'psychic reality', of which Deirdre English gave us an example: the male-psychical reality of woman as a threat. But there still is a danger, according to Mitchell and Gallop, of lapsing into pre-freudianism:

> Distortion of Freud always seems to go in the direction of some sort of biologism. Hence his descriptions of man's inscription in culture are interpreted as prescriptions for normality based on nature. One of the first to fall back into biologism, in an attempt to go beyond Freud, specifically on the question of women, was Karen Horney.[3]

Horney, like many other feminists opposing Freud, has recourse to a concept of women's 'true nature' which fails to be adequately represented by the freudian theory. Gallop's emphasis is important, since the better part of the chronologically post-freudian era has nevertheless taken Freud's theory as the description of reality and endowed the unconscious with the authenticity of Nature, the source of

Truth. Fredric Jameson calls the unconscious 'one of the two surviving pre-capitalist enclaves of Nature'.[4] Only recent research places Freud in a historical perspective which allows us to relativize the truth content of his work. Feminist work moreover examines Freud through a gender analysis which relativizes the status of the 'human' psyche to that of the male-gendered psyche: Freud's contribution to man's understanding of himself is exactly that, a description of the *male* being in the culture, as he constitutes himself as 'human' subject. From this emphasis on the cultural being in contrast to 'the natural animal', we further derive a congruity between 'psychical reality' and culture, an equation, in other words, between male-gendered psychical reality (fantasy) and culture. The post-freudian perspective clearly no longer permits us to oppose culture as 'fiction' to 'reality', or to distinguish lightly between male 'fantasy' and actual reality. However, we seem more ready to recognize the reality of the psychic than we are to recognize the reality of culture, as the commonsense opposition between 'fact' and 'fiction', the true and the imaginative, demonstrates.

Freud, in other words, was engaged in the description of cultural reality, not in the prescription of a normality reducible to nature and biology. Freud, cultural seismograph, recorded in minutiae the project of the cultural subject constituting himself through sexuality, through language. He read the culture – as we read it – as the self-representation of the Subject, the subject's desire his motor and goal. Freud identified this desire (libido) as the transitive force of a single subject projecting himself on to the world, fixing itself on to objects, the objects interchangeable, never satisfying, always in need of substitution for the renewal of the subject's desire. Desire in the lacanian emphasis, libido in the freudian emphasis, is 'disinterested', that is to say, has no interest in, no cognitive understanding of, the objects of its desire; its interest is purely subject-related, its goal itself, continuing desire, the feeling of life. It is produced by the subject's own internal economy, independently of the objects it temporarily devours. Every object is Object, every other Other.

Freud may have rescued us from biologism and positivism, refining the cultural understanding. This seems to me a very different emphasis, however, from the first one given by Gallop: that Freud's concept of sexuality as the project of the subject 'is not inscribed within the bounds of actual interpersonal relations'. 'Actual interpersonal relations' describe a political reality rather than a biologism. Freud's theory removes the subject from a political realm of interpersonal relations and intersubjectivity, to a psychical reality and a cultural fantasy where the subject is the sole Subject, the rest of the world are objects, representations by the subject. To describe the subject's project, his 'reading' of reality, the word 'representation' (*Darstellung*) is central: representation is the means by which the subject objectifies the world.

In a political perspective, sexuality, like language, might fall into the category of intersubjective relations: exchange and communication. Sexual relations – the dialogue between two subjects – would determine, articulate a sexuality of the subjects as speech interaction generates communicative roles in the interlocutors. Sexuality would thus not so much be a question of identity, of a fixed role in the absence of a praxis, but a possibility with the potential of diversity and interchangeability, and a possibility crucially depending on and codetermined by an interlocutor, another subject.

In the current cultural climate, to see sexual relations as a matter of interpersonal interaction appears as a blunder of the same order as pre-freudian biologism, a lapse into non-freudianism. But to choose a political context of intersubjectivity is not the same as dismissing the cultural insights of Freud, it is to look at the cultural frame within which 'sexuality' is fabricated and to analyse the sexual politics of that subject who inscribes his sexuality within the bounds of his solitary sanctuary. As Stephen Heath emphasizes: ' "sexuality" [is] the construction of something called "sexuality" through a set of representations – images, discourses, ways of picturing and describing.'[5]

In the present dominant cultural representation of sexuality, sex is as monologic as speech, particular roles being assigned and fixed, as the roles of speakers and listeners, individuals and masses, givers and takers are assigned as personal identities. Sex is further a matter of aesthetics, the representation of the subject to himself. 'Your sexual body is "a magnificent work of art",' Heath discovers from the expert source *Total Loving*.[6] '"Sex," wrote the poet Pound, "in so far as it is not a purely physiological reproductive mechanism, lies in the domain of aesthetics."'[7] To that extent, sexual relations become reified as 'sex', the Romantic Image. Where the romantic poet forged an Image of Truth, from himself and for himself, the modern sexual subject forges an orgasm, the Big O, with the same attendant pain and joy. The orgasm is more than sheer physical gratification, the Big O is an aesthetic matter whose representation to the subject produces the feeling of life. As the orgasm becomes reified, its production an art, it also becomes subject to critical analysis; as Heath notes:

> The 'sexual revolution' . . . has produced and been caught up in a whole discourse of 'the orgasm', a whole elaboration and representation, a standard of sexual life . . . Orgasm is a qualitative phenomenon ('true orgasm'), refers to an authentic . . . level of experience and being . . . not the intercourse . . . [but] the real emotional experience.[8]

With an objective set of orgasms, a critical discourse can be developed by the experts, analysing, classifying, describing them. Notice the vocabulary consistent with romantic literary criticism: authenticity, true orgasm, emotional experience, 'sexual maturity', 'natural sexuality'.[9] Heath even tells us of 'An Orgasm Manifesto',[10] in tune with modern artistic movements. An orgasmic sanctuary is being created where everyone is having their own orgasms, working on it for their own subjective fulfilment, for 'individual realization',[11] for *jouissance*. For the modern sexual sensibility, constituting oneself means expressing oneself, through the Big O. Everyone is running for the 'speaking' function, the listening function is not very highly developed. Exemption from political reality has been bought, as with the romantic poet, at the price of a Human Condition now understood exclusively as the prison of solipsism, the sanctuary of the subject, 'psychic reality'.

As we have noted earlier, the 'sexual revolution' has extended the imperative of the orgasm to the woman subject as well: in the era of equal opportunities she is ordered to enjoy herself 'as men do'. Yet the freudian description of psychic reality was still firmly founded on gender asymmetry, the history of 'sexuality' grounded in the nineteenth century understanding of femaleness as disease.[12] Woman identified with 'the Sex' is the problem of man's sexuality. Hence sexuality, the pleasure that is to become her duty, is posited in phallic terms.[13] But there is, in fact, a theoretical necessity for the invitation to women to join the cultural project of the subject (on equal terms, to be sure) which reaches far beyond Freud's own ambiguity towards the 'nature' of female sexuality. The transformation to scenario no. 2 is endogenous in scenario no. 1. This necessity can be traced to Freud's work on female hysteria.

Freud's major stress in his *Studies on Hysteria* was that 'hysterics suffer mainly from reminiscences'.[14] 'The original traumatic event is seduction by an adult.'[15] Freud's 'clinical experience showed overwhelmingly that the incidences of fathers raping their daughters occurred more often than anybody, including Freud, cared to admit.'[16] Other colleagues treating hysterics confirmed Freud's findings.[17] Freud also attended the lectures and demonstrations at the morgue in Paris given by Paul Brouardel, and owned the book by Brouardel, which dealt with the rape of children by their parents and others in authority over them.[18] 'Freud's personal library contained proof that he had known far more about the reality of abuse than he was ever prepared to admit in print.'[19] As is well known in the history of psychoanalysis, Freud abandoned his theory about early seduction in the late 1890s and replaced it by a theory of infantile *fantasy*. As Heath puts it: 'We emerge from a whole world of "scenes" and an external violence of sexual imposition – all those seducers, all those "trouble makers" – into one of a whole imagination of sexuality, the process of the individual's own history.'[20]

Freud's knowledge of a political reality of sexual abuse, of imposition and vexation, was a most unwelcome intrusion into the sanctuary of theory-building and of pure subjective sexuality or 'psychic reality'. In a historic gesture, women – the hysterical Woman – is admitted into the guild of cultural producers as author of fantasy emanating from her own subjectivity. The discharge of the victim is given the status of subjective authorship and of the source of freudian meaning. But that discharge, response to vexation, needs to be authored nevertheless by the Author in charge; the cry in response to rape is reformulated as the pleasurable discharge of the libertine, the *jouissance* of infantile sexuality.

At this crucial stage of the elaboration of the archetype of the scenario, of the orchestration of human sexual destiny, Freud needs to cut out all competition, needs like Sade to be the sole and supreme Author. He decides not 'to admit *in print*'; when Ferenczi 'came to believe that Freud's early theory of seduction was correct, and that Freud was wrong to give it up, Freud did not want to *discuss* this; he simply wanted Ferenczi to *stop talking about it* and to *stop writing about it*'[21] (my emphasis). There can be only one voice, I am the Word, one God, one Patriarch, Sade, Freud.

The author's intervention at this stage is crucial, else the plot might have slipped out of his hands. Allowing the Other subject to speak is taking the grave risk of inviting a political reality to invade the supreme subject's sanctuary. Hence the victim's speech must be channelled into the ear of the Author, under oath to preserve its secrecy, closeted, in private, and the Author will integrate it in a respectable scenario, assign it to the emerging scenario no. 2: sexuality issuing from the subject-*patient*. The invitation to women to speak is kept under strict supervision, embedded in a practice of being caught, submitted as patient: certain well-educated middle-class hysterics, apprenticed already to culture, are the ideal candidates. With others, the Author must retract the invitation and make sure he controls and manages their 'speech'. As Heath reports in a footnote:

> 'Servant-girls', Freud explains to Jung in 1907, are barely worth consideration and the analyst can tell their story without needing to listen: 'Fortunately for our therapy, we have previously learned so much from other cases that we can tell these persons their story without having to wait for their contribution. They are willing to confirm what we tell them, but we can learn nothing from them.'[22]

Fortunately for our therapy, fortunately for our theory, our representation – whose dominance is thus assured, is interaction-proof, immune from any external contribution, in this case, from a recognized and acknowledged gender-class, 'servant-girls'. Instead of listening, we assume the role of telling. In the scenario of their representation – 'their story' – they are willing to confirm, willing to choose an attitude of approval (so we are *told*). They won't have cause to complain of our services, as they won't have access, in the cultural edifice, to any other speaking slot. No need, as Sade thought, to kill them. Soon, moreover, they won't have access to our services any longer, since we shall offer these, in the form of the fortunate therapy, for a fee that will select a more fortunate class. For, the contribution of 'servant-girls' might undermine the representation of hysterics as generic Woman, might relativize that representation as determined by political factors of class affiliation which would invalidate it as the picture of universal femininity (no biologism intended in this, of course).

Feminist research has paid special attention to that sensitivity of Freud's with regard to the gender-class of 'servant-girls'. As Gallop says, 'Psychoanalysis can be and ought to be the place of symbolic inscription of the governess.'[23] And she notes in her analysis of Freud's case history of 'Dora', the 'heroine' of his 'Fragment of an Analysis of a Case of Hysteria': 'Neither Dora nor Freud can tolerate identification with the seduced and abandoned governess.'[24] The governess plays a crucial, yet curiously 'invisible' role in the freudian family drama: she is that other, lowest victim in the chain of victims generated by scenario no. 2 which foregrounds the conversion of the victim into libertine, but which thus spawns a new true victim (compare Said and the women). She is the one most completely objectified, victimized in turn by the Author and his libertine-victim:

> As threatening representative of the symbolic, the economic, the extra-familial, the maid must be both seduced (assimilated) and abandoned (expelled) . . . The nurse is desirable: her alterity is a stimulus . . . Her alterity is not just her femininity, not even just her not belonging to the family, it is her not belonging to the same economic class . . . Dora and Freud cannot bear to identify with the governess because they think there is still some place where one can escape the structural exchange of women. They still believe that there is some mother who is not a governess.[25]

For the times and for the class of Freud and Dora, the governess is a prostitute, the *putain* in Sade's scenario. She prostitutes herself, against payment of money, to perform the services carried out for free by the mother. She threatens the family economy. As with the conventional prostitute, there is tension between gender and class, an intersection between the scenarios of the oppression of women and the oppression of an economic class. The result is a complication of plot: seduction in the sexual scenario (the prostitute is a willing libertine) and expulsion in the social: the prostitute lives 'outside' the bounds of (polite) society. Her desirability augments in proportion: she attracts not just through femininity, but through the doubled opportunity for humili-ation, the doubled yield of the feeling of life, of superiority, to the subject, which accounts for that 'invincible taste for prostitution' (not sex) which the poet shares with 'all men'.

The dirtiest secret at the heart of the freudian family is money, not sex. Within the cosiness of the closed family, prostitution (libertinism, collaboration) can take place without the tarnishing influence of cash, just as in Sade's aristocratic chateau the beautiful prostitution is achieved by the noble-woman who renounces pay. Gallop quotes Sade's Saint-Ange, who is made to explain: ' "As for me, my dear, who for twelve years have worked to deserve [the name of whore], I assure you that far from from taking offence [*loin de m'en formaliser*], I enjoy it." '[26] And Gallop comments:

> The prostitute as subversive force is not she who does it for money, but the woman who, like Saint-Ange, does it for pleasure. 'Everything is exchanged, but without commerce. Between us, neither proprietors nor acquirers, no determinable objects, no prices' . . . By class a noble lady, she does not take on the identity of prostitute; she prostitutes her identity.[27]

In Saint-Ange speaks the libertine-victim, the angel in the bed who plays 'for free', willingly, in return for a shimmer of the glamour reflected on her by her noble patron. She who for twelve years has *worked* thinks that by renouncing the price of her labour ('no prices') she will renounce its name. Willing to sell her fellow victims and to prostitute her (victim-)identity in return for imaginary access to the class privilege of her oppressor, she thinks that as 'a noble lady' she will be part of the noble*men* (remember the daughters of Jefferson, Hancock and Adams). But far from being 'subversive', as Gallop maintains, women's prostitution for 'pleasure', for 'love', for class glamour instead of as commerce is a cornerstone of the freudian family as it is of the sadean aristocracy. Subversion is introduced, precisely, by the contrast of the paid victim: she represents the danger of a juxtaposition of the whore and the wife, the governess and the mother, the 'servant-girl' and the 'noble lady' which reveals the true structural relations of the women in the family and in the aristocracy to their illustrious male hosts. Such juxtaposition, such identification, must not take place, and to prevent it, you control the representation and manage the identifications made by the reading or viewing subject.

Neither Dora nor Freud can tolerate identification with the seduced and abandoned governess. Just as Freud, the scientific researcher, could not ultimately tolerate identification with the female child victim, whom he had seen, and first represented through a quotation from Goethe: 'Poor child, what have they done to you?'[28]

A double victim, the female child is doubly caught by the superimpositions of two kinds of oppression and power disequilibrium, that of adult–child, and that of male–female. Introduce a libertine-victim with carefully constructed 'subjectivity', and thus provide the subject of representation with another locus for identification, that of the willing counterpart to the male aggressor. As Gallop demonstrates for us, Freud has to search around a little to find the appropriate representation:

> Unable to accept the possibility of so many perverse fathers, he presses on to the discovery of infantile, polymorphous perverse, sexuality. Not fathers but children are perverse: they fantasize seduction by the father. But his detective work does not stop there. Perhaps because he is a father and was a child, he goes on to locate the guilt where it will not besmirch him . . . In the 1933 lecture 'Femininity' he writes, 'And now we find the phantasy of seduction once more in the pre-Oedipus . . . but the seducer is regularly the mother. Here, however, the phantasy touches the ground of reality, for it was really the mother who by her activities over the child's bodily hygiene inevitably stimulated, and perhaps even roused for the first time, pleasurable sensations in her genitals'.[29]

Where the 'reality' suits, it is allowed again to touch the fantasy sanctuary and supply it with 'scientificity'. Where the girl child 'fantasizes' (reports) seduction by a male adult, it is certainly fantasy. Where 'she' (with Freud's help) fantasizes seduction by the mother, a more fantastic imaginative effort, it is reality. The imaginative representation (to himself) of female nursing work as seduction we know to have stimulated and roused the fantasy of many *men*, who have an invincible taste not only for prostitutes (the commercial variant of the wife) but also for 'servant-girls' (the commercial variant of the mother), a particularly Victorian predilection.[30]

But what interests us here above all is Freud's disinterested search for an acceptable form of representation. He invents the 'phallic mother', the libertine in the scenario of the phallic vexation, a scenario which conveniently excludes its frame of a larger scenario in which the mother is caught in a patriarchal practice of exchange where she is assigned the work of nurse. And Dora, a true daughter of Freud's family, jumps at the new option for identification (for understandable reasons, under the vexation): 'In the imaginary, the "mother", unlike the maid, is assumed still to be phallic; omnipotent and omniscient [participating as guest in the rank of Parent], she is unique . . . neither Dora nor Freud wanted to see . . . that Frau K. and Dora's mother are in the same position as the maid.'[31] Dora, like Freud, refuses to recognize the category of gender, 'a term that represents a class', whose members 'are in a position of substitutability and economic inferiority',[32] where mother and maid share a common destiny. Just as today, the Human Rights lobbyists and their Doras do not wish to recognize a gender-class of victims where mother and maid, wife and prostitute, share a common destiny of pornographic representation.

Freud's arduous search has a further benefit. With the discovery of the 'phallic mother', the need to grant full fantasizing authorship to female subjectivity has disappeared again. The female child does not create fantasy as a full expression of her subjectivity, but returns to the fold of victims who ejaculate in response to a vexation, this time the hygienic regimen inflicted by the phallic mother. All is well in the psychic sanctuary and a fundamental gender asymmetry has again been restored, one of which Lacan in turn takes full advantage.

Jane Gallop asks: 'Why does Lacan insist upon using the phallic, sexually unreasonable, unbalanced term "castration" for the general relation of the subject to signifier? This question rejoins [Ernest] Jones's unexpected discovery of the phallocentrism of symbols.'[33] The 'subject's relation to the signifier' is where the project of sexuality and the project of verbal self-representation (writing) join together. It is a crucial point at which to insist that 'desire, the Freudian libido, is masculine.'[34] For in the beginning, Lacan had 'talked about subject, language and desire without specifying the sexual differentiation of his schemes', just as 'Freud did not get around to writing about the "psychical consequences" of sexual difference – about the ways in which female sexuality might differ from the model of "human" sexuality he had generated from the little boy's history – until later in his career.'[35] But Lacan, like Freud, is a cultural seismograph, and after a little humanist hesitation concerning the asymmetry of gender relations, comes out full force with the assertion of the phallus's 'unreasonable privilege':[36] not only is desire itself masculine, but the phallus is 'the signifier intended to designate as a whole the effects of the signified, in that the signifier conditions them by its presence as signifier'.[37]

Language, for Lacan (as for Freud), is as important as is sexuality, as important in constituting male subjectivity and in constituting gender asymmetry. Subdue not only through sex, but through representation. The 'general relation' is precisely not a general relation, but the relation of the *male* subject to the signifier. Lacan is extraordinarily sensitive to language. He realizes that desire (libido) is transitive, a vexation engendered by the subject and projected on to an object world. And he discovers a further structure of hierarchical disequilibrium and consequent domination: in the relationship of the signifier to the signified. One is active, an agent, the other passive, acted upon. The signifier designates, the signifier conditions. The signifier must needs be masculine, like desire. Its symbol shall be the Phallus. As with every supreme authority we have encountered in patriarchal scenarios, be it poet-author or unique master-piece, nobleman or king, the very distillation of power through the elite structure always implies another, higher, often invisible authority, the guarantor of power on earth: kingship is given by God, male supremacy by Nature, the Romantic Image, the 'beatific vision' 'is received' (from whom?), and 'the signifier *intended* to designate': whoever by?

We have already seen Lacan ask 'What does woman want?' He is trying to get it out of her, her pleasure, her *jouissance* his need in more than one way. It is his need as male sexual subject inflicting the phallic vexation designed to force her response, but his need also as cultural subject, as psychoanalyst who theorizes and writes her pleasure. For it is his phallus-signifier that shall 'designate as a whole' (Woman rather than women) 'the desired effects of the signified, condition them by its presence'.

More is at stake, however, in Lacan's quest than in the apparently homologous quest of the sexual liberation hero who wills his woman's pleasure. For Lacan has realized that 'phallic pleasure [*jouissance*] is the obstacle through which man does not succeed . . . in taking possession of and revelling in [*jouir de*] the woman's body, precisely because he takes possession of and revels in [*jouit de*] the organ's pleasure.'[38] What any 'servant-girl' could have told him, had he not insisted on telling her 'her story'. Sexuality as a project of the male subject may lead to orgasm, but it fails to give the subject full possession of the Other, the goal of the subject's every move and vexation. The possession and patronage of which the male subject has so successfully convinced himself through the ages turns out to be a trick of rhetoric, a particular appearance forged through representation. The woman is objectified, her body used, the orgasm achieved, yet with the systematic annihilation of woman's subjectivity, the male subject has robbed himself of the possibility of possessing her, owning her body and soul. Lacan discovers the failure of the phallic project: a failure of 'the sexual relation as relation between the sexes', 'a failure to reach the Other', in Gallop's paraphrase.[39]

Throughout *Encore* Lacan returns to this failure, beginning with the reflection that courtly love or chivalry is 'the only elegant way to pull out of the absence of any sexual relation' for the man 'whose lady was entirely, in the most servile sense, his subject [victim-object]'.[40] Courtly love is a 'refined way of supplementing the absence of sexual relations, by pretending that it is we who put the obstacle there'.[41] It appears, according to Lacan, 'at the level of political degeneracy [when] it had to become evident that on a woman's side . . . there was something that could no longer work at all'.[42] The temporal perspective, perhaps, applies to the phallic subject's discovery rather than any 'objective' historical dimension: having defined, described and analysed the subject's project of sexuality – everything, incidentally, working very well – Lacan chooses to leave his sanctuary and take a peek at a political reality where he sees women, not those so successfully represented back in his sanctuary, but women with a subjectivity of their own, for whom something 'no longer' works. He assumes, of course, that it still worked for them while he was in the sanctuary, since any simultaneity of vision is denied the singular subject. And on this excursion from the sanctuary to political reality, Lacan also (re-) discovers something called 'sexual relations' – what Freud abandoned when he turned to 'sexuality'.

Women not only perceive that 'something . . . could no longer work' for them, they locate, rather more precisely, what does not work in the subjective sanctuary of the male psyche. Gallop finds that Luce Irigaray, once apprenticed to lacanian vision, 'has discovered that phallic sexual theory, male sexual science, is homosexual, a sexuality of sames, of identities, excluding otherness. Heterosexuality, once it is exposed as an exchange of women between men, reveals itself as a mediated form of homosexuality.'[43] Interaction, for the male subject, is interaction between male subjects – 'human interaction'; exchange is exchange between guardians, of commodities and of women. Language is the means by which 'man recognizes man'; man communicates to man through representation, where author and viewer are male. The prohibition of incest attempts to prevent the exchange of one's women with oneself.

Irigaray, in her search to uncover the underlying structure

of phallocracy, finds in 'the Sadian scene . . . a certain redeeming value'.[44] like Carter and other literary critics appreciating the overt quality, the unashamed 'showing forth', of the sadean text. 'Maybe, by dint of exhibiting, without shame, the phallocracy reigning everywhere, another sexual economy will become possible?'[45] The tone is that of a first discovery, the question a hope produced by shocked amazement. Yet the question is uncertain in its address: who will see with her, and who will, on the basis of what they see, want 'another sexual economy'? But Sade has seen already, and his descendants have seen too – they are the very subjects of cultural seeing. What they do, on the basis of what they see, is not want another, fairer, more egalitarian economy, but profit from the one that institutionalizes their advantage: 'Like Lacan, the knowledgeable libertine profits from phallocracy, in such an unabashed manner as to reveal [to whom it needs revealing] the homosexual closed circuit which underlies our supposed heterosexual culture.'[46] Or rather Lacan, like the knowledgeable libertine, profits from it too: 'Lacan too lauds the progress Sade makes by "bringing to light the 'anal-sadistic'"'.[47]

Lacan relies on the scriptural, the virtue of 'showing forth' and 'bringing to light' which, moreover, leads to an aesthetic orientation of contemplation rather than the 'normal human orientation towards action'. Just so Irigaray's question, curiously without logical subject, expresses the hope that another sexual economy 'will become possible' on the basis of people's seeing, rather than suggesting that anybody do anything to bring that change about. Yet Irigaray's criticism tries at least to break through the boundaries and asks beyond the sanctuary's own terms. Gallop positively advocates infidelity, that is, not sticking to the rules of the game, the law of the sanctuary, the Name-of-the-Father:

> Infidelity then is a feminist practice of undermining the Name-of-the-Father. The unfaithful reading strays from the author, the authorized, produces that which does not hold as a reproduction, as a representation. Infidelity is *not* outside the system of marriage, the

symbolic, patriarchy, but hollows it out, ruins it, from within.[48]

Critique with gender, adultery being the sin of the female spouse.

But what is it that Lacan wants? To what end does he seem to subvert the sanctuary with an unauthorized glance at a political reality? As Gallop suggests:

> A real ladies' man, there is nothing he wants more than to be with the women . . . Lacan is with the women to try to get at their response . . . 'For a long time now I have desired to speak to you while strolling a bit among you . . .' Lacan derives a phallic enjoyment from his lectures . . . yet Lacan would talk from the audience, 'with the women', in an attempt to get at the other enjoyment, that which responds to the phallic.
>
> This satisfaction is denied him. He cannot talk from the audience. He cannot talk and at the same time be in the audience. Yet that is his longstanding desire.[49]

You might consider this the ultimate consequence: auto-eroticism, auto-communication, narcissism. Lacan does not want to exchange the women with the other men, he wants to exchange them with himself. He would like to make himself a gift of them. The discovery of the absence of a 'sexual relation' does not make him want to make 'another sexual economy . . . possible', as Irigaray hopes; it makes him want to make the best of this absence and draw the conclusion to the homosexual closed circuit. He knows what the libertine's response to the phallic vexation is worth, knows it is not the other half of the 'sexual relation' but a part of his self-authored and authorized creation. Rather than waste it, he wants to receive the magnificent gift of the phallus himself, just as he would love to be his own audience. He fulfils the promise latent in the subject's distillation of power: instead of just being supreme amongst the supreme, instead of making love to the other men via the exchange of women, he wants to be the Supreme, and make love to himself.

# Postscript

I do not really wish to conclude and sum up, rounding off the argument so as to dump it in a nutshell on the reader. A lot more could be said about any of the topics I have touched upon, many more examples could be adduced, further connections be made. I have meant to ask the questions, to break out of the frame in which the picture of pornography and cultural representation in general is presented, and to make us look at it in other ways. The point is not a set of answers, but making possible a different practice, of seeing, of questioning, of critique, of infidelity to the dominant vision, of hollowing out from within.

The subject–object relation is at the core of this dominant way of seeing. The individualistic perspective of our culture has insistently focused on the necessity of this pair, denying any capacity of the human individual for collectivity and intersubjectivity. It is the fundamental axiom of the justification of inequality, domination and power.

The *New Statesman* (what's in a name?) treats us to the following view on torture by 'provocative historian and philosopher' husband of Susan Barrowclough:[1] 'Torturers' motives would only be a moral puzzle if we supposed humans to possess a natural empathy for the suffering of others. But why should we assume any such thing?'[2] Why should we assume any such things when it is so much easier to harp on the well-tried solipsism of the subject and assume that 'we have little natural empathy for each other'[3] (as if the cultural and political organization of society had to depend on the 'natural')? Why should we assume, as Berger did, that the fact of language can bridge the abyss between men, when the argument applied to animals and the gender of women – that the superficial differences outweigh the fundamental similarities – can be applied to all individuals: 'we value our differences as individuals more than our similarities as a species . . . Each fault line of difference . . . can be widened . . . into an abyss across which screams cease to signify'?[4] Why assume any social potential of the human individual when the allegation of this 'natural' leads to the 'right question to ask about torture', namely 'not why it exists [it is 'natural'] . . . but why so normal [natural?] an instrument of power has become a scandal'?[5]

Torture, from this provocatively familiar perspective, 'is the most intimate of all relations between strangers: eye to eye, hand to hand, breath on breath, torturer and victim are as close as lovers.'[6] And hardly any less close is the man who offers this view, the white man behind the Instamatic who frames a picture of the proximity of two humans, eye to eye, breath on breath, a view so naturalized, so disinterested, so aesthetically accomplished as to obliterate any distinction between the torturer–victim pair and the pair of lovers, the hand that hurts and the hand that suffers. From the male viewing perspective with its focus through the active subject, there is no difference between the hero-torturer and the hero-lover: each has his own object from whom he derives his pleasure. 'Torture works, torture pleases'[7] – perhaps it depends on your point of view and your role in the torture scenario. But the male analyst identifies 'naturally', obsessionally, with the subject: 'Such an approach may be criticised for ignoring the centrality of the victims' suffering,' writes another contributor to the *New Statesman*, reviewing another male analyst's book on torture, 'but the important point, surely [surely?], is to comprehend *why* there are victims at all'.[8] Such an approach may be criticized for its elision of the victims' subjectivity, but rather than criticize it, we make a spirited apology for it. And whilst we are at it justifying the fascination with the acting torturer, we employ the right words that will lead to the answer we already know: we ask why there are victims. And we know why there are victims (even if we wonder why there are torturers): they make themselves victims because they choose to scream; if, under the same vexation, they were to discharge and ejaculate, they would cease to be victims and become libertines of torture, they would become lovers. Far from ceasing to signify, the screams across the abyss are the beginning of choice, of sadean meaning, of the feeling of life and of pleasure produced in the ear of the torturer attuned to response. It is the signal of power. 'Torture', says the man of the *New Statesman*, 'is power's answer to the collapse of legitimacy'.[9] Collapse? Legitimacy? Answer? A *response*, like men's violence against women, of the powerful to the threat of the powerless?

The article is accompanied by artistic woodcuts: the first shows a screaming victim, of indeterminate sex under the artistic treatment, with breasts that could be a man's or a woman's. A (male) hand (with the cultural gender signs of suit and cuff), intruding into the picture from the left foreground, applies an electric instrument to the nipple of the represented victim: an image familiar from pornographic representations. The pictorial focus, the loving gaze, is on the victim, the torturer symbolized, like Thomas Kasire's torturer, by the intruding arm, his subjectivity confirmed by the victimization of the victim. The second illustration shows the victim's face in a state of comparatively relaxed exhaustion, a hand intruding from the same corner, touching, caressing, without instrument. With lovers like men, who needs torturers?

Communication, sex, exchange (and yes, in a sense, even torture) are practices where the individual engages in sociality: they involve at least two subjects. Yet the cultural outlook prefers to frame these as practices of the subject, of the individual. By turning social practices into transitive processes, the social partners in the practice are represented as objects and the practice is predicated upon a single subject. The individual subject is regarded as the unit of society, which then becomes the simple conglomeration of individuals, and social practice the multiplication of individual practices.

Our analysis has tried to bring these 'individual' practices into relation with larger cultural practices. If the individual looks with a one-way gaze at women, if he monologues at his interlocutor, if he pursues his Big O or the pleasure of torture, the larger social practice is not just the sum total of individuals gazing, monologuing, orgasming, torturing. Rather, the social whole 'divides itself' – is divided by forcible organization – into subject groups and object groups, the male gender and the female gender, speakers and listeners, exploiters and exploited. Women are the generic object of culture, culture is the monologue of the male gender. There is a dialectic not between subject and object, master and slave, but between these 'individual' practices and cultural practice, since individual practice, involving at least two subjects, is the minimal unit of social practice.

The relationships of domination and oppression are played out on the 'individual' level: men hold forth at women, silence their wives, demand that they be linguistically available to them as listeners. On the macro-level, we have a cultural discourse that is monologic, a self-representation of a dominant group, and a distribution of roles that reflects the inequality of the subject and object. On the macro-level we (the 'masses') are, like women, spoken to in authoritative voices, and if we look at who is speaking culturally, it is experts and 'contributors' (professionals), governments, and industries. The rest of society, those excluded from Raymond Williams' 'many kinds of ruling groups', are silenced into a passive and consuming attitude that is read as consent. The communication model is the same at both levels, one endorses the other, but whilst individual men use it at the individual level, they resent it when it is used against them at the macro-level. Or perhaps the contradiction points the other way: whilst resenting it at the macro-level – the power of the state, the social elite, capital – they see no contradiction in employing it at the personal level. The naturalization of monologic forms of intersubjective practices is what ensures the management and control of democracy (without any apparent contradiction), ensures, that is, the passivity and lack of participation of the 'masses' (of individuals) and prevents the foundation of collectivity and solidarity. (See for instance the breakdown of attempted collectivity in left-wing groups due to 'individual' practice: e.g. 'men will make the revolution and make their chicks'.)[10]

Social cultural practices do not evolve 'culturally'. As the case of gender demonstrates, the cultural distribution of gender roles and gender values is dependent on and supported by social and political organization: the silence of women can be developed on the cultural level only on the basis of coercive discriminatory measures in the social organization. Conversely it is true that social changes cannot be achieved through changes in organization only: we have seen that attainment of political rights and theoretical legal equality by women or by black people has not led to their social equality, because no cultural change in social practices (and their conception) has accompanied the legal changes. On the contrary, the cultural understanding of these 'individual' practices, the values evolved and maintained through cultural practice (the arts, media, advertising, free-market economy) ensure that any changes in the legal status of the members of society remain without fundamental effect on the social and economic organization. It is, in fact, *impossible* that women, black people, the working classes and consumers attain anything like their 'democratic' rights, anything like full human rights and liberty within the present cultural system of values. Society as we know it, social, political and economic organization as we know it, and power as we know it, do not allow for freedom and equality for all: there must be a class or classes of people who are the objects for the subject. For, the liberty and the rights that are the cultural ideals are the liberty to cause suffering rather than suffer, and the right to dominate rather than be dominated. As Simone de Beauvoir writes, basing herself on the 'individual' subject–object pair:

> Thus it is that no group ever sets itself up as the One without at once setting up the Other over against itself

. . . Things become clear . . . if, following Hegel, we find in consciousness itself a fundamental hostility toward every other consciousness; the subject can be posed only in being opposed – he sets himself up as the essential, as opposed to the other, the inessential, the object.[11]

History is a continuous illustration of this principle. Yet this particular picture with its particular frame of the individualist perspective on the 'human condition' as usual shows us some aspect and obscures another. It does not really make things clear, but on the contrary obscures a significant dimension belonging to groups: the fact that the very same structure of opposition and hostility also builds a group, a partial community, through solidarity. The individual consciousness as part of a group is hostile only towards the members of the Other group, but bonds with the members of its own whom it recognizes as 'same'.

The question to ask is why such solidarity and lack of hostility seems possible only on the basis of a simultaneous opposition to another class, but the hegelian hostility of consciousness to every other consciousness is no explanation. It would, if anything, prove the impossibility of the formation of any group whatsoever. But if the individual consciousness is capable of bonding with another consciousness, then there is no reason why it cannot do so in the absence of a simultaneous hostility elsewhere. The hegelian explanation – the reduction of the minimal social unit of two subjects to an individual relation of subject to object – should be seen, rather, as a convenient excuse for the establishment of oppressive social systems, as a cultural justification of the privileges and power of a ruling group. The culture of men, the dominant gender (each one a ruler at least in his 'individual' context) – all those narratives, all those pictures constructed on scenarios no. 1 and no. 2, seek to convince us of the necessity of power disequilibria, oppression and domination as 'fundamentally' human ('natural') phenomena.

Women – like members of other oppressed groups – are living an experience under the very noses of our philosophers of the human condition which disproves the fundamental necessity of the human consciousness's hostility toward every other consciousness. The only way the dominant group – here the male gender – can accommodate such forms of intersubjectivity and collective solidarity is to deny, through cultural representation, that these are forms of consciousness. Thus women's lack of hostility towards other consciousnesses is represented as a complete renunciation of selfhood. The bond between woman and man, glorified in romantic love, and the bond between mother and child, glorified in the Madonna, are reduced to biological instincts on the one hand, and to make sure, represented as a virtuous abnegation of self on the other. Ultimate Madonna status is achieved in selflessness, where the woman has graduated to angel and ceases to be part of the human condition. For the perspective of the male's relation to the woman, the cultural effort, as we have seen, is to deny that women have any subjectivity at all, so that they become objects, and so that their example of lack of hostility towards every other consciousness in the absence of any simultaneous hostility towards an Other group, need not be taken as an example, or as a counter-example to the theory. The woman-to-woman bond thus ceases to be any bond at all, and escapes glorification.

This is not to say that women are 'naturally' more loving than men. The phenomenon just described – the lack of fundamental hostility toward every other consciousness – is typical of anyone not part of a ruling group. For the 'fundamental' hostility towards a group of Others is a necessity not of human consciousness, but of ruling groups. It is the ruling group that needs to defend its status, needs to regard the group it rules as fundamentally hostile to its power and as contesting its 'legitimacy', or needs to go on the offensive as it takes possession of the group it wants to dominate. The individual of the ruling group, already one step up in the distillation of power, sees himself as 'fundamentally' opposed to every other consciousness, since the ultimate goal of the ruler of the ruling group is to become the one and only ruler. He does not even care to represent the temporary absence of hostility towards his fellow rulers. As concerns the members of the oppressed class, we have seen that they come under the pressure of the dominant ideology, and may either become the carbon-copies of their rulers as the would-be revolutionaries who turn their rulers into their own Other group, or they may retain their consciousness and direct hostility at the power structure itself.

If women, black people, workers, listeners were allowed to contribute to the culture's description of 'its' condition, Hegel might be challenged, the dominant versions of the partial collectivities of the family, of the brotherhood, of the mafia, of the nation, of the first world, might be rejected as unacceptable models of groups that are based on self-interest rather than solidarity. Part of a feminist strategy must be the elaboration of a concept of collectivity that differs from male bonding over commodities and enemies. Feminist critique must evolve forms of communication that are neither ego-trips nor solid objects, but forms of exchange. A feminist psychology will negotiate the relationship of the individual with the collective, the subject with sociality, not with an objectified other. The personal is political, because the personal is the minimal social unit. Hence feminist critique will envisage intersubjectivity: revolution, not *coup d'état*.

# Practical Perspectives

I have just finished reading *How to Suppress Women's Writing* by Joanna Russ, who also cannot finish her book: after an 'Epilogue' there is an 'Author's Note' and then an 'Afterword'. Perhaps there is too much to say, perhaps the form of a 'well-written book', a fine composition, with a finishing flourish does not suit the urgent need of a feminist multi-logue. Consider this section a compromise: it will be the last, but it is not the end.

A good book, like a good girl, spells out the implications at the end, so that there is nothing left to do but close the book and buy another. My argument has not been concerned with practical measures which we could take today or tomorrow in order to get rid of the problem of pornography. I have tried to show that there is no such isolated problem as 'pornography'. I have aimed, rather, to build up a critique of the underlying assumptions which make a pornographic practice of representation 'natural'. With these assumptions in place, it seems to me pointless to embark on a quick programme of reforms that would patch up the status quo in the hope of silencing the women who are so angry. My analysis suggests that you cannot remedy the situation by appointing more women pornographers or more male victims, i.e. by achieving a more equitable quota of exploitation. Equal opportunities are out when what they are equal to is undesirable.

It is also worth stating what I am *not* implying. I am *not* suggesting that besides 'pornography' all other representations of women including 'art' should be censored. The question of censorship has been addressed already (e.g. by Deirdre English), and the appeal to a cultural police force seems to me the opposite of what a feminist politics envisages. For the same reasons I do not believe in the possibility (or desirability) of laying down a programme of 'feminist aesthetics', a charter of ideologically 'correct' procedures, a catalogue of 'positive images'. The concept of 'aesthetics' is fundamentally incompatible with feminist politics.

This is not to say that women should abstain from any 'artistic', i.e. creative practice: on the contrary, the active participation of women (and other non-experts) in cultural practice is essential to the process of transforming the structure of representation, the conventions of viewing and the conception of creativity. But it is decidedly not enough to have female genitals and take over the means and forms (not to say 'tools') which the culture holds ready today. Nor is it enough to change the 'point of view' and tell the tale (paint the picture) of male violence and domination from the victim's point of view, since that perspective has already been formed, painted and elaborated *ad nauseam* under existing conventions. It is a stock in trade, for instance, of the tabloid press. The cultural representation of women's subjectivity will not be easily evolved, and it is certainly not there to be picked up by women Artists ready for a reversal of roles, letting men instead of women pass in front of the speculum. Inversion is the swing of Sade's pendulum.

Women's 'artistic' practice must therefore be experimental in the largest sense of the word – not an avant-garde experiment with technique, which has been the hallmark of western art for so long – but experimenting with respect to the practice itself: a practice which will not produce Art for the museums and products for the market place. If anything is to be done about pornography, if a cultural shift in consciousness (revolution, not *coup d'état*) will eventually move away from pornographic structures of perception and thought, then the arts themselves will necessarily also have to change, Art will have to go. The necessity of giving a voice to our female perspective, to female vision, understanding and critique is beyond question, but we should seriously ask why we should wish to offer these to aesthetic contemplation in fiction, in make-believe forms designed for leisure consumption. The committed intention of the feminist (or any other political) writer is irreconcilable with the attitude required of art and artists, that is, their irresponsibility towards political reality.

A feminist cultural practice, then, would be one that arises from a changed consciousness of what culture and its practices are, and it would arise from a different social and economic organization. It would not be commercially produced by a set of 'contributors' – white, male, educated professionals. It would be a practice in the interest of communication, not representation. It would be dialogic, multilogic, an end to the pornologic.

So how do you go about changing consciousness? But you already know that. You are doing it.

# Notes

*Problem 1*

1 Aslak Aarhus and Ole Bernt Froshaug, 'A Murder in Namibia', *The Guardian Weekly*, 8 January 1984, p. 7. Namibia has been administered by South Africa since 1915. In 1971 the International Court of Justice ruled this an 'illegal occupation' and demanded that South Africa withdraw. It has refused to do so. SWAPO is the national liberation movement fighting to end South African rule in the country.

 Van Rooyen is only one example of a white settler in Namibia who got away with murdering a black worker.
2 Ibid.
3 Ibid.
4 Ibid.
5 Ibid.
6 Raymond Williams, *Keywords: A Vocabulary of Culture and Society* (London, Fontana, 1976); see especially 'Literature' and 'Fiction'.
7 See, e.g. Frank Kermode, 'Obscenity and the Public Interest', in his *Modern Essays* (London, Fontana, 1971).
8 'Dr Sharon Satterfield (at the University of Minnesota human sexuality program) . . . has given us serious testimony that there is no correlation between pornography and violence against women' *Minneapolis Star and Tribune*, 31 December 1983, p. 4A.
9 Roland Barthes, *Sade, Fourier, Loyola* (Paris, Editions du Seuil, 1971), p. 164.
10 Marquis de Sade, quoted in *Time Out*, 1–7 March 1984, p. 11.
11 Aarhus and Froshaug, 'A Murder in Namibia', p. 7.

*Problem 2*

1 *Minneapolis Star and Tribune*, 31 December 1983, p. 1.
2 Ibid., p. 4A.

3 Ibid.

4 Ibid.

5 Ibid.

6 *Emma* (August 1978), 8.

7 Aslak Aarhus and Ole Bernt Froshaug, 'A Murder in Namibia', *The Guardian Weekly*, 8 January 1984, p. 7.

8 Ibid.

9 Ibid.


*Problem 3*

1 Dale Spender, *Man Made Language* (London, Routledge & Kegan Paul, 1980), p. 150.

2 Deirdre English, 'The Politics of Porn: Can Feminists Walk the Line?', *Mother Jones* (April 1980), 22.

3 *Report of the Committee on Obscenity and Film Censorship* (London, HMSO, 1979), Cmnd 7772, reprinted 1981.

4 Bernard Williams, 'Pornography and Feminism', *London Review of Books*, 17–31 March 1983, p. 23.

5 Susan Barrowclough, 'Not a Love Story', *Screen* 23 (Nov./Dec. 1982), 26–36.

6 Williams, 'Pornography and Feminism', p. 23.

7 Ibid.

8 Ibid.

9 Ibid.

10 Ibid.

11 *The Guardian*, 29 June 1983.

12 Ibid.

13 Williams, 'Pornography and Feminism', p. 23.

14 Ibid.

15 Ibid.

16 Ibid.

17 Ibid.

18 Ibid.

19 *Report on Obscenity and Film Censorship*, p. 160.

20 Ibid., p. 27.

21 Ibid., p. 9.

22 Ibid., p. 159. There is still, however, no significant shift in the conception of 'harm'. As Liz Bradbury points out, gender is rarely a factor considered in research on the effects of or responses to pornography (Liz Bradbury, 'Pornography the

Theory, Rape the Practice?', unpublished B.A. dissertation, Cambridge College of Art and Technology, 1985).

23 Ibid., p. 112 *passim*.
24 Ibid., pp. 106, 116.
25 Ibid., p. 117.
26 Ibid., p. 122 *passim*.
27 Williams, 'Pornography and Feminism', p. 23.
28 *Report on Obscenity and Film Censorship*, p. 131.
29 Ibid., p. 131. Exploitation, according to the Report, may also include (ab)use of a person against their will or without their knowledge; the concept of exploitation is thus centred entirely on the actor in the scenario of representation.
30 Henry Schipper, 'Filthy Lucre: A Tour of America's Most Profitable Frontier', *Mother Jones* (April 1980), 62.

## Problem 4

1 Deirdre English, 'The Politics of Porn: Can Feminists Walk the Line?', *Mother Jones* (April 1980), 20.
2 Ibid., p. 22.
3 Ibid., p. 20.
4 Ibid., p. 22.
5 Ibid.
6 Ibid.
7 Ibid., p. 49.
8 Ibid., p. 48.
9 Ibid., p. 49.
10 Ibid., p. 48.
11 Ibid.
12 Ibid., pp. 48–9.
13 Ibid., p. 48.
14 Ibid., p. 49.
15 Ibid.
16 Virginia Woolf, *A Room of One's Own* (London, Granada Publishing, Panther Books, 1979), p. 27. See also Simone de Beauvoir, 'Introduction' to *The Second Sex*, in Elaine Marks and Isabelle de Courtivron (eds), *New French Feminisms* (Brighton, The Harvester Press, 1981), p. 43.
17 Ray A. Killian, *The Working Woman: A Male Manager's View* (New York, American Management Association, 1971), pp. 16–21.

18 English, 'The Politics of Porn', p. 22.
19 For a rare but excellent examination of the issues raised by Chicago's *Dinner Table*, see Michèle Barrett, 'Feminism and the Definition of Cultural Politics', in Rosalind Brunt and Caroline Rowan (eds), *Feminism, Culture and Politics* (London, Lawrence and Wishart, 1982). A later version of the same article appeared as a review, 'Top Girls', in *New Socialist* (June 1985), 18–19.
20 English, 'The Politics of Porn', p. 23.
21 Ibid., p. 48.
22 Ibid.
23 Ibid.
24 Gloria Steinem, 'Erotica and Pornography: A Clear and Present Difference', in *Ms* (November 1978), 53f.
25 Ibid., p. 53.
26 Ibid.
27 Ibid., p. 54.
28 Ibid., p. 78.
29 Ibid.
30 English, 'The Politics of Porn', p. 49.
31 Ibid., p. 50.
32 Ibid.
33 Ibid.
34 Ibid.
35 Ibid.
36 Ibid.
37 Ibid., p. 22.
38 Ibid., p. 50.
39 Ibid.
40 John Berger, *Ways of Seeing* (Harmondsworth, Penguin, 1972), p. 47.
41 Immanuel Kant, 'From Critique of Judgement', in William Handy and Max Westbrook (eds), *Twentieth Century Criticism: The Major Statements* (New York, The Free Press–Macmillan, 1974), tr. J. C. Meredith, p. 9.
42 Ibid.
43 Ibid., p. 11.
44 Ibid., p. 12.
45 English, 'The Politics of Porn', p. 22.
46 Germain Greer, *The Obstacle Race: The Fortunes of Women Painters and Their Work* (London, Secker & Warburg, 1979).
47 Marquis de Sade, quoted in Angela Carter, *The Sadeian Woman* (London, Virago, 1979), p. 37.

48 Henry Schipper, 'Filthy Lucre: A Tour of America's Most Profitable Frontier', *Mother Jones* (April 1980), 60.


*Problem 5*

1 Henry Schipper, 'Filthy Lucre: A Tour of America's Most Profitable Frontier', *Mother Jones* (April 1980), 60.
2 Simone de Beauvoir, 'Introduction to The Second Sex', in Elaine Marks and Isabelle Courtivron (eds), *New French Feminisms* (Brighton, The Harvester Press, 1981), reprinted from *The Second Sex* (Vintage, 1974), p. 44. The English edition of de Beauvoir's *The Second Sex* appeared in Penguin, 1972.
3 Compare Mary Vetterling-Braggin (ed.), *Sexist Language* (New York, Littlefield Adams, 1981), which is a collection of essays on 'sexism in language' by language philosophers who treat the concept of 'sexism' as symmetrical.
4 Immanuel Kant, 'From Critique of Judgement', in William Handy and Max Westbrook (eds), *Twentieth Century Criticism: The Major Statements* (New York, The Free Press 1974), tr. J. C. Meredith, p. 12.
5 Ibid.
6 Ibid.
7 Ibid., pp. 12–13.
8 Ibid., p. 13.
9 Walter Pater, *The Renaissance* (New York, The New American Library, Mentor Books, 1959), p. 97.
10 Roland Barthes, *S/Z* (Paris, du Seuil, 1970), p. 18.
11 Brian Doyle, 'The Hidden History of English Studies', in Peter Widdowson (ed.), *Re-Reading English* (London, Methuen New Accents, 1982), p. 25.
12 Schipper, 'Filthy Lucre', p. 32: 'Lick it for a dollar', 'another customer starts to finger a dancer', the dancer 'being tongued'.
13 Andrea Dworkin, *Pornography: Men Possessing Women* (London, The Women's Press, 1981), p. 13.
14 Dale Spender, *Women of Ideas (And What Men Have Done to Them)* (London, Ark, 1983); Joanna Russ, *How to Suppress Women's Writing* (London, The Women's Press, 1984); Tillie Olsen, *Silences* (London, Virago, 1980).
15 Schipper, 'Filthy Lucre', p. 60.
16 *The Guardian Weekly*, 23 December 1984, p. 3.
17 Ibid.

18 Bell Hooks, *Ain't I A Woman: Black Women and Feminism* (London, Pluto Press, 1981), p. 107.


*Problem 6*

1 John Berger, *Ways of Seeing* (Harmondsworth, Penguin, 1972).
2 John Berger, 'Why Look at Animals?', in John Berger, *About Looking* (London, Writers and Readers Cooperative, 1980), pp. 1–2. I shall henceforth give page references to this chapter in brackets following the quotations.
3 Ariana Stassinopoulos, *The Female Woman* (London, Fontana, 1974); Government White Paper *Equality for Women* (London, HMSO, 1974), Cmnd 5724.
4 *United Nations Report*, 1980.
5 Quoted in Dale Spender, *Man Made Language* (London, Routledge and Kegan Paul, 1980), p. 41.
6 See, e.g. Kate Young, Carol Wolkowitz and Roslyn McCullagh, (eds), *Of Marriage and the Market* (London, CSE Books, 1981); Lydia Sargent (ed.), *Women and Revolution: The Unhappy Marriage of Marxism and Feminism* (London, Pluto Press, 1981); Elizabeth Whitelegg et al. (eds), *The Changing Experience of Women* (Oxford, Martin Robertson in association with The Open University, 1982); Angela Davis, *Women, Race and Class* (London, The Women's Press, 1982).
7 Henrik Ibsen, *A Doll's House*, in Henrik Ibsen, *Plays Vol. II* (London, Methuen, 1980), tr. Michael Meyer, p. 98.
8 Cf. Lorna Duffin, 'The Conspicuous Consumptive: Woman as an Invalid', in Sara Delamont and Lorna Duffin, *The Nineteenth-Century Woman: Her Cultural and Physical World* (London, Croom Helm, 1978); Barbara Ehrenreich and Deirdre English, *For Her Own Good: 150 Years of the Experts' Advice to Women* (London, Pluto Press, 1979).
9 *Actuel* (December 1984), 28, my translation.
10 See any analysis of the consciousness of race oppression and its gender differences, e.g. Bell Hooks, *Ain't I A Woman: Black Women and Feminism* (London, Pluto Press, 1981); or black fiction, e.g. Alice Walker, *You Can't Keep a Good Woman Down* (London, The Women's Press, 1982), Buchi Emecheta, *Adah's Story* (London, Allison and Busby, 1983).
11 *Actuel* (December 1984), 44–5.
12 Henry Schipper, 'Filthy Lucre: A Tour of America's Most

Profitable Frontier', *Mother Jones* (April 1980), 32.
13 Ibid.


*Problem 7*

1 Bernard Williams, 'Pornography and Feminism', *London Review of Books*, 17–31 March, 1983, p.23.
2 Ibid.
3 Ibid.
4 Henry Schipper, 'Filthy Lucre: A Tour of America's Most Profitable Frontier', *Mother Jones* (April, 1980), 60.
5 Williams' 'Pornography and Feminism', p. 23.
6 Schipper, 'Filthy Lucre', p. 62.
7 D. M. Thomas, 'Different Voices' (An Interview), *London Magazine* (February, 1982), 27.
8 Susan Sontag, 'The Pornographic Imagination', in *A Susan Sontag Reader* (New York, Farrar, Straus and Giroux, 1982), pp. 205–33.
9 Susan Griffin, *Pornography and Silence* (London, The Women's Press, 1981), p. 227.
10 D. M. Thomas, *The White Hotel* (Harmondsworth, King Penguin, 1981), p. 3.
11 Thomas, 'Different Voices', pp. 32–3.
12 Ibid., p. 33.
13 Thomas, *The White Hotel*, pp. 19–29.
14 Ibid., pp. 19–30.
15 *Susan Sontag Reader*, p. 222.
16 Ibid., p. 220.
17 Ibid.
18 Roland Barthes, quoted in Andrea Dworkin, *Pornography: Men Possessing Women* (London, The Women's Press, 1981), p. 94. The original French source is Roland Barthes, *Sade, Fourier, Loyola* (Paris, Seuil, 1971), p. 147.
19 Thomas, *The White Hotel*, pp. 19, 23 and 22 respectively.
20 See, e.g. Fatna Ait Sabbah, *La femme dans l'inconscient musulman* (Paris, Le Sycomore, 1982), esp. pp. 47–59.
21 George Levine, 'No Reservations', *The New York Review of Books*, 28 May 1981, p. 20.
22 *Susan Sontag Reader*, p. 214.
23 Thomas, 'Different Voices', pp. 28, 30 and 30.
24 Levine, 'No Reservations', p. 20.
25 Ibid.

26 Ibid.
27 Ibid.
28 Thomas, *The White Hotel*, p. 220.
29 Ibid., p. 221.
30 Levine, 'No Reservations', p. 20.
31 Ibid.
32 Ibid.
33 Ibid.
34 Ibid.
35 Ibid.
36 Ibid.
37 Ibid.
38 Ibid., p. 22.
39 Ibid., p. 23.
40 Ibid.
41 Ibid., p. 21.
42 Ibid., p. 23.
43 Ibid., pp. 21, 23 and 23.
44 Ibid., p. 21.
45 Ibid., p. 23.
46 Ibid., pp. 23 and 20.
47 Thomas, 'Different Voices', pp. 31–3.
48 Ibid., p. 36.
49 Ibid.
50 Levine, 'No Reservations', p. 23.
51 Ibid., pp. 20 and 23.
52 Ibid., p. 23.

## Problem 8

1 Raymond Williams, *Communications*, 3rd edn (Harmondsworth, Pelican, 1982), p. 109.
2 Matthew Arnold, *Culture and Anarchy*, in Lionel Trilling (ed.), *The Essential Matthew Arnold* (London, Chatto & Windus, 1949), p. 473.
3 Ibid.
4 See, e.g. A. Olrik, 'Epische Gesetze der Volksdichtung', *Zeitschrift für Deutsches Altertum*, 51 (1909), p. 5; or Vladimir Propp, *Morphology of the Folktale*, 2nd edn (Austin and London, University of Texas Press, 1979), tr. Laurence Scott, pp. 63, 79 f.

5 Propp, *Morphology*, p. 107.

6 Vladimir Propp, 'Transformationen von Zaubermärchen', tr. Karl Eimermacher, in his *Morphologie des Märchens*, ed. Karl Eimermacher (Frankfurt am Main, Suhrkamp Verlag, 1975), p. 168. See also Alison Lurie, *Clever Gretchen* (London, Heinemann, 1980).

7 Roland Barthes, 'The Death of the Author', in his *Image, Music, Text* (London, Fontana, 1977, tr. Stephen Heath, p. 142.

8 Althusser proposes a 'trilogy of the superstructure' which includes 'Art' as a given entity. For a critique, see Tony Bennett, *Formalism and Marxism* (London, Methuen, 1979), esp. pp. 120–6. Raymond Williams tells us: 'I am sure that *Lady Chatterley's Lover* is in a wholly different class, *as art*, from the great bulk of popular work' (my emphasis) (*Communications*, p. 122).

9 Frank Kermode, 'Obscenity and the Public Interest', in his *Modern Essays* (London, Fontana, 1971), p. 76.

10 Michèle Barrett, 'Feminism and the Definition of Cultural Politics', in Rosalind Brunt and Caroline Rowan (eds), *Feminism, Culture and Politics* (London, Lawrence and Wishart, 1982), p. 49.

11 *The Observer Colour Supplement*, 6 December 1981.

12 Raymond Williams, *Keywords: A Vocabulary of Culture and Society* (London, Fontana, 1976), p. 151.

13 Sculley Bradley et al. (eds) *The American Tradition in Literature*, 4th edn (Grosset & Dunlap, distributed by W. W. Norton & Co., Inc., 1956), vol. II, pp. 1539–40.

14 Ibid., p. 1562.

15 Ibid.

16 Ibid., p. 1740.

17 Ibid., p. 1741.

18 Ibid., p. 1749.

19. Ibid., pp. 1692–757.

20 Ibid., p. 1707.

21 Ibid., p. xvii.

## Problem 9

1 All quotes concerning this episode are taken from an interview with Doris Lessing in *Actuel* 62 (December 1984), pp. 138–9, my translation from French. Here, p. 138.

2 Ibid., p. 139.

3 Ibid.

4 Ibid.

5 Ibid.

6 See Judith Williamson, *Decoding Advertisements: Ideology and Meaning in Advertisements* (London, Boyars, 1978).

7 Raymond Williams, *Communications*, 3rd edn (Harmondsworth, Penguin, 1982), p. 104.

8 Tony Bennett, *Formalism and Marxism* (London, Methuen, 1979), p. 58.


*Problem 10*

1 Roland Barthes, *Image, Music, Text* (London, Fontana, 1977), tr. Stephen Heath, p. 142.

2 Angela Carter, *The Sadeian Woman* (London, Virago, 1979), p. 37.

3 Ibid., p. 36.

4 Roland Barthes, *Sade, Fourier, Loyola* (Paris, Editions du Seuil, 1971), p. 147. English translation based on that by Richard Howard, quoted in Andrea Dworkin, *Pornography: Men Possessing Women* (London, The Women's Press, 1981), p. 94.

5 Joseph Heller, *Something Happened* (London, Corgi, 1975), pp. 360–1.

6 Barthes, *Sade, Fourier, Loyola*, p. 147 (my translation).

7 Ibid., p. 148 (my translation).

8 Ibid. (my translation).

9 See, e.g. Roland Barthes, 'The Death of the Author', in his *Image, Music, Text*, pp. 142–8; Michel Foucault, 'What Is an Author?', in Josué V. Harari (ed.), *Textual Strategies: Perspectives in Post-Structuralist Criticism* (London, Methuen, 1980), pp. 141–60.

10 Jane Gallop, *Feminism and Psychoanalysis: The Daughter's Seduction* (London, Macmillan, 1982), p. 33.

11 Ibid.

12 Barthes, *Sade, Fourier, Loyola*, p. 155 (my translation).

13 *The Guardian Weekly*, 3 February 1985, section reprinted from *Le Monde*, p. 14.

## Problem 11

1 Kate Millet, *Sexual Politics* (London, Virago, 1977), p. 350.
2 Ibid., p. 359.
3 See Bell Hooks, *Ain't I A Woman: Black Women and Feminism* (London, Pluto Press, 1981).
4 Hooks, *Ain't I A Woman*, p. 127.
5 Ibid.
6 Ibid., p. 20.
7 Except in the works of black feminists already mentioned, which include a critique of the historiography of slavery.
8 See Sandra Harding, 'What Is the Real Material Base of Patriarchy and Capital?', in Lydia Sargent (ed.), *Women and Revolution: The Unhappy Marriage of Marxism and Feminism* (London, Pluto Press, 1981), pp. 135–63.
9 Fatna Ait Sabbah, *La femme dans l'inconscient musulman* (Paris, Le Sycomore, 1982), esp. 'La femme omnisexuelle ', pp. 47–76.
10 See Sandra Findley, 'Pornography and British India: *Venus in India*', unpublished M.A. thesis, University of Essex, 1979.
11 Andrea Dworkin, *Pornography: Men Possessing Women* (London, The Women's Press, 1981), chapter 7: 'Whores', pp. 203–24.
12 When I sent my analysis of *The White Hotel* (chapter 7) in article form to *New Left Review*, the letter of rejection included the suggestion that I consider 'possible counter-examples to [my] general thesis (perhaps the novels of Erica Jong?)'.
13 Julia Swindells, 'Falling Short With Marx: Some Glimpses of 19th Century Sexual Ideology', *Literature, Teaching, Politics* (*LTP*) 3 (1984), p. 57.
14 Ibid.
15 Ibid., p. 58.
16 Hooks, *Ain't I A Woman*, p. 25.

## Problem 12

1 Raymond Williams, *Communications*, 3rd edn (Harmondsworth, Pelican, 1982), p. 6.
2 Ibid., p. 12.
3 Ibid., p. 9.
4 Roland Barthes, *Image, Music, Text* (London, Fontana, 1977), tr. Stephen Heath, p. 146.
5 Susanne Kappeler, *Writing and Reading in Henry James* (London, Macmillan, 1980), chapter 7, 'A Literary Taboo', pp. 75–82.

6 P. Bogatyrev and Roman Jakobson, 'Die Folklore als eine besondere Form des Schaffens', *Donum natalicum Schrijnen* (Nijmegen and Utrecht, 1929). For a French text, see Roman Jakobson, *Questions de poétique* (Paris, Seuil, 1973).

7 Frank Kermode, *Romantic Image* (London, Fontana, 1971), p. 14.

8 Ibid., p. 15.

9 Quoted in Kermode, *Romantic Image*, p. 19.

10 Ibid., p. 37.

11 Ibid., p. 16.

12 Quoted in Kermode, *Romantic Image*, p. 18.

13 Ibid.

14 Ibid.

15 Ibid., pp. 32, 15, 20 and 39 respectively.

16 Ibid., p. 19.

17 Ibid., p. 33.

18 Ibid., pp. 36 and 37.

19 Ibid., p. 17.

20 Ibid.

21 Quoted in Kermode, *Romantic Image*, p. 19.

22 Ibid., p. 24.

23 Marion Glastonbury, 'Holding the Pens', in Sarah Elbert and Marion Glastonbury, *Inspiration and Drudgery: Notes on Literature and Domestic Labour in the Nineteenth Century* (London, Women's Research and Resource Centre (WRRC), 1978), p. 34.

24 Ibid., p. 35.

25 Ibid., pp. 35–6.

26 Ibid., p. 36.

27 Ibid.

28 Ibid.

29 Ibid., p. 30.

30 Ibid., p. 36.

31 I have analysed this at greater length in my *Writing and Reading in Henry James*.

32 Kermode, *Romantic Image*, p. 17.

33 Ibid.

34 Ibid., p. 33, quoting Walter Pater.

35 Terence Hawkes, *Structuralism and Semiotics* (London, Methuen, 1977), p. 112.

36 This is not exclusively Barthes's invention, but already

grounded in the romantic and symbolist tradition; cf. Kermode, *Romantic Image*, p. 170.

37 *The Guardian Weekly*, 8 January 1984, section reprinted from *Le Monde*, p. 13.

38 Ibid., p. 13.

39 Julia Swindells, *Victorian Writing and Working Women* (Cambridge, Polity Press, 1985), p. 176.

40 Cf. E. P. Thompson, *Writing by Candlelight* (London, Merlin, 198), Introduction.

41 Williams, *Communications*, p. 13.

42 Ibid., p. 123.

43 Ibid., p. 124.

44 Ibid., pp. 124–5.

45 Ivan Illich, quoted in Swindells, *Victorian Writing*, p. 15.

46 Swindells, *Victorian Writing*, ibid.

47 Glastonbury, 'Holding the Pens', p. 30.

48 Williams, *Communications*, p. 125.

49 Ibid.

50 Ibid., pp. 128 and 134 respectively.

51 Swindells, *Victorian Writing*, p. 15.

52 Williams, *Communications*, p. 164.

53 Robert Sherrill, 'Where There's Smoke, There's Money', *The Guardian Weekly*, 23 December 1984, p. 18.

54 Ibid.

55 *The Guardian Weekly*, 23 December 1984, p. 6.

56 Ibid.

57 Ibid.

58 Ibid.

59 Ibid.

60 Ibid.

61 Anne Karpf, 'Oh, really? How Interesting! Grrr . . .', *The Sunday Times*, 25 September 1983, p. 38.

62 Ibid.

63 Ibid.

64 Dale Spender, *Man Made Language* (London, Routledge & Kegan Paul, 1980), p. 46.

65 Ibid., p. 43.

66 Ibid., p. 42.

67 Ibid.

68 Pamela Fishman, quoted in Spender, *Man Made Language*, p. 49.

69 Karpf, 'Oh, really?', p. 38.
70 Ibid.


*Problem 13*

1 Jane Gallop, *Feminism and Psychoanalysis: The Daughter's Seduction* (London, Macmillan, 1982), p. 2.
2 Ibid., p. 3.
3 Ibid.
4 Fredric Jameson, 'Pleasure: A Political Issue', in Formations Collective (ed.), *Formations of Pleasure* (London, Routledge & Kegan Paul, 1983), p. 3.
5 Stephen Heath, *The Sexual Fix* (London, Macmillan, 1982), p. 3.
6 Ibid., p. 1.
7 Ibid., p. 145.
8 Ibid., p. 66.
9 Ibid.
10 Ibid., p. 68.
11 Ibid., p. 4.
12 See, e.g. Barbara Ehrenreich and Deirdre English, *For Her Own Good: 150 Years of the Experts' Advice to Women* (London, Pluto, 1979).
13 Heath, *The Sexual Fix*, p. 46.
14 Ibid., p. 40.
15 Ibid., p. 41.
16 Jeffrey Masson, 'The Persecution and Expulsion of Jeffrey Masson', *Mother Jones* (December 1984), p. 43.
17 Ibid., pp. 43–4.
18 Ibid., p. 44.
19 Ibid.
20 Heath, *The Sexual Fix*, p. 43.
21 Masson, 'Persecution and Expulsion', p. 44.
22 Heath, *The Sexual Fix*, footnote on p. 43.
23 Gallop, *Feminism and Psychoanalysis*, p. 146.
24 Ibid., p. 147.
25 Ibid.
26 Ibid., p. 89.
27 Ibid., pp. 89–90.
28 Masson, 'Persecution and Expulsion', p. 43.
29 Gallop, *Feminism and Psychoanalysis*, p. 143.

30 See, e.g. Heath, *The Sexual Fix*, footnote pp. 12–13; Liz Stanley (ed.), *The Diaries of Hannah Cullwick, Victorian Maidservant* (London, Virago, 1984).
31 Gallop, *Feminism and Psychoanalysis*, pp. 147–8.
32 Ibid., p. 148.
33 Ibid., pp. 19–20.
34 Ibid., p. 20.
35 Ibid., p. 15.
36 Ibid., p. 21.
37 Lacan, quoted in Gallop, *Feminism and Psychoanalysis*, p. 20.
38 Ibid., p. 34.
39 Gallop, *Feminism and Psychoanalysis*, p. 34.
40 Lacan, quoted in Gallop, *Feminism and Psychoanalysis*, p. 44.
41 Ibid.
42 Ibid.
43 Ibid., p. 84.
44 Ibid.
45 Ibid., pp. 84–5.
46 Ibid., p. 85.
47 Ibid.
48 Ibid., p. 48.
49 Ibid., pp. 33–4.

*Postscript*

1 *New Statesman*, 13 September 1985, p. 3.
2 Michael Ignatieff, 'Torture's Dead Simplicity', *New Statesman*, 20 September 1985, 'Weekend' section, p. 24.
3 Ibid.
4 Ibid.
5 Ibid., p. 25.
6 Ibid., p. 24.
7 Ibid.
8 Tony Beeton, *New Statesman*, 13 September 1985, p. 32.
9 Ignatieff, 'Torture's Dead Simplicity', p. 24.
10 From Robin Morgan, *Going Too Far* (New York, Random House, 1977), p. 127, quoted in Lydia Sargent (ed.), *Women and Revolution: The Unhappy Marriage of Marxism and Feminism* (London, Pluto Press, 1981), p. xiii.
11 Simone de Beauvoir, *The Second Sex* (Harmondsworth, Penguin, 1972) tr. H. M. Parshley, p. 17.

# Index

8948